Essays
on
Traditional Korean Music

Essays
on
Traditional Korean Music

by
LEE, Hye-Ku

Translated and Edited
by
Robert C. Provine

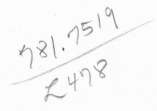

Published for the Royal Asiatic Society
Korea Branch
by Seoul Computer Press

First published July 6, 1981

Copyright © 1981 by the Royal Asiatic Society, Korea Branch
Published for the RAS-KB
by
Seoul Computer Press
Registration No. 15-21
Seoul, Korea

Designed by Norman R. Sibley
Dragon's Eye Graphics

Inquiries should be addressed to the author
care of: The Royal Asiatic Society, Korea Branch
C.P.O. Box 255, Seoul 100, Korea
Printed in Korea.

To my wife
Who knows why.

TABLE OF CONTENTS

AUTHOR'S PREFACE

There are very few books on Korean music in Western languages. In view of this, the present book attempts to characterize Korean music through translations of my articles on traditional music. These articles have been chosen for their emphasis on the unique features of native Korean music; except for instances of Koreanized pieces, the Chinese music preserved in Korea has been avoided. Sources for the articles are my *Han'guk ŭmak yŏn'gu* 韓國音樂研究 (Studies in Korean Music, 1957), *Han'guk ŭmak sŏsŏl* 韓國音樂序説 (Topics in Korean music, 1967), and *Han'guk ŭmak nonch'ong* 韓國音樂論叢 (Essays on Korean Music, 1976).

The first two articles, "A Short History of Korean Music" and "Characteristics of Korean Music," are designed to give the uninitiated reader a general introduction to the history and flavor of Korean music. The "Introduction to Traditional Music Notation Systems" provides a basis for technical studies with traditional sources. Four articles, "Modes in Early Korean Music Sources," "*Ujo* in Modern *Kagok*," "*Kyemyŏnjo* in Modern *Kagok*," and "*Yŏngsan hoesang*," treat the concepts of mode and key as used in Korea. The article on "*Chung-yŏngsan*" concerns the method of variation by which this piece was derived from its parent, *Yongsan hoesang*. The articles on "Appreciation of *Sijo*" and "*Sujech'ŏn*" deal with the relationship of aesthetics to dynamic shading in slow music. "*Yukchabaegi*" reveals the presence of a regular rhythmic pattern, despite an impression of free rhythm. Three articles, "Creative Activity in Traditional Korean Music," "*Ssanghwajŏm*," and "*Hyumyŏng*," show how Korean music may be modified toward Chinese style when it is adapted to a newly written Chinese text. Conversely, "*Nagyangch'un*: Chinese *tz'u* Music" shows the extent to which imported Chinese music has been subject to Koreanization. "Left and Right Music" explores the early Korean court music repertoire and its relations with Chinese and Japanese music.

The above-mentioned purpose of this volume is accomplished through the beautiful translations of Mr. Robert C. Province, Jr. His mastery of both the Korean and Chinese languages, as well as his deep knowledge of Korean music, has produced translations that the Korean author finds not only satisfactory, but pleasantly surprising and worthy of re-reading in English. Two articles, "A Short History of Korean Music" and *"Yukchabaegi,"* were kindly translated by Dr. Martina Deuchler before work on this volume began; Mr. Provine has made a few editorial revisions in these, for the sake of overall consistency.

Lee, Hye-Ku
College of Music
Seoul National University

Seoul, Korea
October, 1980

ACKNOWLEDGEMENTS

The author acknowledges with gratitude the financial help given by the Korean Culture and Arts Foundation. I am very grateful to Professor Barbara B. Smith for her sympathetic concern for the publication of the present work. I also wish to thank the Royal Asiatic Society, Korea Branch, for preparing a volume of such complexity in less than two months. My appreciative thanks go to my colleagues of the Korean Musicological Society for their dedicated help and devoted interest.

L. H. K.
May 1981

TRANSLATOR'S INTRODUCTION

Dr. Lee Hye-ku is one of the titans among scholars of East Asian music. Until recently, he was the only Korean musicologist whose name was known outside Korea; his reputation in the West, however, has rested upon a few articles in English and not on his important and voluminous contributions in the Korean language. Although Dr. Lee has played an important role in the introduction of Korean music to the West, it is more significant that for over three decades he has also been the leading voice of support for traditional Korean music in its native country. During Korea's rampant modernization since 1945, Westernization has often been equated with worth, and Western music now dominates the Korean musical scene. Dr. Lee has unswervingly dedicated himself to the preservation and study of the best in the traditional Korean music he deeply loves, and it is in no small part a result of his efforts that this music still thrives both in performance and scholarship.

A description of Dr. Lee's achievements would fill a volume, and the following is only a brief outline. Born in 1909, he graduated from Keijo [Seoul] Imperial College in 1931, with a major in English literature. He began his career in radio, and for over a decade and a half he was an announcer and programmer in charge of music and drama. His love for Korean music grew during this period, and his profession gave him the opportunity to confront problems of dissemination and modernization, and to form numerous contacts with traditional musicians. During this period, Korea was a colony of Japan, and advocacy of things Korean was not always a politically secure course of action. Dr. Lee's dedication, however, won him respect among both Korean musicians and Japanese scholars.

After Korea's liberation in 1945, Dr. Lee turned to academia. From 1947 to the present, he has taught music at Seoul National University, which until recently had the only academic department devoted to traditional Korean music. In the early years of the new nation, a career based entirely on scholarship in Korean music was economically impossible, and Dr. Lee had to support himself and his family by teaching concurrently in several schools, generally offering courses in English literature. During the Korean War, Dr. Lee spent much of his time teaching English in high schools and colleges and acting as a translator for the military. He suffered the loss of his entire library.

Soon after the war, the Korean Musicological Society (*Han'guk kugak hakhoe* 韓國國樂學會) was founded, and Dr. Lee has served as its president from 1954 to the present. His first book, *Han'guk ŭmak yŏn'gu* 韓國音樂研究 (Studies in Korean Music), appeared in 1957 and is a collection of essays written between 1943 and 1956. In 1958, he travelled to Europe and the United States, making contacts with noted scholars and visiting many universities. He contributed introductions to Korean music and absorbed Western musicological ideas in return. In 1959 he received the Doctor of Literature degree with a dissertation on modes in Korean music; this, one should note, was his fiftieth year.

Since 1960, Dr. Lee has continued to be unceasingly active in teaching, writing, and broadcasting. He has served on innumerable committees, both governmental and private, and his influence on the current state of Korean music is unrivaled. In 1961 and 1962, he again visited the United States, exchanging ideas and information with the eminent composer Lou Harrison. He completed a book on Korean musical instruments, *Han'guk akki torok* 韓國樂器圖録 (Illustrated Description of Korean Musical Instruments), in 1962.

Essays written after 1957 were collected and published in 1967 as *Han'guk ŭmak sŏsŏl* 韓國音樂序説 (Topics in Korean Music). To honor his sixtieth birthday in 1969, friends and colleagues presented him a remarkable *festschrift* in five languages, *Umakhak nonch'ong* 音樂學論叢 (Essays in Ethnomusicology: A Birthday Offering for Lee Hye-ku). Dr. Lee gathered his shorter contributions (newspaper articles, reviews, etc.) in *Mandang munch'aerok* 晩堂文債録 (Essay Collection of Mandang [Lee Hye-ku]) in 1970. His most recent collection of articles, *Han'guk ŭmak nonch'ong* 韓國音樂論叢 (Essays on Korean Music), appeared in 1976.

I first met Dr. Lee in 1968, when I was in Korea on the federal involuntary travelling fellowship program. At that time, I knew no Korean language or music, and the impression made by this gracious man was an important factor in my decision to pursue the study of Korean music. I returned to Korea in 1973 with a Fulbright-Hays grant and some book knowledge of Korean language and culture. Dr. Lee welcomed me as a colleague rather than a student and gave unhesitatingly and generously of his knowledge, patiently correcting my endless mistakes and uninformed notions. We shared three "offerings of wine" at each session. These meetings with Dr. Lee were invaluable and often moving experiences; few young scholars can claim such treasured memories. It is largely as a tribute to these personal contacts with Dr. Lee that I undertook the preparation of this volume.

Translation of the articles presented a number of difficulties. I have always found Dr. Lee's articles informative and engaging in Korean, but their organization often results from the inspiration of the moment. One often feels that Dr. Lee's dedication to so many worthy causes has prevented him from spending an extra measure of time on organization and analytical approach in his writing, though the principal ideas, clearly, are fully formed. I soon discovered that literal renderings in English could neither reflect the nature of Dr. Lee's inspiration nor do justice to his achievements: a Western reader unfamiliar with Korea could well mistake apparent problems of organization for weakness of thought. For this reason, I undertook substantial editorial alterations, adding and omitting passages as necessary for Western readership. Explanatory phrases have been liberally inserted, terminology has been made consistent, and Western terms have been used when appropriate. Material which originally was duplicated in more than one article has been eliminated or abbreviated, and cross references have been added.

Since Chinese was the written language of Korea until the recent past and is still quoted frequently in scholarly writing, Dr. Lee often cites an orginal text without translation into modern Korean, much as Western musicologists pass around European languages and phrases with an assumption of common knowledge. It has been necessary here to translate both the Chinese original and any Korean commentary, a procedure which destroys the stylistic effect of the original scholarly technique. Those readers who can deal with the languages are encouraged to go to the original articles.

My editorial alterations in these articles are intended solely to transfer Dr. Lee's presentation to a more viable international format, and I have endeavored to leave his intentions and results intact. At the distance of half a globe, Dr. Lee and I have consulted on matters of presentation; although he has given his approval to all changes, the responsibility for any unwitting misrepresentations of his thought is mine.

Written between 1943 and 1974, these articles display a wide variety of styles. "Characteristics of Korean Music," for example, is rather an impressionistic account, while "*Chung-yŏngsan*" picks apart a piece almost note by note. Two of the articles were given to me in English ("A Short History of Korean Music" and "*Yukchabaegi*"), and these have been revised only slightly, for consistency of terminology.

Modes have been described with the movable-do system. Thus, a "fa-mode" is one with a Lydian scale structure, the tonic note being fa; any pitch may serve as fa. Romanization is according to the McCune-Reischauer system.

In the course of translation, I have been struck with the continuing freshness of this great scholar's work. It is unlikely that Dr. Lee will ever cease being youthful. His dedication to his rich cultural heritage and his qualities as a gentleman make him a humanist in the deepest sense of the word.

Robert C. Provine
Faculty of Music
University of Durham

Durham, England
October 1980

A SHORT HISTORY OF KOREAN MUSIC

THE EARLY PERIOD

The earliest literary source on Korean music is the chapter on Korea in the *San-kuo chih* (The History of the Three Kingdoms) by Chen Shou (-297 A.D.). According to it, in the state of Mahan (Southwest Korea) sacrifices were offered to the deities after the planting and the harvest, and people sang, danced and drank day and night. It may well have resembled the exuberant music still performed by peasants today with gongs and drums. The same source records that in the Pyŏnjin area (southern Korea) an indigenous string instrument resembling the Chinese *chu* was already in use. This earliest Korean string instrument must have fallen into disuse, however, by the time the *kayago* (*kayagŭm*) was invented in the state of Kaya (southern Korea) in the sixth century. The crude yet powerful music of the third century may well have its counterpart in the black, somewhat crude pottery excavated in the remains of Silla.

The mural paintings of Tomb No. 3 in Anak (bearing the inscribed date of 357 A.D.) depict several Chinese musical instruments. On one wall of the anteroom are represented a standing drum (*ku*), panpipes (*hsiao*), and a singer, characteristic of the ceremonial music (*ku-ch'ui*) of the Han dynasty. On the corridor wall a grand procession is painted. In the rear a band on horseback plays a drum, panpipes (*hsiao*), a horn (*chiao*) or aulos (*chia*), and a hand-bell (*nao*). This band may be said to represent a military band of the Han dynasty (*tuan-hsiao nao-ko*). On the wall of the rear room three seated musicians are shown accompanying a dancer with a zither (*kŏmun'go* or

1

cheng), a lute (*yüan-hsien*), and a long vertical flute. These wall paintings in Anak show that these Chinese musical instruments of the Han dynasty were used in north Korea. These musical instruments as well as the bronze jug with the long handle (*chiao-tu*) excavated in Korea are characteristic of Han culture. The *ku-ch'ui* music must have been adopted at the courts of the Three Kingdoms in Korea for the royal nobility, and the word *ku-ch'ui* is often found in the *History of the Three Kingdoms*.

PERIOD OF THE THREE KINGDOMS (UP TO 668 A.D.)

In the Koguryŏ period Wang San-ak invented a zither, the *kŏmun'go*. It is a remodelled Chinese *ch'in* which was sent to the court of Koguryŏ, presumably from Eastern Chin (317-420 A.D.). This four-stringed zither had about 16 frets which were struck with a pencil-like stick. It is represented on the wall of the Koguryŏ Tomb of the Dancers in T'ung-kou and is assumed to be the original *kŏmun'go*. Later the number of strings was increased to the present number of six.

King Kasil of the state of Kaya received the Chinese *cheng* and remarked that when the languages of the countries are different, the music cannot be one and the same. He thereupon invented the *kayago* using the *cheng* as a model, and ordered the musician U Rŭk to compose music for the new instrument. Later, when Kaya was about to fall, U Rŭk escaped with the *kayago* to the neighboring kingdom of Silla. The invention of the *kayago* must predate the year 551 A.D., when U Rŭk met King Chinhŭng of Silla. The old twelve-stringed *kayago* was little different from the one in use today. This is illustrated by the *kayago* held by a clay figure musician found in Kyŏngju and the *shiragi-koto* (Japanese for "Silla zither") preserved in the Shōsō-in at Nara, Japan.

The music and instruments of the Three Kingdoms were introduced to the Japanese court where, in 684 A.D., *Koma-gaku* (Japanese for "music of Koguryŏ"), *Kudara-gaku* (Japanese for "music of Paekche"), and *Shiragi-gaku* (Japanese for "music of Silla") were performed. The music of the Three Kingdoms must have been brought to Japan earlier, however, for in 554 A.D. (two years after the introduction of Buddhism to Japan from Paekche), four musicians from Paekche returned home from Japan and were replaced by others. According to the *Nihon Goki* (*History of Japan*), in the year 809 A.D. there were four teachers of Koguryŏ music in Japan, one for flute, one for *kunko* (presumably Japanese for *kŏmun'go*), one for *makumo* (not identified yet), and one for dance. Four Paekche musicians fulfilled the same role. But there were only two teachers of Silla music, one for *kin* (presumably Japanese for *kayago*) and one for dance. The difference between the musical instruments of Koguryŏ and Paekche and those of Silla seems to represent a general difference in culture. The tombs of Koguryŏ and Paekche have the same structure, while those of Silla are distinctly different.

However, after Buddhism was introduced into Koguryŏ from north China in 372 A.D., and to Paekche from south China in 384 A.D., the music of Koguryŏ and Paekche developed along less similar lines. This difference is recorded in the chapter on Korea in the *History of the Sui Dynasty* (*Sui-shu*, 622 A.D.). According to this chapter the musical instruments of Koguryŏ included the five-stringed lute (*wu-hsien-ch'in*) and the cylindrical oboe (*p'iri*), both of which are Central Asian in origin, though both were prevalent in north China before the Sui dynasty. On the other hand, the dominant musical instruments of Paekche were the harp (*k'ung-hou*) and, more significant, the flute with a mouthpiece (*ch'ih*) which is found only in the *ch'ing-yueh* music favored in south China. Further evidence of the separate evolutions of Koguryŏ and Paekche music can be seen in the fact that Koguryŏ musicians wore the boots typical of northern China, while Paekche musicians wore the shoes of southern China. Thus, Koguryŏ probably imported its musical instruments from north China, and Paekche from south China.

The five-stringed lute, the oboe, and the harp mentioned above are Indian or Central Asian instruments. The lute differs from the instruments of the Han dynasty represented on the walls of Tomb No. 3 in Anak, as well as from the four-stringed lute of the T'ang dynasty. The five-stringed lute was mistakenly called the Korean lute (*hyang-pip'a*) in contrast to the four-stringed lute (*tang-pip'a*), and the oboe was wrongly called the Korean *p'iri* (*hyang-p'iri*) in contrast to *tang-p'iri* which is shorter but thicker. The harp which came from Central

Asia through south China to Paekche and passed on to Japan was mistakenly called *kudara-koto* (Japanese for "Paekche zither)" in Japan. This error in nomenclature suggests that those musical instruments had already existed in Korea before the introduction of the musical instruments of the T'ang dynasty. This suggestion is confirmed by the passages in the *Sui-shu* mentioned above.

The music of Koguryŏ (*kao-li-chi*), enriched by these newly adopted Central Asian instruments, was played at the Sui court as one of the seven national types of music (*ch'i-pu-chi*) and subsequently as one of the nine kinds of music (*chui-pu-chi*), and continued to be performed at the T'ang court, there constituting one of ten national types of music (*shih-pu-chi*). The music of Paekche, incomplete compared with that of Koguryŏ, was not performed at the Chinese court until the T'ang dynasty and did not constitute one of the ten types of music (*shih-pu-chi*).

The music as well as the musical instruments of Central Asia must have been introduced to the Three Kingdoms, for by 612 a Paekche musician named Mimashi (in Japanese), who had learned the mask play (*gigaku* in Japanese) in south China (Wu), taught it at the Japanese court. The facial features (particularly the high noses) of the masks used in the mask play indicate their Central Asian origin. Moreover, the fact that the mask dances of Central Asian origin were called Korean music by Ch'oe Ch'i-won (857-) in his *Five Poems on Korean Music* (*Hyangak chabyŏng osu*) suggests that Central Asian music had already been in use before the new T'ang music reached Korea. The subjects of the five poems are as follows: (1) The lion dance is obviously of Hsiliang or Kueitsu origin. (2) *Soktok* (or *Sotoku,* the Japanese equivalent), a kind of Korean music played at the Japanese Court (*Koma-gaku*), probably means Sogdiana, one of the countries of Central Asia. (3) *Wŏljŏn*—described as a comic mime of drunkards fighting for wine—probably means Khotan, a country of Central Asia. (4) *Taemyŏn* is described as a man in a golden mask exorcizing evil spirits with a whip in his hand. It evidently means the *Ta-mien* of Northern Ch'i (550-577 A.D.). (5) *Kŭmhwan* is described as an acrobatic game of tossing up several balls and catching them one by one.

Kŭmhwan and *Taemyŏn* belonged to the *san-yueh* (entertainments) which, in China, were performed to the flute and the hourglass drum (*yao-ku*). In Japan the accompaniment of the Japanese *sotoku* (equivalent to the Korean *soktok*) included the oboe as well as these two instruments. Most dances in Korea today are performed to the fiddle (*haegŭm*), and the three instruments mentioned above. The poem, however, only mentions the drum as loud and lively. After all, a lively dance to lively music of Central Asian origin is as different from an elegant Chinese dance with soft music as the slender gilt bronze Buddhas of the period of the Three Kingdoms are different from the life-size statues of Buddha of the Unified Silla period.

UNIFIED SILLA PERIOD (669-936 A.D.)

The most important event in the musical history of this period is the importation of the new T'ang music, probably early in the ninth century. After its introduction T'ang music was performed together with Korean music until the period of the Yi dynasty. Strictly speaking, Chinese music of Koryŏ and Yi dynasties is the music of Sung China, but in a broad sense it is called T'ang music (*tangak*). Sources on T'ang music of this period are scant, and the music is no longer performed in Korea or China, although it can still be heard in Japan (*Tōgaku*). Before the importation of T'ang music, the four-stringed lute (*Tang pip'a*), the shorter and thicker oboe (*Tang p'iri*), the iron slabs (*fang-hsiang*), and the clapper (*p'o-pan*) were not used.

The oboe (*Tang p'iri*) and the iron slabs (*fang-hsiang*) have a range from *c* to *g'*. In comparison, the lowest tone of the Korean oboe is A^b. This suggests that T'ang music was played in a higher register. Judging from its function in the Koryŏ period, the clapper (*p'o-pan*) probably punctuated the phrases of Chinese music. Its phrasing and rhythm must have been regular and serene.

Korean music of this period combined Silla musical instruments and some of non-Silla origin: the former being the *kayago* and three sizes of the flute (*taegŭm*, *chunggŭm* and *sogŭm*), and the non-Silla instruments being the *kŏmun'go* of Koguryŏ, the five-stringed lute (*hyang-pip'a*) of Central Asia and the clapper (*pak*) of T'ang China. The use of the clapper in Korean music suggests that the music of Unified Silla was sophisticated, and the use of the *kŏmun'go* indicates that it still preserved its power. This Korean music is quite different from the old Silla music which had used only the *kayago*. It is also to be noted that the long tradition of distinct classes of Korean music (*hyang-ak*) and T'ang music (*tangak*) begins from this period.

KORYŎ PERIOD (936-1392)

When King T'aejo founded the Koryŏ dynasty he inherited two Silla institutions: the *p'algwan-hoe*, a ceremony during which a priest (*hwarang*) prayed for the peace of the country, and the *yŏndŭng-hoe*, the Buddhist lantern-lighting ceremony. The two ceremonies, which were performed until the end of the Koryŏ dynasty, are important because they not only included Korean and T'ang music, but also preserved the associated dances and acrobatics (*paek-hŭi*).

However, the year 1116 A.D. stands out in the musical annals of Koryŏ. In that year Emperor Hui-Tsung of Sung sent *a-ak* (Chinese *ta-sheng ya-yüeh*) to King Yejong of Koryŏ. *A-ak* was performed for the first time in the Royal Ancestral Shrine with such rare instruments as the bronze bells (*pien-chung*), stone chimes (*pien-ch'ing*), trough (*chu*), and tiger (*yü*), among others. By 1188 A.D. this foreign archaic ritual music was mixed with the more familiar Korean music (*hyangak kyoju*), and it was not until the 15th century that the pure Chinese music was restored.

Another important event was the introduction into Korea of the music of the Sung dynasty which eventually replaced the T'ang music. By the tenth century Chinese musicians and musical instruments had found their way to Koryŏ. In 1073 the group dances of the Sung dynasty, *T'a-sha-hang* and *P'ao-ch'iu-yüeh*, were incorporated into the *yŏndŭng-hoe* and the *p'algwan-hoe* at the Koryŏ court. The latter, a dance game during which balls are thrown through a hole in a gate-like frame, is still performed. In 1076 T'ang music used iron slabs (*fang-hsiang*), lute (*p'i-pa*), mouth organ (*shêng*), flute (*T'ang-ti*), oboe (*p'iri*), hourglass drum (*changgo*) and clapper (*p'o*), most of which are the same as those of Unified Silla. The musical instruments sent by King Hui-Tsung of Sung to Koryŏ in 1116 included such rare instruments as the stone slabs (*shih fang-hsiang*) and the two-stringed instrument (*shuang-hsien*), as well as special musical instruments for *a-ak,* such as the flute with mouthpiece (*ch'ih*), panpipes (*hsiao*) and the globular flute (*hsün*).

All the Chinese music performed at the Koryŏ court was music for *tz'u* (a form of poetry in irregular lines). The *History of Koryŏ* records forty-one Chinese *tz'u* and no other Chinese poems. Of these, eight poems have been identified as the work of the Chinese poet Liu Yung (eleventh century), a fact which helps date the introduction of *tz'u* music into Koryŏ. The poem *Loyang-ch'un,* consisting of two four-line stanzas, was written by the Chinese poet Ou-Yang Hsiu (1000-1072), and its music is notated in *Sogak wŏnbo,* an 18th century music book. Eight columns of Korean notation are set regularly to one line of the poem, with the clapper regularly providing punctuation in the fourth and eighth columns. Each column of notation is usually set to one syllable of the text, except for the eighth column, which is a prolonga-tion of the preceding note of the seventh column. Therefore, the Chinese music may be called syllabic, or at most, neumatic. Chinese *tz'u* music has neither a prelude nor an interlude.

Korean music of the Koryŏ dynasty is included in old music notations such as the *Taeak hubo* and the *Siyong hyangak-po.* Accord-ing to them, Korean poems are composed of either three (e.g. *Kasiri*) or five lines (e.g. *Ch'ŏngsan pyŏlgok*) instead of the customary four lines found in Chinese poems, and have an irregular number of syllables to the line. In Korean music the clapper is struck at the beginning of the phrase, while in Chinese music it is struck at the end of the phrase. The rhythm of Korean music is much more irregular. In Korean music the cadence drops gradually to the lowest note (an octave below the central tone), while in Chinese music the last note is drawn out. Korean music has, with only a few exceptions, a prelude and an interlude.

The Chinese court dances such as *P'ao-ch'iu-yüeh* were performed as follows. Two pole bearers (*chu-kan-tsu*) heralding the dance troupe proceed to the king, accompanied by the orchestra. As soon as they take their positions in front of the king, the orchestra stops. They then recite the name of the dance to be performed, whereupon the dance begins, accompanied by the orchestra. The dancers interrupt the dance and sing a song without accompaniment, then resume the dance until the pole bearers announce the end of the dance. Thereupon they retreat.

On the other hand, Korean court dances such as *Tongdong* begin with dancers prostrating themselves in front of the king. Accompanied by the orchestra, the still prostrate dancers raise their heads and sing a song that prays for the happiness of the king. Then they rise and dance without interruption, accompanied by the orchestra and a female chorus. At the end the dancers again prostrate themselves in front of the king and then retreat.

Korean music and dance alternated with Chinese music and dance at royal banquets. Korean music of the Koryŏ dynasty couples simple but noble Chinese music with its own lively music. This liveliness of Korean music is largely a result of the irregular rhythm. The florid Korean song with orchestral accompaniment may be compared with the beautiful decorations of Koryŏ celadons.

EARLY YI DYNASTY (1392-1593)

At the beginning of the Yi dynasty, Koryŏ music was still largely used. However, from the reign of King Sejong, when Confucianism began to exercise great influence, some modifications were introduced. Confucianism drew much attention to *a-ak*, a form believed to have been brought to perfection in the Chou dynasty, the golden age. The exploration of the works of the Chinese scholar Chu Hsi (1130-1200) led to the study of Ts'ai Yüan-ting's *A New Treatise on Regulating the Pitch Pipes* (*Lü-lü hsin-shu*, 1174-1189) in 1430. This, in turn, stimulated an unsuccessful attempt to determine the pitch of *huang-chung*. However, many musical instruments for *a-ak*, e.g. the bronze bells (*pien-chung*), stone chimes (*pien-ch'ing*), zithers (*ch'in* and *se*), mouth organ (*shêng*), and panpipes (*hsiao*), which had hitherto been imported, were now made in Korea. The *a-ak* of the Koryŏ dynasty which had contained elements of Korean music was completely purified. *Yang* (male) tones and *yin* (female) tones had mistakenly been used for the orchestra on the terrace (*teng-ko*) and the orchestra on the ground (*hsüan-chia*) respectively, and this was corrected. Even the very music of *a-ak*, the source of which was obscure, was questioned as to its authenticity and was finally replaced by Lin Yü's music for the temple of Confucius, which is preserved in the *Chronicles of King Sejong* (*Sejong Sillok*). The *a-ak* perfected under King Sejong continues to be performed today. The *t'zu* music which had hitherto been used for court ceremonies was also replaced by *a-ak* based on the music from *A General Survey of Ritual* (*I-li ching-chuan t'ung-chieh*). However, the use of *a-ak* for court ceremonies was short-lived. *T'zu* music was soon reestablished.

Confucianism not only contributed to the perfection of *a-ak*, but also changed the concept of music in general: music should not be merely pleasant to the ear, but should also be healthy for the mind. With these criteria the Chinese *tz'u* msuic of the Koryŏ dynasty was re-examined. Most of these Chinese songs were love songs. Several of them, for example *Shui-lung-yin*, *Hsia-yun-feng*, and *I-ch'ui-hsiao*, were accepted because they were regarded as more or less conforming to the Confucian ethic. Their original texts, however, were abolished and poems from the *Shi-ching* were substituted for singing at the royal banquet.

The Korean songs of the previous dynasty which sang of love were rejected as unfit for the formal ceremony at the court. In some cases only the text was rewritten and the music left untouched (e.g. *Manjŏn-ch'un*), and in some cases where the text was changed from Korean into Chinese, the music was also slightly changed (*e.g. Ssang-hwa-gok*).

In addition to the already existing songs, new songs were written. After the Korean alphabet was invented in 1443, the long poem *Flying Dragons Rule the Heavens* (*Yongbi-ŏch'ŏn-ga*) was written in the Korean alphabet and printed in 1447 and sung by many people. The "dragon" is a symbol for a great man destined to be king: "flying up" means ascending to the throne, and "rule the heaven" means ruling the country. The song describes the difficulties of founding the dynasty and concludes by charging its dynastic successors to develop it. This Korean poem was set to two different melodies: one called *Ch'i-hwap'yŏng* (in three movements), the other *Ch'uip'unghyang* (in a single movement). Both of them are pentatonic and in *p'yŏngjo* (*sol* mode). The same poem translated into Chinese was set to Chinese music (hexatonic) and called *Yŏmillak* (meaning "the king shares the pleasures with his people"). While the former two songs are no longer sung, the latter is still performed today in an orchestral version.

Pot'aep'yŏng is a song suite which praises the civil achievements of the kings of the Yi dynasty, and *Chŏngdaeŏp* is a song suite which praises their military achievements. Both of them were written in Chinese during the reign of King Sejong. The music for these songs was borrowed from already existing Korean songs or *ku-ch'ui* music. For example the melodies of *Hwat'ae* and *Sunŭng* of *Chŏngdaeŏp* were borrowed from the music of *Sŏgyŏng pyŏlgok* and *Manjŏnch'un* of the Koryŏ dynasty. *Pot'aep'yŏng*, consisting of eleven songs, all in *p'yŏngjo*, and *Chŏngdaeŏp*, consisting of fifteen songs all in *kyemyŏnjo* (*la* mode), were shortened and adopted as the music for the Royal Ancestral Shrine in 1464. They are still performed today. In addition to its function as ritual music, *Huimun* from *Pot'aep'yŏng* is appreciated as art music today.

All six pieces mentioned above were notated in the *Chronicles of King Sejong*. This musical notation (fifteenth century), comprised of columns of thirty-two squares (each square representing one metrical unit), is the earliest mensural notation in Korea and is still in use today, although since the reign of King Sejo the 32-square columns have been divided into two columns of 16 squares each.

In 1493 the first treatise on music (*Akhak kwebŏm*) was written. It covers the theory of music (the determination of tones), the arrangement of the orchestral players, choreography, musical instruments, costumes and properties. Its detailed descriptions and the illustrations made it possible to restore the old music after the court musicians had fled to the countryside and the musical instruments had been destroyed at the time of the Japanese invasions at the end of the 16th century.

During the first half of the Yi dynasty the theory of music was mastered, mensural notation was invented, and a treatise on music was published. Moreover, the simple but noble *a-ak* was brought to perfection, and Korean music was influenced by the Confucian ideal of simplicity.

LATER YI DYNASTY (1593-1910)

Although the old court music was eventually restored, the new orchestra for *a-ak* was much smaller than the old one. The orchestra for Chinese music (*tangak*) was no longer separated from the orchestra for Korean music (*hyangak*) in the manner of east and west, but the two were merged (*hyangdang kyoju*). The Chinese *tz'u* music still in existence includes the pieces *Pu-hsu-tsu* and *Loyang-ch'un*. The former contains so many figurations that it is hard to identify the original melody as Chinese except for its intervals and heptatones, while the latter, being performed during the court ceremony, underwent less change, but is no longer performed as notated in *Sogak wŏnbo*. Its rhythm was irregular and a few figurations were added to the original notes. Thus the two Chinese pieces are close to the Korean musical style.

On the other hand, Korean court music underwent a great deal of change. The music for the Royal Ancestral Shrine, orginally Korean music, was changed to Chinese style. The Korean instruments *kŏmun'go* and *kayago* were excluded from the orchestra and consequently Chinese instruments such as the bronze bells, the stone chimes, the trough (*chu*), and the tiger (*yü*) acquired a more prominent position. The music was more or less changed into the Chinese syllabic style (compare for example *Sogak wŏnbo* and *Taeak hubo*). Korean music, influenced by the Confucian ideal, was not supposed to be played fast. Thus Korean court music, especially *Chŏngŭp* (or *Sujech'ŏn*) with its long melody, its sustained notes, its subtle dynamics, and the special orchestral color produced by *yŏnŭm* (equivalent to antiphone) is characterized by majesty and magnificence.

However, outside the court, Korean music tended to be fast, emotional and informal. *Yŏngsan hoesang*, originally a Buddhist chant, was transformed into an instrumental ensemble. To the original music (*Pon-yŏngsan*) was added its variations (*Chung-yŏngsan, Chan-yŏng-san,* and *karak tŏri*). Later popular dance music (*Samhyŏn todŭri, Hahyŏn, Yŏmbŭl, T'aryŏng* and *Kunak*) was added to these four movements. A still later addition was the fast and gay music (*kyemyŏn karak todŭri, Yangch'ŏng* and *Ujo karak todŭri*). Thus, the chamber music begins with dignity and ends with humor.

The lyric song, *kagok*, is the only song which retained the old style. Its rhythmic pattern and cadential formula were the same as those in the old musical notations. The original song notated in *Taeak hubo* (15th century) was very slow and leisurely (*kin hanip*). To this the moderate (*chung hanip*) and the more or less fast song (*chajin hanip*) were added. However, from the early 19th century the slow song was considered old-fashioned and was discontinued. In the late 19th century the moderate song shared the same fate, and only the comparatively fast songs survive today. Later on, songs in faster tempo and songs in popular style were added to the original songs. They freely sang of love with a sense of humor.

Another lyric song, the *sijo*, which adopted the text of the *kagok* but discontinued the melismatic style, was loved by the literati. The earliest *sijo* music is included in a work for the dulcimer, *Kura ch'ŏlsa-kŭmbo* by Yi Kyu-gyŏng (early 19th century).

The long dramatic song, *p'ansori*, sung by lower class musicians (*kwangdae*), was prevalent in southern Korea in the early 18th century. It was first mentioned in the *Manhwa-jip* (1754). Of the twelve songs the story of *Ch'unhyang* is the most popular due to its dramatic story: a virtuous girl named Ch'unhyang, rejecting the amorous overtures of the local magistrate, was about to be executed, when she was rescued by her lover who returned from the capital as a secret inspector. This dramatic song which freely expressed human passion gained a great deal of popularity.

The solo music for *kayago* (*kayago sanjo*) has been ascribed to Kim Ch'ang-jo (ca. 1842-1897). Though it consists of slow, moderate and fast movements according to the classical style, its music is as expressive as the dramatic song, and therefore it may be called the instrumental version of the dramatic song.

The second half of the Yi dynasty was thus characterized by the rise of popular music which combined dignity with much humor.

CHARACTERISTICS OF KOREAN MUSIC

There are two basic categories of Korean music: the first, including such types as ancient aristocratic music (*chŏngak* 正樂) and ritual music (*a-ak* 雅樂), is serene, with emotion restrained; the other, including such types as story-singing (*p'ansori* 판소리) and folksong (*minyo* 民謠), is passionate and given to free emotional expression.

I

The special character of aristocratic music derives largely from its slow and nonpulsatile rhythm. Generally speaking, a slow melody is leisurely, like a flock of clouds floating in the sky; it is not always melismatic, and a long drawn-out melody is like a breeze sweeping over fields.

Sang-yŏngsan 上靈山 , the first movement of the chamber suite called *Yŏngsan hoesang* 靈山會相, basically has a tempo of twenty-five beats per minute. This would be a metronome setting of 25, or a tempo almost twice as slow as 40, the normal lowest metronome setting. As a performance continues through the several movements of this suite, the tempo picks up to about M.M. 45, still only slightly faster than the metronome's lowest setting.

It is said that the orchestral piece *Haeryŏng* 解令 is in a slow, free rhythm, expressed as sixteen breaths. The tempo of such slow music is indeed more easily grasped if measured by breaths rather than strict pulsations. In the introductory words to the notation book for the *kŏmun'go* 玄琴 (six-string zither) called *Hakp'o kŭmbo* 學圃琴譜 , the ten beats of the slowest piece of *kagok* 歌曲 (aristocratic vocal chamber music), *Isudaeyŏp* 二數大葉 , are indicated as five breaths. This source cites a work on medicine which says that one breath of an adult male corresponds to six heartbeats. In the abovementioned *Sang-yŏngsan,* one rhythmic pattern consists of twenty beats, and it is said that the *p'iri* 觱篥 (oboe) player performs it mostly in four breaths; this comparison allows us to recognize the genuine slowness of the music.

Music which is slow to this extent requires a special hand technique, just as in the case of drawing huge strokes with a writing brush, not a pen, in gigantic calligraphy. First of all, a long, drawn-out note normally commences with a strong appoggiatura, just as the calligrapher begins his long lines with a sharp jab of the brush onto the paper. In the case of *Yŏngsan hoesang,* mentioned above, a *kŏmun'go* solo extends for ten introductory beats. The first real melody note is a low B^b (*tung* 둥), but it is preceded with a strong *ssŭl* 슬(open first string, E^b) and *ki* (E^b an octave higher), which lasts only a fraction of a beat. The *Yanggŭm sinbo* 梁琴新譜 , a *kŏmun'go* handbook of 1610, explains that one must go by way of the open first string so that the tone can slow down. In fact, the very slow *Sang-yŏngsan* has eighteen such open first-string appoggiaturas, and the comparatively fast movement *Karak tŏri* has only two.

Second, the production of a drawn-out note might be compared to the strength required for lifting a heavy object from the earth over one's head. When we say a *sijo* 時調 (lyric song with long notes predominant) is weighty and leisurely, what we mean by "weighty" is like lifting a heavy object: the movement requires great strength if it is done slowly. Thus, the long-held note is quite the opposite of lethargic or languid, but rather like the wind sweeping smooth fields; it acquires strength like the sound of huge waves driving onto a beach.

Just as a long, bold stroke of the writing brush has variations in width, a long, drawn-out note is accompanied by dynamic shading. That is, when the brush first attacks the paper, there is great strength; the line begins wide and copiously inked. As it proceeds, the line gradually weakens, becoming thinner and weaker in coloration; but from the middle of the line toward the end, it again widens and thickens. This is like singing two tones in one breath. An example is *sijo*, where the first five beats are sung in a single breath: the first three beats have one pitch emphasized with great strength, like lifting a heavy object over the head, beginning *sforzando* and diminishing to *piano;* after this, another pitch is on the next two beats, and, like returning the heavy object from overhead back to the ground, the strength diminishes and the energy of the tone is dispersed in vibrato. If we compare this singing of two tones in one breath to a slow-motion movie of a pole vault, the first tone starts when the pole is thrust into the ground, being sung with great strength. The long, spread-out first note corresponds to the jumper approaching the bar, the grace of his motion being like the note's dynamic shading. Like the relaxation of the jumper passing over the bar and returning to ground level, the second tone is sung with less tension. The end of the tone comes in slow vibrato, like the impact of the feet of the jumper touching earth while his motion subsides.

Further, in the abovementioned *sijo,* a tone which stretches over five beats forms a slight arch, the summit being a melodic height of about 3/4 tone at the second beat. In the case of the writing brush making a huge stroke, the resultant line tends to have a slight convexity like the entasis of a column in Greek architecture. That is, when a single tone lasts through an entire breath, the end is weaker than the beginning, and because this would leave the impression of falling pitch, the actual pitch of a long tone is raised slightly in the middle to avoid this suggestion.

Music with this degree of slowness, only one or two notes to a breath, is simple in terms of melodic pitch motion, but it substitutes a special beauty in its subtle dynamic and microtonal shading.

Finally, this kind of music with a slow tempo ends abruptly. For example, in the three sections (lines) of a *sijo,* the last tone of the first section is drawn out for over five beats, "like a wisp of smoke from a solitary lamp". The final tone of the second section is drawn out over two beats, but then sinks down a fourth on the third beat, like "a sea gull gliding down on a sandy beach." The final tone of the last section, however, just drops abruptly a fourth, "like a heavy boulder." Quite the opposite of this slow music with an abrupt final note is the comparatively long note used to conclude pieces of folk music, in which a beat length ranges from M.M. 80 to 200.

In contemplating this music in slow tempo with long tones, subtle dynamic and microtonal shading, and gentle changes in nuance, one finds it possible to forget the disease of modern life with its sick hurry. One thinks of music such as the chamber suite *Yŏngsan hoesang*, like the tolling of a bell in a distant Buddhist monastery, *T'aep'yongga* 太平歌, a vocal duet singing of the harmony in Elysium; the lyrical *sijo*, like a swelling wave; dignified court orchestral music, *Sujech'ŏn* 壽齊天 , like a moutain with its peak shining serene in the sun above the cloud of passion.

II

The preceding type of music, which restrains emotion, has a slow tempo, like the swell of a wave, as an important characteristic. However, passionate Korean music is characteristically fast, like the rushing, dashing, thumping, bumping, swirling, whirling cataract. Of course, even among the folksongs there are some plaintive songs, like the *Arirang* 아리랑 from the *Chŏngsŏn* 旌善 locality, which have a tempo as slow as M.M. 40, but normally the range is from M.M. 80 to M.M. 200. For the most part, folksongs come in pairs, one slow and one fast; the slow one has a tempo around M.M. 80 and the fast one may be as fast as M.M. 200.

For example, there is a folksong sung during rice planting activities in the southern area, slow *Nongbuga* 農夫歌 , which has a tempo of M.M. 92 for each beat. After this song is a fast *Nongbuga* with a tempo of M.M. 198. In other words, many Korean folksongs are written in triple meters; the slower ones, in the rhythmic pattern *chungmori* 중모리 (moderate 3/4), use one breath for each occurrence of the rhythmic pattern. For the fast ones, in the rhythmic pattern *chajinmori* 자진모리 (fast 12/8), two occurrences of the rhythmic pattern require a single breath.

In this fast music, unlike the slow music discussed above, clear rhythm and meter emerge. On the other hand, this fast music cannot have the same sort of subtle dynamic and microtonal shading as the slow music. Rather than variations in dynamic shading, the fast music characteristically derives its vital strength from variations in rhythm.

The most complex rhythms are to be found in the dramatic music called *p'ansori*. In this genre, a single vocalist presents a long story (such as the well-known Ch'un-hyang 春香 or Sim Ch'ŏng 沈清 stories) through song, speech, and gesture; one other person, a drum player, accompanies. One example of tremendous rhythmic variety takes place when the performers describe the appearance of the inspector in the course of the Ch'un-hyang story. In order to explain the nature of the music, it is necessary briefly to introduce the scene.

Dressed in threadbare clothes, a royal inspector manages to get in amongst the local officials sitting at a banquet held to honor the birthday of the corrupt provincial magistrate who is the object of the royal inspection. When the inspector writes a poem with the line, "The golden goblet of sweet wine is the blood of a thousand people," the entire company recognizes the beggar as a royal inspector. Immediately, the faces of all the local officials turn pale; they frantically give orders for welcoming preparations, and, frightened, they all rush off to their offices.

The music of this scene is set in the rhythmic pattern called *chajinmori*. This pattern consists of four beats with triple subdivision (12/8), and more than two patterns are sung with a single breath. The basic pattern is presented by the singer alone in the first line. This is because the singer and drummer do not have all performance matters worked out in advance, and the details of the story may change unpredictably; at the beginning of a song, therefore, the singer gives the first line in the basic rhythmic pattern as a cue to the drummer, who then begins accompanying at the second occurrence of the pattern.

The basic rhythmic pattern, in the case of a seven-syllable line of text, is a follows:

Example 1

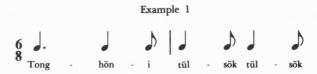

The basic rhythmic pattern when the royal inspector appears on the scene is that of Example 1. It is transformed in such a way that in the course of the song, which lasts for ninety-three occurrences of the pattern, the exact original version never once recurs.

For eight and six-syllable lines, the structures are as follows:

Example 2

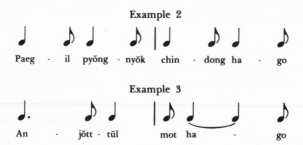

Paeg - il pyŏng - nyŏk chin - dong ha - go

Example 3

An - jŏtt - tŭl mot ha - go

The many transformations of the basic rhythmic structure may be divided into three types:

1) Music which starts not during a pattern, but on the first beat: Observe the caesura in the middle, varying only within the triplet subdivisions of the beats. For example:

Example 4.

Sa myŏn - ŭl tul - lŏ po - ni

Example 5

i - ri chŏ - ri ta - ni - nŭn - de

In this way, the triplet divided into long and short notes gives a bouncy, dancing effect. The following examples show division of the triplet into equal short notes, giving the impression of scurrying about rapidly.

Example 6

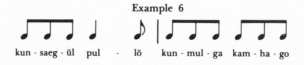

kun - saeg - ŭl pul - lŏ kun - mul - ga kam - ha - go

Example 7

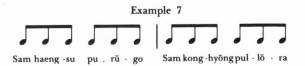

Sam haeng -su   pu . rŭ - go   Sam kong -hyŏng pul - lŏ - ra

In the above examples, each note represents one syllable of text. Accordingly, eleven notes are set to eleven syllables (Example 6). More generally speaking, fast Korean music belongs to a syllabic style; and in this sort of fast music, examples of a text syllable being set to two or three notes are rare. The rhythm of fast music is essentially the same as the rhythm of the text.

2) Music which does not start on the first beat:

Example 8

kak ch'ŏng - i   twi -   num - nŭn   -   da

Example 8, like Example 1, has three notes in the first half of the pattern, but as mentioned above, the exact rhythmic structure of Example 1 occurs only once in the piece. On the other hand, the exact rhythm of Example 8 occurs several times. In other words, the most common manner of setting the first three syllables of a seven-syllable line of text in *chajinmori* is with the first quarter-note time silent. The reason for this might be to allow the singer to take a breath; this is deduced on the basis of the following facts. In a song in *chajinmori*, a singer performs two to four rhythmic patterns without breathing, and there is no other purpose for having the silent beat than taking a breath.

Comparing Example 8, which has the silent opening quarter-note, with Example 1, both have the same number of syllables, three, in the first half of the rhythmic pattern. The time distance between the first and second notes has been diminished, producing an effect of somewhat greater speed. Accordingly, Example 1 is more like dance rhythm and Example 8 more like speech rhythm. This is also often evidenced by other passages in the story of Ch'un-hyang.

Thus, if the text has three syllables in the first half pattern, the first quarter-note is silent. Similarly, if there are two syllables, the entire first beat (dotted quarter) is left silent:

Example 9

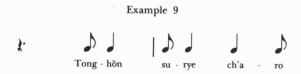

In exceptional cases, a three-syllable first half may be set neither like Example 1 nor 8, but as follows, with the full first beat silent:

Example 10

The rhythm of Example 10, of course, gives an impression of even greater speed than Example 8, and depicts the rapid flight of the *kisaeng*, "still with their arms open wide in dancing postures."

Finally, in cases where the first eighth note is silent and the singing starts on the second eighth note, the text has two syllables in the first full beat. Combined with two syllables in the second full beat, this almost gives an impression of duple rather than triple meter:

Example 11

This example gives the impression of being faster than Example 10; the rhythm well reflects the panic of the officials who, in their haste, are kicking and breaking drums and knocking over wine cups. If this text were set to the rhythm of Example 1, it would have to be rewritten from smashing drums to dancing a dance.

3) In the last type of rhythmic transformation, the central caesura

may be violated and even the entire metrical shape may be broken down. Only the drummer can sense the basic framework; he adheres to the four-beat framework, while the singer makes fundamental transformations.

An example of the violation of the central caesura follows:

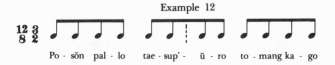

Example 12

Po - sŏn pal - lo   tae - sup' - ŭ - ro   to - mang ka - go

Here the twelve syllables of text are divided into three groups of four syllables each, not four groups of three, so that the resultant music has been changed from triple meter (12/8) to duple (3/2), destroying the central caesura. In this way, the driving rhythm of the steady series of rapid notes well matches the content of the text, "the local officials are panic-stricken and flee for a bamboo grove in their stocking feet." This passage is almost closer to speech than music. The caesura of the normal pattern is broken down by the driving rhythm, and this provides a musical comic touch, illustrating the frantic officials.

In the most extreme cases of this sort of transformation, even the length of the pattern can be broken down:

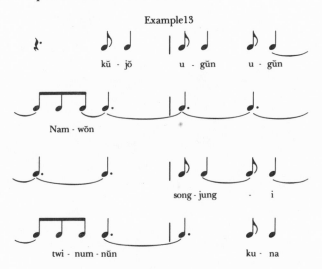

Example13

kŭ - jŏ   u - gŭn   u - gŭn

Nam - wŏn

song - jung - i

twi - num - nŭn   ku - na

Here the rhythmic chaos resulting from destruction of the fixed metric framework paints well the scene of confusion described in the text: "The whole town of Namwon was swaying from the wild swarming."

Thus, the fast-tempo rhythmic pattern *chajinmori* and its diverse transformations can paint the confused scene of attacking, running away, shouting, and yelling. It provides a great contrast to the previously described slow music with dynamic shading that was "like a mountain with its peak shining serene in the sun above the cloud of passion."

INTRODUCTION TO TRADITIONAL MUSIC NOTATION SYSTEMS

INTRODUCTION

Rhythm and pitch are treated more independently in traditional Korean notation systems than in Western staff notation. While there are several pitch notations from tablature (*Hapja-po*) to neumes (*Yŏnŭmp'yo*), depending on the genre involved, Korea has only a single mensural notation; due to its graphic construction, this mensural notation can be used in conjunction with almost all the various pitch notations.

As with all notation systems, there are problems of detail in the various Korean notations: the present article is intended only as an introduction to the types of notation and not as a guide to the interpretation of difficult passages. From time to time, reference will be made to written sources of Korean music, but they will not be described in detail. For bibliographic information on these sources, the reader is referred to the following publications:

1) Sŏng Kyŏng-nin 成慶麟 , "*Han'guk akpo haejae*" 韓國樂譜解題 , in *Han'guk yesul ch'ongnam (Charyo-p'yŏn)* 韓國藝術總覽 (資料篇) (Seoul, 1965), pp. 126-177.

2) Chang Sa-hun 張師勛 , "*Ko-akpo haejae*" 古樂譜解題 , in his *Kugak non'go* 國樂論攷 (Seoul, 1966), pp. 572-614.

3) Bang-song Song, *An Annotated Bibliography of Korean Music* (Providence, 1971), *passim*. (In English)

I. YULJA-PO 律字譜 (LETTER NOTATION)

Yulja-po uses twelve Chinese characters to indicate the twelve pitches in the octave. The twelve characters are taken from the Chinese names of the twelve pitches (*lu* 律) (pronunciations shown are Korean, not Chinese):

1.	*Hwangjong*	黃鐘	C
2.	*Taeryŏ*	大呂	C#
3.	*T'aeju*	太簇	D
4.	*Hyŏpchong*	夾鐘	D#
5.	*Kosŏn*	姑洗	E
6.	*Chungnyŏ*	仲呂	F
7.	*Yubin*	㽔賓	F#
8.	*Imjong*	林鐘	G
9.	*Ich'ik*	夷則	G#
10.	*Namnyŏ*	南呂	A
11.	*Muyŏk*	無射	A#
12.	*Ŭngjong*	應鐘	B

For pitch notation purposes, only the first character of each pair is used. This is an absolute pitch notation system, but historically the indicated pitches have changed considerably, and for convenience we have simply assigned *hwangjong* to C.

Example 1 is taken from the treatise *Akhak kwebŏm* 樂學軌範 (1493) 2.15b. The third lined column from the right, under the title *Hwangjong-kung* 黃鐘宮 , gives the pitches of a piece of ritual music; succeeding columns (i.e. to the left) show transpositions of the same piece to different pitch levels. In each case, the larger characters in the columns (read top to bottom, right to left) give the *Yulja-po* characters, 32 for each transposition. The smaller characters to the right of the *Yulja-po* are a second (Chinese) notation in a movable-*fa* solmization system (they are the same in all transpositions). The transcription shows only the first piece.

Example 1

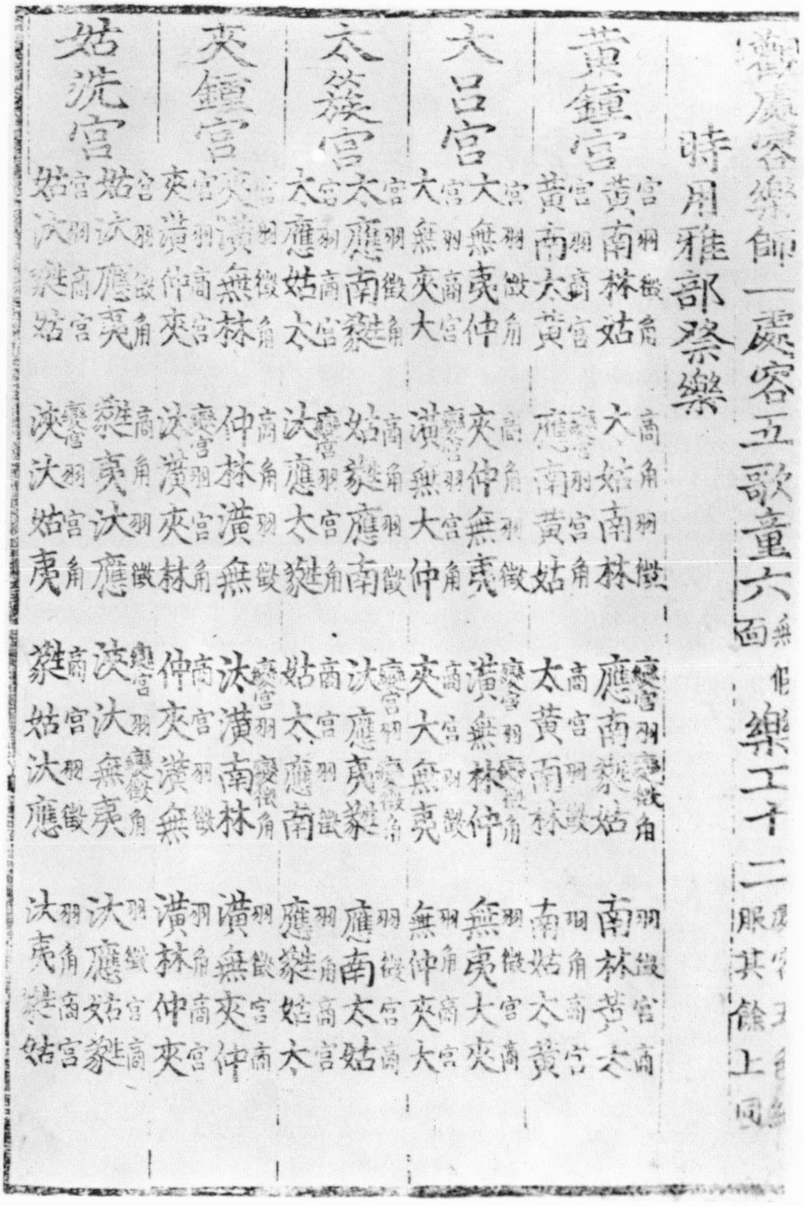

時用雅部祭樂

黃鍾宮

大呂宮

太簇宮

夾鍾宮

姑洗宮

Transcription 1

1)

Hwang Nam Im Ko

Yulja-po is a notation imported from China which has been used in Korea to notate ceremonial music of Chinese origin (*a-ak* 雅樂). It was also used to notate native court music (*hyangak* 鄉樂) in the *Annals* of King Sejong (*Sejong sillok* 世宗實録, covering the years 1418-1450). Shortly thereafter, however, *Yulja-po* was abandoned for the latter purpose; in the *Annals* of King Sejo (*Sejo sillok* 世祖實録, covering the years 1455-1468), it was replaced by *Oŭm yakpo* (Section III below). However, *Yulja-po* is being used even today for *a-ak*.

Yulja-po was apparently used only for court music, since there is no evidence that it was ever employed in folk music. Furthermore, when court musicians memorized pieces of court music, they used the *Yulja-po* syllables as a sort of solmization. But there were many errors: the syllables helped in the memorization process, like a song text, but were not accurately used as pitch indicators. Hence, it is clear that *Yulja-po* presented difficulties even for court musicians, and this may be the reason that King Sejo abolished its use in *hyangak*.

II. *KONGCH'ŎK-PO* 工尺譜
(SIMPLIFIED LETTER NOTATION)

Like *Yulja-po*, *Kongch'ŏk-po* is a letter notation, but with fewer and simpler symbols; as used in the *Akhak kwebŏm* and the *Annals* of King Sejo, the symbols are as follows:

hap	*sa*	*il*	*sang*	*ku*	*ch'ŏk*	*kong*	*pŏm*	*yuk*	*o*
合	四	一	上	勾	尺	工	凡	六	五
c;	c#, d;	d#, e;	f;	f#;	g;	g#, a;	a#, b;	c';	c#', d', d#';

Example 2 is taken from the *Annals* of King Sejo 48.3a. It shows several pieces of ritual music, or rather, several texts set to the same melody. The third column from the right gives the title of the first piece (*Yongsin* 迎神), the mode (*hyŏpchong-kung* 夾鐘宮, "E^b is *fa*"), and the number of repetitions (6). The next column gives the text of 16 syllables. The fifth column gives two pitch notations: *Yulja-po* on the right and *Kongch'ŏk-po* on the left. The remainder of the page gives three more texts set to the same music.

Example 2

(Transcription 2)

il   yuk pŏm ch'ok

As Example 2 implies, *hap* 合 is associated with *hwang* 黃 (c) of *Yulja-po*. In China, however, the *sa* was also associated with c# and d#, not being fixed. But in any case, it is clear that *Kongch'ŏk-po* was intended to indicate absolute pitches and was not a solmization system.

The first mention of *Kongch'ŏk-po* in Chinese sources is in the *Meng-shi pi-t'an* 夢溪筆談 (1093), written by Shen Kua 沈括 (1031-1095) of the Northern Sung 北宋 dynasty. The notation was used in China for popular music, but in Korea it was used rarely, and then only for ceremonial music and theoretical purposes. It is used in conjunction with *Yulja-po* to notate ritual melodies in the *Annals* of King Sejong and King Sejo. In Chapter 7 of the *Akhak kwebŏm*, it is utilized in the explanations of playing techniques for instruments used in performing *tangak* 唐樂 (Koreanized music of Chinese origin): *tang pip'a* 唐琵琶, *tang chŏk* 唐笛, *tang p'iri* 唐觱篥, and *t'ongso* 洞簫 . This may suggest that *tangak* was largely notated in *Kongch'ŏk-po*.

In *Kongch'ŏk-po*, the symbols 四, 一, 工, 凡, and 五 each stand for more than one pitch, so that, unlike *Yulja-po*, the notation is incapable of showing all pitches with equal precision. Since it has only eight symbols within the octave, it can only be used accurately for two *fa*-modes: the *hap* mode (合. 四. 一. 勾. 尺. 工. 凡) and the *sang* mode (上. 尺. 工. 凡. 合. 四. 一). For this reason, it must be used in conjunction with *Yulja-po* when notating melodies transposed to other pitches.

In the so-called *Minshin-gaku* 明清樂 ("Ming and Ch'ing music") preserved in Japan, *Kongch'ŏk-po* is employed. The mnemonic sounds they use for the symbols are: 乙 *yi*, 上 shang, 尺 ch'eh, 工 *k*ung, 凡 *f*an, 六 *l*iu, 五 *w*u, 合 *h*o, and 四 *s*su. In this mnemonic aspect, *Kongch'ŏk-po* is more convenient than *Yulja-po*.

III. *OŬM YAKPO* 五音略譜 *(SCALE DEGREE NOTATION)*

Beginning with the central (basic) tone *kung* (not to be confused with the *kung* of the Chinese notation *kung* 宮 (*fa*), *sang* 商 (*sol*), *kak* 角 (*la*), *ch'i* 徵 (*do*), and *u* 羽 (*re*)), the notes are indicated by a number and direction. Thus, the first scalar tone above *kung* is *sang il* 上一 ("above by one"), the second is *sang i* 上二 ("above by two"), and so forth, using the Chinese numerals *il* 一 (1), *i* 二 (2), *sam* 三 (3), *sa* 四 (4), and *o* 五 (5).

Sang o 上五 ("above by five") is the note an octave above *kung*. The pitches below *kung* are notated in similar fashion, using *ha* 下 ("below") instead of *sang*. In other words, the notation corresponds to the cipher notation 1.2.3.4.5.6.7 in common use today.

Example 3, from the *Annals* of King Sejo 48.17a, shows part of the piece *Huimun* 熙文. The page contains three sets of five columns each (for the rhythmic meaning of the squares, see Section VII below). The first (right) column in each set shows, in *Oŭm yakpo*, the melody played by string instruments; the second gives the part played by wind instruments; the third contains drum strokes; the fourth has the part of the wooden clappers, *pak* 拍; and the last column gives the text. The transcription is of only the string instruments' melody.

Example 3

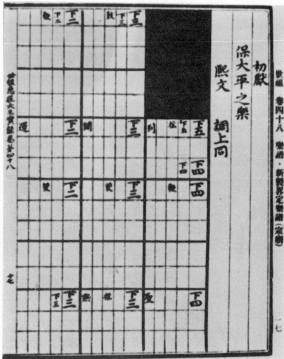

Transcription 3

Thus, *Oŭm yakpo* can notate only five notes in the octave. While Chinese music (*a-ak* and *tangak*) is heptatonic, native Korean music (*hyangak*) is pentatonic, and it is the latter for which *Oŭm yakpo* is appropriate. The *Annals* of King Sejo occasionally use *Oŭm yakpo* for notating music of Chinese origin, like *P'unganjiak* 豊安之樂 (48.14b-16b), and borrows the symbols 一 and 凡 from *Kongch'ŏk-po* to fill in the remaining two notes of the scale.

In *Yulja-po* and *Kongch'ŏk-po*, it is necessary to be able to read Chinese characters, but even court musicians were not always sufficiently educated. On the other hand, *Oŭm yakpo* gives relative pitches by number and is readable at a glance. Its convenience is its strong point, but since it has only five pitches per octave, it is less complete than the other two notations.

Two things must be known before *Oŭm yakpo* can be deciphered: 1) the pitch (absolute) of *kung*, which is usually specified at the beginning of the piece in a prescription like "*hwangjong-kung*" 黃鐘宮 ("*kung* is *C*"); and 2) the mode of the piece, since the scalar intervals vary according to whether the piece is in *p'yŏngjo* 平調 (*do*-mode) or *kyemyŏnjo* 界面調 (*re*-mode):

		do	re	fa	sol	la	do
p'yŏngjo:	宮	上一	上二	上三	上四	上五	
		Maj 2	min 3	Maj 2	Maj 2	min 3	

		re	fa	sol	la	do	re
kyemyŏnjo:	宮	上一	上二	上三	上四	上五	
		min 3	Maj 2	Maj 2	min 3	Maj 2	

In *p'yŏngjo*, the intervals 宮 to 上一 and 上三 to 上四 are major seconds, but they are minor thirds in *kyemyŏnjo*. Unless the mode is given, therefore, it is impossible to know the correct intervals.

Originally conceived in the reign of King Sejo (1455-1468), *Oŭm yakpo* was used in the *Annals* of King Sejo, the *Taeak hubo* 大樂後譜 (1759), *Siyong hyangak-po* 時用鄉樂譜 (early 16th century?), *Isu samsan chaebon kŭmbo* 二水三山齋本琴譜 (17th century, lost in the Korean war), and *An Sang kŭmbo* 安瑺琴譜 (1572). It came to be replaced in the *kŏmun'go* 玄琴 books (*kŭmbo* 琴譜) by tablature (*Hapcha-po*; see Section V), remaining only as a notation for the flute *chŏk* 笛 (see Example 4 below). Later on, it disappeared from use entirely.

IV. *YUKPO* 肉譜 *(MNEMONIC NOTATION)*

According to the *Annals* of King Sejo, "Formerly there was only the use of mnemonic sounds, called the *Yukpo*. There is an individual set for each of the following instruments: *pip'a* 琵琶, *kŏmun'go* 玄琴, *kayagŭm* 伽倻琴, *chŏk* 笛, and *p'iri* 觱篥. The complexities are difficult to comprehend, and there is no notation for vocal sounds." (48.1b). *Yukpo*, then, is a set of mnemonic sounds imitating the sounds of the instruments being notated.

Example 4, from the now lost *Isu samsan chebon kŭmbo*, shows *Yukpo* for *kŏmun'go* and *chŏk* in the beginning of the piece *Mandaeyop* 慢大葉. The first column, on the right, gives tablature for the *kŏmun'go* (see Section V); the second, *Yukpo* for *kŏmun'go*; the third, *Oŭm yakpo* for the *chŏk*; the fourth, *Yukpo* for *chŏk*; and the fifth, the singer's text. The sets of five columns are then repeated twice in this example.

Even today such mnemonic sounds are used, as follows:

> *Kŏmun'go* and *kayagŭm*: *tŏng* 덩, *tung* 둥, *tang* 당, *tong* 동, and *ting* 딩.
> *P'iri*: *rŏ* 러, *ru* 루, *ra* 라, *ro* 로, and *ri* 리, often pronounced *nŏ* 너, *nu* 누, *na* 나, *no* 노, and *ni* 니.
> *Haegŭm* 奚琴: *ka* 가, *ke* 게, *ki* 기, etc.
> *Taegŭm* 大笒: *tte* 떼, *ru* 루, *tta* 따, *tto* 또, etc.

Example 4

Transcription 4

In each case, the vocal sounds resemble the sounds of the particular instrument; in other words, there is a separate set of *Yukpo* for each instrument.

The modern syllables used for the hammerdulcimer *yanggŭm* 洋琴 and their corresponding pitches are as follows: *hŭng* 흥 (A^b), *tung* 틍 (B^b), *tŭng* 틍 (c), *tang* 당 (e^b), *tong* 동 (f), *chi* 지 (g^b), *ching* 징 (a^b), *tang* 당 (b^b), *tong* 동 (c'), *ti* 디 (d^b'), *ting* 딩 (e^b'), *t'ing* 팅 (f'), and *tchong* 쫑 (a^b').

The example of the *yanggŭm* might seem to indicate that a fairly strict correspondence exists between syllable and pitch. But if we examine, for example, the *Yukpo* for *kŏmun'go* in the *Yanggŭm sinbo* 梁琴新譜 (1610), it is clear that the syllables *tang* 당, *tong* 동, *ting* 딩, and so forth refer to more than one pitch each. *Tang*, for example, can refer to both the note produced at the 4th fret of the second string (e^b) and the note produced at the 5th fret of the third string (B^b).

Also, *Yukpo* does not refer to scale degrees like *Oŭm yakpo*, since it is inconsistent in this regard. It might be thought that the syllables refer to playing techniques, such as the fingers of the left hand used to press a string at a fret: for example, *tang* is used when the ring finger presses the second string at the 4th fret (e^b), or 5th fret (f), or 7th fret (a^b). But there are also strong counter examples: in the *Yanggŭm sinbo*, the thumb pressing the second string at the 6th fret (g) is called *tong* ten times and *ting* twenty times. *Yukpo* is also not a tablature. The *Annals* of King Sejo were quite correct in saying that "the complexities are difficult to comprehend."

Fortunately, *Yukpo* was normally used in conjunction with another notation, usually *Hapcha-po* (Section V), which clarifies the pitch (as in Example 4). Most likely, its mnemonic nature provided an aid to memorization, and this is the manner in which it survives in the folk tradition today.

The origins of *Yukpo* are unclear. Due to its nature, it is unlikely that it was in some way derived from another known notation system such as *Yulja-po* or *Kongch'ŏk-po*. Similar notations exist in Japan for the *shakuhachi* 尺八 (ro, tsu, re, ch'i, ri, hi), *samisen* 三味線 (ten, tsuru, shan), and *koto* 箏 (ton, shan, tsun, ten). It is unclear at this point whether there are any connections between the Korean and Japanese systems (there are some similar syllables) or whether the notation was invented in Korea and exported to Japan.

V. HAPCHA-PO 合字譜 (TABLATURE)

The *Akhak kwebŏm* indicates that there was *Hapcha-po* for *kŏmun'go, kayagŭm, tang pip'a,* and *hyang pip'a*. Only that for *kŏmun'go* survives today. (There is *pip'a* tablature recorded in the *An Sang kŭmbo*, but it is essentially the same as that for *kŏmun'go*.) *Hapcha-po* gives playing instructions rather than pitch names; that is, it supplies information about the left hand (pressing strings onto frets) and right hand (plucking strings). This information is conveyed by simplified Chinese characters:

  A. Strings:

        文 : abbreviation of 文絃, 1st string
        方 : abbreviation of 遊絃, 2nd string
        大 : abbreviation of 大絃, 3rd string
        清 : abbreviation of 清絃, 4th or 5th string
        止 : abbreviation of 武絃, 6th string

  B. Frets:

        Chinese numerals indicate fret number: 一 (1), 二 (2), 三 (3), . . . up to 十六 (16).

  C. Left hand fingers:

        フ : left thumb
        イ : index finger
        レ : long finger
        タ : ring finger

D. Plucking:

     ➤ : play the string by pulling inward with the plectrum

     ✓ : play the string by pushing outwards with the plectrum

     ❘ : play the open 1st string, followed immediately by a stopped 2nd or 3rd string

     ∟ : arpeggio from the 1st string through the 6th string.

Example 5. from the *Yanggŭm sinbo* 13b shows the opening of the piece *Chungdaeyŏp* 中大葉 in the mode *ujo kyemyŏnjo* (see page 000). In each set of three columns, the middle one gives the *Hapcha-po*, the left one shows *Yukpo*, and the right one gives the Chinese solmization system mentioned above in Section III.

Example 5

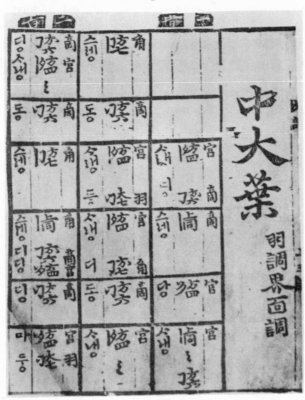

Transcription 5

The matter of the various *kŏmun'go* tunings is a complex one and will not be examined here. Clearly, it is necessary to know the appropriate tuning before transcribing *Hapcha-po*.

The introduction to the *An Sang kŭmbo* says, "If a person lives in a secluded area and wants to learn *kŏmun'go*, it may be difficult to get a teacher; but this notation book is just as good as having a teacher sitting in front of one and pointing things out. There are no difficulties." In other words, this is an understandable notation.

According to the *Oju yŏnmun changjŏn san'go* 五州衍文長箋散稿 (ca. 1840) (Chapter 20), Sŏng Hyŏn 成俔 (primary author of the *Akhak kwebŏm*) became director of the government music office, and together with the musician Pak Kon 朴楗 and the official Kim Pok-kun 金福根 , he quoted the ancient precepts, based on the *Shih-lin kuang-chih* 事林 廣記 (ca. 1270) and the *Ta-ch'eng yüeh-p'u* 大成樂譜 (1349). After careful consideration of these precepts and the structure of the *kŏmun'go*, they joined various characters to create the notation called *Hapcha-po*. Since that time, most *kŏmun'go* books have been notated with this system, and there have been various alterations and eliminations of symbols, probably due to the complicated nature of *Hapcha-po* in its full form.

VI. YŎNŬMP'YO 連音譜 (NEUMATIC NOTATION)

Yŏnŭmp'yo is a notation which graphically shows the rise and fall of the pitches and turns of a melody. It resembles the neumatic notation which was used for Gregorian chant and the Japanese notations for *Noh* singing (*Yōkyoku-fu* 謠曲譜), *Heike biwa* (*Heike biwa-fu* 平家琵琶譜),

and Buddhist chant (*Shōmyō-fu* 聲明譜). Of the Japanese notations, that for *Heike biwa* is closer to *Yŏnŭmp'yo* than that for *Noh* singing is.

Like some forms of Gregorian chant notation, *Yŏnŭmp'yo* seems to be more a memory aid than a precise notation, and transcription can only be tentative at best. *Yŏnŭmp'yo* was used only for vocal music. The symbols of the notation are as follows:

A. Symbols related to height of opening pitch:
  ╱ : opening high pitch (e.g., a^b)
  ╲ : opening low pitch (e.g., B^b)
  ◻ : opening level pitch (e.g., f)
    (above is true when central tone is e^b)

B. Symbols for two pitches:
  ᴜ̃ : from low with vibrato to high (e.g., from B^b with vibrato to f)
  ᴜ : from low without vibrato to high (e.g., from e^b to f)
  ᘔ : from low to high (e.g., from e^b to f at the beginning of phrase)

C. Other symbols:
  ⟩ : two notes are connected, no break between
  • : punctuation, phrasing
  ⋮ : addition of eight beats (one half-cycle of the rhythmic pattern)

Example 6, from a late 19th-century source of vocal texts called *Kagok wŏllyu* 歌曲源流 , shows *Yŏnŭmp'yo* placed to the right of the columns of text of Korean lyric songs called *kagok* 歌曲.

The imprecise nature of *Yŏnŭmp'yo* makes it clear that it was not a notation for beginning singers, but a shorthand method of prodding the memories of experienced singers. In the case of Gregorian chant, Guido (1050) added four lines to improve the precision of neumes, thereby setting the foundation for the modern staff notation. Such a development did not take place in Korea.

Example 6

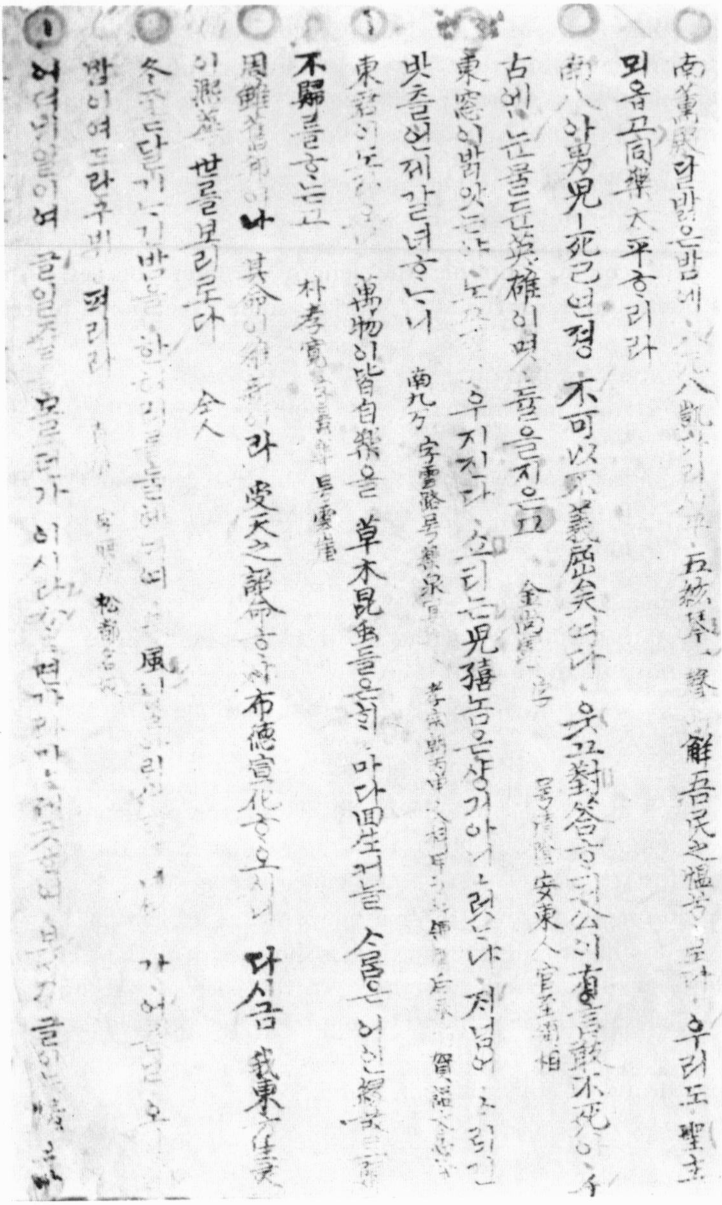

VII. *CHŎNGGAN-PO* 井間譜 *(MENSURAL NOTATION)*

Chŏnggan-po is a graphical notation made up of columns of small squares, read in the east Asian fashion of top to bottom, right to left. The time value of tones is shown by relating one beat to one square, and notation of pitches (in *Yulja-po, Hapcha-po*, etc.) is placed in the appropriate squares. Typically, there are 16 squares to a column, divided into a meter of $3+2+3+3+2+3$ beats. These six groupings of the beats are called the six *taegang* 大綱 . The early *Annals* of King Sejong have columns double the length of later sources, using 32 squares per column. In the later sources, some exceptional pieces have 20 squares per column.

Pieces do not always begin in the first square of a column, though they always begin in the first square of a *taegang*. The choice of beginning square varies from piece to piece and even from source to source for the same piece. This latter problem is one deserving more study. Examples 3, 4, and 5 above illustrate a few uses of *Chŏnggan-po*.

Before the invention of *Chŏnggan-po*, notations showed only pitch, not duration, so the results were very incomplete. The appearance of *Chŏnggan-po* in the mid-fifteenth century was indeed epochal, but it is unclear who invented it. The *Annals* of King Sejo attribute its invention to him, but the notation was already in use in the *Annals* of his father, King Sejong. Examples of a similar mensural notation exist in China, but only from much later date and substantially less developed. Nonetheless, it is possible that such a notation existed earlier in China and was exported to Korea; or perhaps the reverse was true.

In Europe, rhythmic notation began around the twelfth century and reached basically its present form in the fifteenth and sixteenth centuries. *Chŏnggan-po* first appeared in Korea in the *Annals* of King Sejong, showing copies of notations purportedly written down in 1447. To the author's knowledge, this precedes any other example of real mensural notation in east Asia.

Chŏnggan-po is a convenient notation, as it can be used in conjunction with any Korean pitch notation except *Yŏnŭmp'yo*. But it delivers much less rhythmic information than Western mensural notation, the primary deficiencies being the depiction of fast notes and the fact that the precise time value of a square is unknown.

CONCLUSIONS

In Europe, Guido improved the existing neumatic pitch notation in 1050 by adding a lettered four-line staff. By the twelfth century, mensural notation and the five-line staff configuration had been added. The theory and practice of mensural notation had become immensely complex by the sixteenth century, so in the seventeenth, bar lines were added to distinguish measures. That system served its purpose well and has continued to the present in basically the same format. Tablature disappeared at the beginning of the nineteenth century, and today only the five-line staff is used. Thus, in the West, improvement has been added to improvement, and the resultant notation reveals at a glance an intuitive grasp of the melodic and rhythmic structure of a piece of music. Because of this ability to yield an intuitive grasp of the music, staff notation is more effective than *Yulja-po, Kongch'ŏk-po, Yukpo,* and *Hapcha-po.* Because the pitches are precise, it is more exact than *Oŭm yakpo* or *Yŏnŭmp'yo.* Its precision in time values is better than *Chŏnggan-po.*

At first, Korean notations included letter notations, tablature, and neumes, like Western notation; but later developments and improvements were minimal, so we might say that Korean notations are on a level with Western notations of the twelfth or thirteenth centuries. The reasons why developments did not occur are not clear, but there are two factors playing important roles:

A. Each type of music in Korea had its own notation system: *Yulja-po* for *a-ak, Kongch'ŏk-po* for *tangak, Yukpo* for native instrumental music, and so forth. Since notation systems were specific, it was difficult to develop universality of a single notation.

B. In Korea, music is traditionally learned by rote, directly from a teacher and with no use of notation. Occasionally, one writes down something for his own eyes only, as a memory aid; this, of course, is not intended to be a complete score. Typically, also, the teacher forbids his students to use written materials. Thus, the need for written scores is minimal.

It seems unlikely that many more old notation books will surface in Korea; also, there are sources of notation in China and Japan of substantially greater age than those in Korea, Korea's earliest notations dating from the mid-fifteenth century. Despite their imperfections, the old Korean written notations are valuable sources for exploring the background and content of our traditional music. A single page of notation is worth more than volumes of explanatory words, just as a single painting is better than endless description.

MODES IN EARLY KOREAN MUSIC SOURCES, WITH SPECIAL CONSIDERATION OF THE *YANGGŬM SINBO*

INTRODUCTION

The description of melodic modes in Korean traditional music is a matter of fundamental importance, but it is also a particularly complex undertaking. The difficulty arises from the fact that the use of modal terminology was historically inconsistent, varying from period to period. The present article examines several written sources and attempts to deduce an outline of the early development of Korean modal terminology; the following two articles trace particular modes down to the present time.

The *Yanggŭm sinbo* 梁琴新譜 [Yang's New Handbook for the *Kŏmun'go*], written by the music master Yang Tŏk-su 梁德壽, is an instructional handbook for the Korean six-string zither, *kŏmun'go* (or *hyŏn'gŭm*) 玄琴. A postface (p. 22ab), written by Kim Tu-nam 金斗南 and dated 1610, explains the background of the work as follows:

> The former court musician, Yang Tŏk-su, was widely renowned for his playing of both the *pip'a* 琵琶 and the *kŏmun'go*. During the [Hideyoshi] invasion [of 1592] he fled to the [southwest] town of Namwŏn 南原 .Wishing to avoid the affairs of men, he devoted himself solely to the *kŏmun'go*. His house was isolated, but there were plum trees and bamboo within his courtyard; his instrument was always on his knee.
>
> He was an old friend of mine, so when I went south I searched him

out. He was destitute, and I invited him here. Day after day. I heard his playing; even though I am not versed in music, the limpid tones of the strings were evidently a genuine inheritance from high antiquity.

I said to him, 'Not only are you a superlative performer, but you also are literate. Is it not your responsibility to write a book of notations to pass on your techniques to later generations?'

He consented, and thereupon sketched a *kŏmun'go* on a piece of paper. First he described the various finger techniques, and then described the pitches of the five tones and the rhythm. Everything applied to pieces of music. The presentation was fully detailed and clear, making it easy to comprehend everything.

He was a past master of the instrument, and I subsequently named the book *Yanggŭm sinbo* [Yang's New Handbook for the *Komun'go*]."

The *Yanggŭm sinbo* is the second oldest source containing string tablature notation (see page 34), the oldest being the *An Sang kŭmbo* 安瑺琴譜 of 1572. There is preserved, however, a single older piece in the work *Isu samsan chaebon kŭmbo* 二水三山齋本琴譜 ; this piece, in tablature, is *Mandaeyop* 慢大葉 in the version of Cho Sŏng 趙晟. Cho Sŏng was a famous performer, active during the reign of King Myŏng-jong 明宗 (1545-1567), so this page represents an older tradition than the *Yanggŭm sinbo* or the *An Sang kŭmbo*.

Example 1 shows the opening page of *Mandaeyop* as it appears in the *Yanggŭm sinbo* (p. la; for the Cho Sŏng version, see Example 4 on page 32).

The tablature notation is mentioned in the *Akhak kwebŏm* 樂學軌範 of 1493 (7. 7a), and thus it could not have been invented by Yang Tŏk-su a century later. (For more information, see page 34).

The *Yanggŭm sinbo* notates nine items of *sogak* 俗樂 ("popular music"):

1. *Mandaeyŏp* 慢大葉 in *naksijo* 樂時調   (pp. la- 4b)
2. *Pukchŏn* 北殿   (pp. 5a- 6b)
3. *Chungdaeyŏp* 中大葉 [in *p'yongjo* 平調]   (pp. 7a- 9a)
4. *Chungdaeyŏp* [in *p'yŏngjo*]   (pp. 9a-11a)
5. *Chungdaeyŏp* in *ujo* 羽調   (pp. 11a-13a)
6. *Chungdaeyŏp* in *ujo kyemyŏnjo* 羽調界面調   (pp. 13b-15b)
7. *Chungdaeyŏp* in *p'yŏngjo kyemyŏnjo*   (pp. 15b-17b)
8. *Choŭm* 調音   (pp. 18a-19b)

(Example 1)

9. *Kamgunŭn* 感君恩 in *p'yŏngjo*   (pp. 20a-21b)

Of these, the first, second, and ninth pieces are also to be found in the *An Sang kŭmbo* and the *Taeak hubo* 大樂後譜 of 1759, which preserve music from the reign of King Sejo 世祖 (1455-1468). *Chungdaeyŏp*, however, appears in the *Yanggŭm sinbo* for the first time; since it is recorded in four modes, it is a fruitful piece for study.

In this article, the four modes in the *Yanggŭm sinbo* (*p'yŏngjo, ujo, ujo kyemyŏnjo,* and *p'yongjo kyemyonjo*) will be examined and compared with modal nomenclature of earlier and later date. A primary problem is determining whether these terms refer to modes (as in major and minor modes) or keys (as in "the key of *A*"). The study of modes is somewhat obscured by historical writings which attempt to make affective distinctions between the modes, as in the "grandeur of *ujo*," "harmony of *p'yŏngjo*," and "poignancy of *kyemyŏnjo*."

THE FOUR MODES OF THE YANGGŬM SINBO

A. Four modes:

In the *Yanggŭm sinbo*, the mode of *Mandaeyŏp* is given as *naksijo;* in the *Taeak hubo*, the same piece has the mode *p'yŏngjo*. From this, it is clear that *naksijo* and *p'yŏngjo* here have the same meaning. *Pukchŏn* and the first two versions of *Chungdaeyŏp* do not have modes listed in the *Yanggŭm sinbo*, but comparison with other pieces in the book makes it clear these three pieces are in *p'yŏngjo*.

Choŭm is the Sino-Korean term for the native word *tasŭrŭm* 다스름 , meaning an instrumental prelude played before the main piece. It serves a tuning purpose, and is played in the mode of the main piece which follows.

Thus, a division of the *Yanggŭm sinbo* pieces by mode shows that only four modes are used:

1. *P'yŏngjo*:   *Mandaeyŏp*
                                          Pukchŏn
                                          Chungdaeyŏp
                                          Kamgunŭn

2. *Ujo*:   *Chungdaeyŏp*
3. *P'yŏngjo kyemyŏnjo*:   *Chungdaeyŏp*
4. *Ujo kyemyŏnjo*:   *Chungdaeyŏp*

B. The instrument:

Before proceeding with technical details on the four modes, we must take a quick glance at the *kŏmun'go* and its tuning. There are six strings, of which three are stretched over a set of sixteen frets; these three extend from the first fret, as from a violin bridge. The other three strings are stretched from V-shaped movable bridges.

For purposes of analysis, we number the strings with Roman numerals and the frets with Arabic numbers. Thus, the fifth fret of the third string is represented as III. 5. (For traditional string names, see page 34.) One particular technique involves lateral push of a string, increasing its tension and raising its pitch a half step; this will be written as +.

Chart 1 shows the string and fret structure of the *kŏmun'go*:

C. The Five Chinese Modes:

Korea inherited from China a way of describing the five basic anhemitonic pentatonic modes. This system of "Five Modes" (*ojo* 五調) is frequently employed by Korean historical sources to explain the several modes actually practiced in Korea. We shall refer to these Chinese modes by means of Western solmization equivalents (movable-*do*), as shown in Chart 2. Thus, for example, the Chinese mode *Kungjo* 宮調 will be called "*fa*-mode."

D. The secondary notations in the *Yanggŭm sinbo*:

As shown in Example 1, the *Yanggŭm sinbo* contains two pitch notations in addition to the tablature. The notation to the left of the tablature is mnemonic (*yukpo*; see page 31) and need not concern us here. The notation on the right of the tablature uses the same characters as those shown in Chart 2; that is, it appears to be the Chinese five-tone notation specifying intervallic relationships (*kung* = *fa*, *sang* = *sol*, etc.). However, comparison with the tablature quickly reveals that the

(Chart 1)
Kŏmun'go

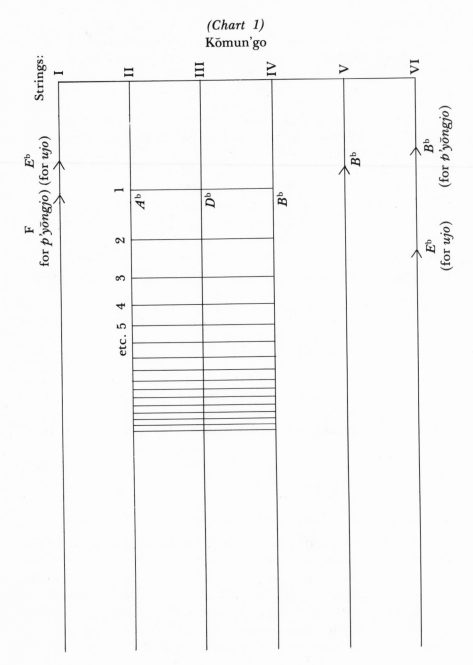

(Chart 2)
Five Chinese Modes

Chinese Name	Western Name	Intervallic Structure						
Kung 宮	fa-mode	fa	sol	la		do	re	
Sang 商	sol-mode	sol	la		do	re		fa
Kak 角	la-mode	la		do	re		fa	sol
Ch'i 徵	do-mode	do	re		fa	sol	la	
U 羽	re-mode	re		fa	sol	la		do

intervals are inconsistent amongst the several modes; the interval from *kung* to *sang,* for example, is a major second in *p'yŏngjo* and *ujo* and a minor third in both forms of *kyemyŏnjo.* In other words, the *Yanggŭm sinbo* does not employ these characters with their original precise intervallic Chinese usage, but rather as a scale degree notation (*kung* being tonic, *sang* being the first scale degree above the tonic, etc.). In other words, this is exactly equivalent to the other Korean scale degree notation, *Oŭm yakpo* (for details, see page 28). Chart 3 shows the relationship:

(Chart 3)
Scale Degree Notations

Kung 宮 Kung 宮	Sang 商 Sang 上一 il	Kak 角 Sang 上二 i	Ch'i 徵 Sang 上三 sam	U 羽 Sang 上四 sa

When Maurice Courant, in his "Essai historique sur la musique classique des Chinois avec un appendice relatif a la musique Coréene" (in Albert Lavignac, ed., *Encyclopédie de la Musique et Dictionnaire du Conservatoire* (Paris, 1913)), transcribed *Mandaeyŏp* into staff notation, he erroneously used the Chinese intervals in transcription because of the identical names. Nevertheless, his efforts were pioneering and command our respect.

E. *P'yŏngjo*, a *do*-mode of the Five Chinese Modes:

The identification of *p'yŏngjo* with the Chinese *ch'i* mode, or *do*-mode, is clearly made by the *Akhak kwebŏm* (1.24b), *Yanggŭm sinbo* (introduction, 3a), and the *Sejo sillok* 世祖實録 (48.2a). If we extract the notes used in the tablature for *Kamgunŭn* and chart them together with a line of half-steps, it is clear that the resulting intervallic structure is indeed a *do*-mode, as shown in Chart 4. The tonic note is shown on the far left.

(Chart 4)

P'yongjo

Half steps:	X X X XX X X X X X XX X					
P'yongjo of *Kamgunun*:	III.5	III.6	III.8 II.4	III.2 II.5	III.3 II.6	III.5
Do-mode:	*do*	*re*	*fa*	*sol*	*la*	*do*

This chart shows that the skips of a minor third between *re* and *fa* and between *la* and *do* in the *do*-mode correspond to skipping frets on the *komŭn'go* from III.6 to III.8 and from III.3 to III.5. The other pieces in the *p'yŏngjo* mode (*Mandaeyŏp*, *Pukchŏn*, and *Chungdaeyŏp*) have exactly the same tonal supply. Chart 4 reveals that these four pieces are all pentatonic, as is normal for Korean *sogak;* heptatonic structures are normal for Chinese ritual music (cf. *Sejo sillok* 48.1b).

F. *Ujo*, a *do*-mode of the Five Chinese Modes:

The *ujo* tuning chart of the *Yanggŭm sinbo* (introduction, p. 3b) identifies *ujo* with the Chinese *sol*-mode. However, if we extract the notes from the tablature of *Chungdaeyŏp* in the mode *ujo*, these do not agree.

(Chart 5)

Ujo

Half steps:	X	X	X	X X	X	X	X	X	X	X X	X
Sol-mode:	sol		la		do		re			fa	sol
Ujo of	III.8		III.2		III.4		III.5		III.6		III.8
Chungdaeyop:	II.4		II.5		II.7		II.8		II.9		
Do-mode:	do		re		fa		sol		la		do

If, on the other hand, the intervals of the *do*-mode are lined up on the same chart, it becomes clear that *ujo*, like *p'yŏngjo*, is a *do*-mode. The *Yanggŭm sinbo* is evidently in error on this theoretical point.

G. *Kyemyŏnjo*, a *re*-mode of the Five Chinese Modes:

Kyemyŏnjo occurs in the *Yanggŭm sinbo* in two forms: *p'yŏngjo kyemyŏnjo* and *ujo kyemyŏnjo*. Chart 6 shows the *kŏmun'go* notes used in *Chungdaeyŏp* for both modes, together with a *re*-mode. It is clear that both *kyemyŏnjo* modes are *re*-modes. Documentary support for this conclusion is given by the *Sejo sillok* (48.2a) and *Akhak kwebŏm* (1.24b).

(Chart 6)

Kyemyonjo

Half steps:	X	X X	X	X	X	X	X	X	X	X	X	X
P'yongjo *Kyemyŏnjo* of *Chungdaeyŏp*	III.5	III.6+	II.4		III.2 / II.5			III.4 / II.6+		III.5		
Re-mode	re		fa		sol		la			do		re
Ujo *Kyemyŏnjo* of *Chungdaeyŏp*	II.4		III.3 / II.6		III.4 / II.7		III.5 / II.8			III.7		III.8

In sum, from the standpoint of melodic modes (tonic note and intervallic structure) the *Yanggŭm sinbo* has only two types: *do*-mode (*p'yŏngjo* and *ujo*) and *re*-mode (*p'yŏngjo kyemyŏnjo* and *ujo kyemyŏnjo*).

H. Iden⁺ification of the tonic pitch of *ujo*:

As stated earlier, the secondary notation system in the *Yanggŭm sinbo* clearly identifies which note on the *kŏmun'go* is the tonic of a given mode, but it does not identify the actual pitch of the tonic note. Indeed, none of the three notations in the *Yanggŭm sinbo* yields absolute pitch information, but the correct answer may be deduced by consulting other written sources.

Chart 7 shows the piece *Pohŏja* 步虛子 as it appears in two sources: the *Isu samsan chaebon kŭmbo,* mentioned earlier, and the 18th-century—*Sogak wŏnbo* 俗樂源譜 . Comparison reveals that these are two versions of the same piece and that the tonic note in the tablature of the *Isu samsan chaebon kŭmbo* (i.e. II.4) corresponds to *Hwangjong* 黃鐘 (i.e. *e*ᵇ) in the *Sogak wŏnbo*. Both versions are transcribed into staff notation in Example 2.

Since *Isu samsan chaebon kŭmbo* and *Yanggŭm sinbo* have the same tablature and tuning, it is clear that II.4 is also *e*ᵇ in the *Yanggŭm sinbo*.

I. Identification of the tonic pitch of *p'yŏngjo*:

The secondary notation again clearly indicates that the tonic note of *p'yŏngjo* is III.5 on the *kŏmun'go*. A comparison of the differences between *ujo* and *p'yŏngjo* must first be made: according to the *Yanggŭm sinbo* (introduction, p. 4a), "Strings III, IV, and V are tuned to the same pitches in both *ujo* and *p'yŏngjo*." This passage does not mention the second string, but it is clear from the two tuning charts for *p'yongjo* and *ujo* (introduction, p. 3ab) that II is tuned a fifth higher than III in both *p'yŏngjo* and *ujo*; that is, in *ujo*, III.4 to II.4 is *fa* to the higher *do* (see Chart 5), or in *p'yŏngjo*, III.5 to II.5 is *do* up to *sol* (see Chart 4). If, as the *Yanggŭm sinbo* says, III is tuned the same in both *ujo* and *p'yŏngjo*, then II must also have the same tuning in both.

Consequently, if II.4 is *e*ᵇ (see preceding section), then III.4 would be *A*ᵇ and III.5, in turn, would be *B*ᵇ, the tonic of *p'yŏngjo*.

(Chart 7)

Isu samsan chaebon kŭmbo

仲	大四	角
仲		
仲 太黃	上同 大二 上同	角 商 羽
林 仲太	六五 大四大二	徵 角 商
仲 林潢	大四 清方四	角 徵 宮

Sogak wŏnbo

南 南潢	大六	羽
南 南林	上同 上同 方五	羽 羽徵
潢○ 南林	方四 太六 六五	宮○ 羽 徵
林 南汰	大六 方四 方五	羽 宮 商

潢○ 潢	方四	宮○
潢沖沖汰	方四方七方五	宮 角 商
潢 潢	方四方五方八	宮 商 徵
淋沖沖汰	方七上同方五	角 角 商

J. Tonic pitches of *kyemyŏnjo*:

Ujo kyemyŏnjo has the same tuning and tonic pitch as *ujo*; that is, $II.4 = e^b$. *P'yŏngjo kyemyŏnjo*, similarly, has the same tuning and tonic pitch as *p'yŏngjo*; that is, $III.5 = B^b$.

K. Summary:

The *Yanggŭm sinbo* only contains modes on two pitches: e^b and B^b. Specifically, there are two *do*-modes, one on e^b and one on B^b, and two *re*-modes, one on e^b and one on B^b. Chart 8 summarizes the four modes in a vertical grid of half steps.

(Chart 8)

Four Modes of *Yanggŭm sinbo*

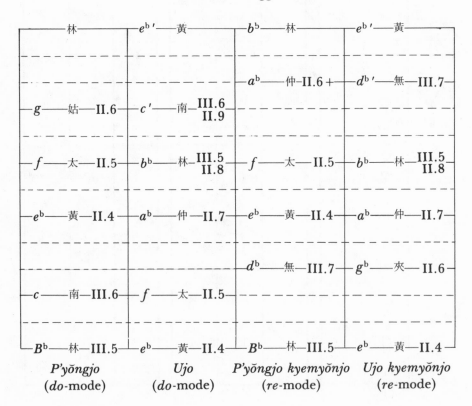

| *P'yŏngjo* | *Ujo* | *P'yŏngjo kyemyŏnjo* | *Ujo kyemyŏnjo* |
| (*do*-mode) | (*do*-mode) | (*re*-mode) | (*re*-mode) |

Example 3 summarizes the pitch information of Charts 4, 5, 6, and 8 in staff notation.

Using Example 3 as a basis, I have made transcriptions of the following *Yanggŭm sinbo* items and appended them to this article. Strings and fret numbers in the original tablature notation are shown below the staff.

1. *Mandaeyŏp*, together with the *Taeak hubo* version for comparison
2. *Chungdaeyŏp* in *p'yŏngjo*
3. *Chungdaeyŏp* in *ujo*
4. *Chungdaeyŏp* in *p'yŏngjo kyemyŏnjo*
5. *Chungdaeyŏp* in *ujo kyemyŏnjo*

THE TERM "UJO" IN EARLY SOURCES

Having explained the meaning of several modal names as they occur in a particular source, the *Yanggŭm sinbo*, we turn to an examination of the use of the terms *ujo* and *p'yŏngjo* in other early written sources.

A. *Ujo* meaning a tonic note on D^b or D:

The Chinese characters used in Korea to write *ujo* are 羽調 ; these happen to be the same as the characters used to signify the *re*-mode of the Five Chinese Modes, also pronounced *ujo* (see Chart 2). However, the Chinese *ujo* and Korean *ujo* are completely different in content.

In 1430, the famous Korean theorist Pak Yon 朴堧 wrote:

> The rules for melody and pitch height in singing were originally based upon the *taegŭm* 大笒 [Korean transverse flute], the performers being unknowledgeable of the precise pitch system of the [Chinese] pitchpipes. What is called '*fa*-mode' (*kungjo*) is not, in fact, *fa* (*kung*). Similarly, what is called '*re*-mode' (*ujo*) is not *re* (*u*) . . . The *ujo* of our country is actually a *fa*-mode on d^b (*muyŏk-kung* 無射宮) . . . Our country happily uses it. (*Sejong sillok* 世宗實錄 47.19a (1430/2).

Much later, Pak Chi-won 朴趾源 (1737-1805) wrote in his *Yorha ilgi* 熱河日記 :

The so-called *re*-mode (*ujo*) is not the *re* of the Five Chinese Notes; the term may also be written *ujo* 雨調 . Our country's *sogak* also uses *kyem-yŏnjo*, which is a conversion of *ujo*.

The *Akhak kwebŏm* of 1493 contains several passages of interest in this matter. One such passage (1.26b-27a) says,

On the *taegŭm*, cover the first, fifth, and sixth holes, leaving the others open. Blow gently, and the note an octave below the tonic of *ujo* will come out. Blowing harder will produce the pitch *D* an octave higher, that is, the tonic note of *ujo*."

In short, the term *ujo* in these early sources does not refer to a *mode* name (*re*-mode), but to a *key* name (*d* or, as we shall see below in Chart 9. *d*ᵇ).

B. *Ujo* as a term complementary to *naksijo*:

The *Akhak kwebŏm* also treats *ujo* as a general term complementary to *naksijo*. The comments in Chapter 7 relating to the *kŏmun'go*, *hyang-pip'a* 鄉琵琶 (five-string lute), and *kayagŭm* 伽倻琴 (twelve-string zither) may be summarized in a scheme of "Seven Tonics," as shown in Chart 9.

(Chart 9)

Naksijo and *Ujo*

Category	7 Tonics	Original Names	Kŏmun'go	Hyang-pip'a, Kayagŭm
Naksijo (tonic on III.5)	1st tonic	*ilji*	Tonic on G^b or C	Tonic on G
	2nd tonic	*iji*	Tonic on A^b or A	Tonic on A^b
	3rd tonic	*samji*	Tonic on B^b	Tonic on B^b
	4th tonic	*hoengji*	Tonic on B or c	Tonic on C
Ujo (tonic on II.4)	4th tonic	*hoengji*	Tonic on B or c	Tonic on c
	5th tonic	*ujo*	Tonic on d^b or d	Tonic on d
	6th tonic	*p'aljo*	Tonic on e^b	Tonic on e^b
	7th tonic	*makcho*	Tonic on e or f	Tonic on f

A passage in Chapter 1 (p. 24b) of the *Akhak kwebŏm* comments upon this system:

Of the Five Chinese Modes, the *do*-mode (*ch'ijo*) is what we popularly call *p'yŏngjo* and the *re*-mode (*ujo*) is what we popularly call *kyemyŏnjo*. The mode of *kyemyŏnjo* originally did not have a fixed pitch as its tonic [i.e. was transposable to various pitches]. Now, of the Seven Tonics, the one after the fourth tonic (*B* or *c*) has *d*ᵇ or *d* as tonic and is called '*ujo*'; the meaning of this is not secure. In the tunings for *komun'go*, if one performs the tonic on string III, the result is called *naksijo*. If the key is changed by performing the tonic on string II, the result is confusingly also termed *ujo*, without specifying the pitch. The mistake is very profound. Some people say that *ujo*羽調 is *ujo*右調 ('right mode'), since the tonic is played on string II, and that *naksijo* is *chwajo* 左調 ('left mode'), since the tonic is played on string III. But this is also imprecise.

In other words, *ujo* in the *Akhak kwebŏm* refers not only specifically to the fifth tonic (on *d*ᵇ or *d*), but also generally to the fourth through seventh tonics (*B*, or *c*; *d*ᵇ, or *d*; *e*ᵇ; *e*, or *f*), as opposed to *naksijo* which includes the first through fourth tonics (the fourth tonic, on *B* or *c*, occurs in both categories). This apparently suggests that *ujo* is either a general name for several keys or for a particular pair of keys but in neither case is it a *mode* name. If it were a mode name, then the terms *ujo p'yŏngjo* and *ujo kyemyŏnjo*, also occurring in *Akhak kwebŏm* 7, would coincide with the terms *p'yongjo* (*do*-mode) and *kyemyonjo* (*re*-mode), and the significance of the longer terms would be unclear.

There is a better explanation: if we consider the four tonics of the general *ujo* to be transpositions up a fourth of the four tonics of *naksijo*, logical results emerge. That is:

a) *ujo* 4th tonic (*B* or *c*) = transposition by fourth of *naksijo* 1st tonic (*G*ᵇ or *G*)

b) *ujo* 5th tonic (*d*ᵇ or *d*) = transposition by fourth of *naksijo* 2nd tonic (*A*ᵇ or *A*)

c) *ujo* 6th tonic (*e*ᵇ) = transposition by fourth of *naksijo* 3rd tonic (*B*ᵇ)

d) *ujo* 7th tonic (*e* or *f*) = transposition by fourth of *naksijo* 4th tonic (*B* or *c*)

Comparison of the tunings of the *kŏmun'go* for *naksijo* first, second, third, and fourth tonics in *Akhak kwebŏm* 7 shows that in every case the relative tuning of the strings is the same and all have the tonic note at III.5. In changing from one *naksijo* tonic to another, then, one simply changes the pitches of all the strings by the same amount, so that the tonic of the new key is still on III.5 and the strings always are in the same intervallic relationship to each other.

There is a limit, of course, to how far the strings may be tightened for upward transposition. This problem is solved by changing the position of the tonic from III.5 to II.4 so that the transposition may be achieved without tightening the strings further. This is the meaning of the "four tonics" of *ujo,* all of which have their tonic note played at II.4. The strings of the *kŏmun'go,* for example, would be tuned the same for *naksijo* first tonic (G^b or G) and *ujo* fourth tonic (B or c), but the tonic notes would be played, respectively, on III.5 and II.4.

This interpretation is supported by the following statement in the *Akhak kwebom* (7.14b): "The original *naksijo* fourth tonic makes the strings excessively tight, so some players now convert to *ujo* to play the, fourth tonic."

Further support comes from the tunings given for the fretless *kayagŭm.* For all of the *naksijo* "tonics," the tonic note is played on the third string; for all the *ujo* "tonics", the tonic note is played on the fifth string. This is summarized in Chart 10.

(Chart 10)

Kayagŭm Tunings

String:	1	2	3	4	5	6	7	8	9	10	11	12
Naksijo:												
1st tonic	C	D	G	A	c	d	e	g	a	c'	d'	e'
2nd tonic	D^b	E^b	A^b	B^b	d^b	e^b	f	a^b	b^b	$d^{b}{}'$	$e^{b}{}'$	f'
3rd tonic	E^b	F	B^b	c	e^b	f	g	b^b	c	$e^{b}{}'$	f'	g'
4th tonic	F	G	c	d	f	g	a	c'	d'	f'	g'	a'
Ujo:												
4th tonic	C	F	G	A	c	d	f	g	a	c'	d'	f'
5th tonic	D	G	A	B	d	e	g	a	b	d'	e'	g'
6th tonic	E^b	A^b	B^b	c	e^b	f	a^b	b^b	c'	$e^{b}{}'$	f'	$a^{b}{}'$
7th tonic	F	B^b	c	d	f	g	b^b	c'	d'	f'	g'	$b^{b}{}'$

Not surprisingly, in view of this interpretation, the words *naksijo* and *ujo* (in this sense) occur in the *Akhak kwebŏm* only in discussions of string instrument tuning, and not in discussions of wind instruments. In other words, the complementary terms are not key or scale names, but categories of string tunings.

This interpretation suggests further an explanation for the etymology of the word *ujo*. Since, as above quotations have shown, *ujo* was written variously in Chinese characters as 羽調 , 右調, and 雨調 , it is clear that the characters are being used simply for their phonetic sound, "*u*", rather than for meaning. In pure Korean, "*u*" can have the meaning "above" or "higher," which corresponds nicely to the idea of the *ujo* tonics as being higher than those of *naksijo*. It can be shown that the names of the six tonics other than *ujo* are also Chinese transcriptions of Korean names:

ilji	一指 = *han-karak*	한가락
iji	二指 = *tu-karak*	두가락
samji	三指 = *se-karak*	세가락
hoengji	横指 = *pit-karak*	빗가락
p'aljo	八調 = *p'alp'aljo*	팔팔조
makcho	邈調 = *mangmakcho*	막막조

The meaning of *mangmakcho*, for example, is like the *mak* in *maktarŭn kolmok* 막다른골목 ("blind alley"), the most extreme or highest tonic; this is indeed the case. If six of these terms are transcriptions of native words, then it is perfectly reasonable that the remaining tonic term, *ujo*, is also a transcription of a native Korean name.

C. Connection to *ujo* in the *Yanggŭm sinbo:*

As explained above, *ujo* was defined in the middle and late fifteenth century as having its tonic note on d^b or d; in the late fifteenth century, additionally, it was used as a term complementary to *naksijo*, that is, as a set of tonic pitches a fourth higher than the tonic pitches in the *naksijo* set. These may be compared with the term *ujo* as used in the *Yanggŭm sinbo*.

First, the tonic pitch of *ujo* in the *Yanggŭm sinbo* is e^b, which differs from the d^b or d of the middle fifteenth century. But basic transpositions of this sort are well known: the piece *Chŏngdaeŏp* 定大葉 , for example, has A as tonic in the Sejong period (1418-1450; see *Sejong sillok* 138.1a) and *c* as tonic in the Sejo period (1455-1468; see *Sejo sillok* 48.32b). It is entirely reasonable that a similar general transposition took place in *ujo*, the pitch moving up a half or whole step from the original d^b or d to e^b.

Second, in the *Yangŭm sinbo*, the tonic pitch of *ujo* is played on II.4 of the *kŏmun'go* and the tonic pitch of *p'yŏngjo* is played on III.5. This is exactly the same as in the *Akhak kwebŏm*, with the observation that several "tonics" are available for *ujo* in the *Akhak kwebŏm*.

Finally, in the *Yanggŭm sinbo*, the term *ujo* has developed the function of both a key name and a mode name; that is, it stands as a complement to the term *p'yŏngjo*, *ujo* being a *do*-mode on e^b and *p'yŏngjo* a *do*-mode on B^b. In the earlier sources, however, *ujo* had been used as a key name, referring specifically to a tonic on d^b or d, and generally to the several higher tonics between B and f. In other words, what would in the older sources have been called *ujo p'yŏngjo*, meaning a *do*-mode (*p'yŏngjo*) on e^b (*ujo*), is simply called *ujo* in the *Yanggŭm sinbo*. The *Yanggŭm sinbo* does retain something of the older practice in the term *ujo kyemyŏnjo*, which would have been the same earlier.

D. *Ujo* in the *Yuyeji*:

The *Yuyeji* 游藝誌 , written by Sŏ Yu-gu 徐有榘 (1764-1845), includes a *kŏmun'go* handbook as part of Chapter 6. The following titles are first encountered in this work: *U-ch'oyŏp* 羽初葉 , *Kye-ch'oyŏp* 界初葉 , *P'yŏng-ujo* 平羽調 , and *P'yŏng-kyejo* 平界調 .

When the notation is deciphered, it is clear that *U-ch'oyŏp* is an abbreviation of *Ujo ch'osudaeyŏp* and, like *Ujo chungdaeyŏp* of the *Yanggŭm sinbo*, has II.4 as tonic and uses a *do*-mode. Similarly, *Kye-ch'oyŏp* is short for *Kyemyŏn ch'osudaeyŏp* and, like *ujo kyemyŏnjo* of the *Yanggŭm sinbo*, has II.4 as tonic and uses a *re*-mode. *P'yŏng-ujo*, like *p'yŏngjo* of the *Yanggŭm sinbo*, has III.5 as tonic and is a *do*-mode; and *P'yŏng-kyejo*, like *p'yŏngjo kyemyŏnjo* in the *Yanggŭm sinbo*, has III.5 as tonic and is a *re*-mode. Thus, the four modes in the *Yuyeji* are the same as those in the *Yanggŭm sinbo*, with the names changed.

THE TERM P'YŎNGJO *IN EARLY SOURCES*

Many of the basic observations about the history of the term *p'yŏngjo* have already been presented in the course of the discussion of *ujo,* and only a short summary will be given in this section.

A. *P'yŏngjo* as a mode name:

Originally, *p'yŏngjo* was a mode name, referring to the Chinese *do*-mode. This is affirmed by the *Sejo sillok* (48.2a): "In the terminology of the Chinese Five Modes, *p'yŏngjo* is the *do*-mode, the *do* note being tonic." This is further confirmed by the *Akhak kwebŏm* (1.24b).

B. *P'yongjo* as a key name:

The use of the term *p'yŏngjo kyemyŏnjo* in the *Yanggŭm sinbo* suggests that *p'yŏngjo* is being used to indicate a key rather than a mode. A comparison of *p'yŏngjo* and *p'yŏngjo kyemyŏnjo* in the *Yanggŭm sinbo* (see Chart 8) shows they are the same in key (B^b), but different in mode. Thus, in fifteenth century sources *p'yŏngjo,* as a mode name, is complementary to *kyemyŏnjo*; later, in the *Yanggŭm sinbo,* it is used as a key name, complementary to *ujo.*

The Chinese character for *p'yŏng* 平調, is often used to mean "lower" or "moderate," as opposed to high or strong. Thus, it is possible that the name *p'yŏngjo* was gradually converted into the counterpart of *ujo,* which means, as explained earlier, "high key." In the *Yanggŭm sinbo,* then, *p'yŏngjo* is the key a fourth lower than *ujo.*

C. *P'yŏngjo* as *naksijo:*

In the *Yanggŭm sinbo,* the tonics of *p'yŏngjo* and *ujo* are separated by a fourth; this is similar to the relationship of the *naksijo* and *ujo* sets of keys in the *Akhak kwebŏm.* The *Yanggŭm sinbo* describes the piece *Mandaeyŏp* as being in *naksijo,* and the *Taeak hubo* has it in *p'yŏngjo,* so it is clear they are the same (both versions of *Mandaeyŏp* are in the appended transcriptions).

Naksijo, as shown in Chart 9, included four tonics, but *p'yŏngjo* in the *Yanggŭm sinbo* has only the tonic of B^b. Perhaps, as indicated in the following comment of Pak Yon, this was because B^b was the most popularly used key for *sogak* (*Sejong sillok* 47.19a):

> But among the keys used in Korean music, there is *naksijo*, which uses either *A*♭ or *B*♭ as tonic. *A*♭ is the second finger note on the *taegŭm*; *B*♭ is the third finger note. The ancients mostly avoided using *A*♭ and for that reason, the pitches they used were not always perfectly in tune. *B*♭ was originally the *do* pitch of heaven and earth and also the pitch used as partition between ruler and minister, each getting in the proper pitch alignment. . . . It is good to use *B*♭ as tonic. I want from now on, in the court banquet music, to chiefly use *B*♭ as the key.

THE TERM KYEMYŎNJO

As mentioned above, *kyemyŏnjo* is the *re*-mode of the Five Chinese Modes. All the sources, from the *Sejo sillok* through the *Yuyeji*, agree in this matter. In other words, in all Korean musical sources, *kyemyŏnjo* remains a mode name. The *kyemyŏnjo* article below discusses the internal changes which have historically taken place in the mode.

CONCLUSIONS

It is clearly recorded in fifteenth-century sources that the terms *p'yŏngjo* and *kyemyŏnjo* refer to modes (the *do* and *re*-modes, respectively). In Chapter 7 of the *Akhak kwebŏm*, there is a passage in which *p'yŏngjo* and *kyemyŏnjo* are used as mode names and *naksijo* and *ujo* are used as collective terms for groups of keys (not as names of particular keys). If, in the nomenclature of these early sources, one wished to clarify key area, it would have to be done by combining terms; thus, the *p'yŏngjo* (*do*-mode) of *naksijo* (lower set of keys from *G*♭ through *c*) would be described as *naksijo p'yŏngjo.*,

Chart 11 summarizes the key names as used in *Akhak kwebŏm*, *Yanggŭm sinbo*, and *Yuyeji*.

(Chart 11)

Key Names

Akhak kwebŏm	*Yanggŭm sinbo*	*Yuyeji*
naksijo p'yŏngjo	*p'yŏngjo*	*p'yŏng-ujo*
ujo p'yŏngjo	*ujo*	*ujo*
naksijo kyemyŏnjo	*p'yŏngjo kyemyŏnjo*	*p'yŏng-kyejo*
ujo kyemyŏnjo	*ujo kyemyŏnjo*	*kyemyŏnjo*

The historical development of mode names is more complex. In the *Akhak kwebŏm*, *p'yŏngjo* and *kyemyŏnjo* referred purely to modes, and *naksijo* and *ujo* referred to keys. In the *Yanggŭm sinbo*, *kyemyŏnjo* continues to be a mode name, but both *ujo* and *p'yŏngjo* have come to be used partially as key names and partially as mode names; indeed, analysis shows that in the *Yanggŭm sinbo*, *p'yŏngjo* is interchangeable with *naksijo*. In the *Yuyeji*, *p'yŏngjo* has become completely transformed into a key name, as in the titles, *p'yŏng-ujo* and *p'yŏng-kyejo*. Conversely, *ujo*, originally a key name, has become in *Yuyeji* a mode name, as in *p'yŏng-ujo*. *Kyemyŏnjo* conveniently remains a mode name from start to finish.

Despite the tremendous complexities of nomenclature explored above, the actual modal structures of pieces of Korean music have remained remarkably constant. It is hoped that this presentation will serve as a reference list for persons exploring old Korean musical sources in the future.

Example 2:
Pohŏja

Example 3:

1. *Mandaeyŏp*

2. Chungdaeyŏp (p'yŏngjo)

3. Chungdaeyŏp (ujo)

4. Chungdaeyŏp (p'yŏngjo kyemyŏngjo)

5. *Chungdaeyŏp (ujo kyemyŏnjo)*

UJO IN MODERN KAGOK

INTRODUCTION

In the preceding article we examined the terms *ujo, p'yŏngjo,* and *kyemyŏnjo* as they were used in various early Korean music sources. The present article traces the further appearance of *ujo* down to its current use in the vocal genre *kagok* 歌曲 (vocal soloist accompanied by chamber ensemble of string, wind, and percussion instruments).

A large portion of the *kagok* repertory is referred to as "*ujo*"; this is distinct from the other portion of the repertory, called "*kyemyŏnjo.*" As suggested in the preceding article, these names might be either mode names or key names. We must exercise caution in using Western methods of mode determination, since there may be substantial differences between Eastern and Western concepts of mode.

With the passage of time, it is likely that internal inconsistencies have accumulated in pieces of *kagok,* so our analysis will not be based solely on the modern pieces, but developed historically. Comparisons with earlier sources will help reveal the historical changes in Korean modal concepts.

The modern repertory is examined here on the basis of the vocal and *kŏmun'go* scores kept at the National Institute of Classical Music; for our purposes, they are transcribed into Western staff notation. The modern *kagok* repertory in *ujo,* for male singer, is as follows:

1. *Ch'osudaeyŏp* 初數大葉
2. *Isudaeyŏp* 二數大葉
3. *Chunggŏ* 中擧
4. *P'yŏnggŏ* 平擧
5. *Tugŏ* 頭擧

71

   6. *Samsudaeyŏp*   三數大葉
   7. *Soyong*   搔聳
   8. *Urong*   羽弄
   9. *Urak*   羽樂
  10. *Ŏllak*   言樂
  11. *Up'yŏn*   羽編

In this article we shall focus primarily upon *Ch'osudaeyŏp* as an example of *ujo*.

UJO *IN MODERN* KAGOK

A. Tonal supply:

Ujo Ch'osudaeyŏp has simply the five following pitches:

   1. e^b (*hwangjong* 黃鐘), II.4 on the *kŏmun'go*
   2. f (*t'aeju* 太簇),   II.5
   3. a^b (*chungnyŏ* 仲呂), II.7
   4. b^b (*imjong* 林鐘),   II.8 or III.5
   5. c' (*namnyŏ* 南呂), II.9 or III.6

As shown by Chart 8 in the preceding article (p. 54), these are the same pitches used in *ujo* in the *Yanggŭm sinbo*.

B. Tonic note:

   We have shown that the tonic note of *ujo* in the *Yanggŭm sinbo* was e^b, but it is not necessarily true that modern *kagok* has the same tonic note, despite the identity of tonal supply. An identification of the tonic pitch might be deduced as follows: certainly the tonic is one of the five scale degrees (*do, re, fa, sol,* and *la*). According to the *Yanggŭm sinbo* and *Yuyeji*, as examined in the preceding article, only *do* and *re*-modes were possible in traditional *kagok*. In modern *kagok*, *ujo* is distinguished from *kyemyŏnjo*, the latter being always a *re*-mode. This leaves only the *do*-mode, with a tonic of e^b, for modern *ujo*.

   However, this deduction should be checked by direct examination of modern *ujo*. For this purpose, we will continue to explore the piece *Ujo Ch'osudaeyŏp*, finding out a) which note is the most frequent pitch, and

b) which note is a cadential tone giving a feeling of stability. This information should enable us to specify the tonic note.

1. Frequency of occurrence:

As time passes, music transmitted in oral tradition tends to gather ornamental notes which fill in the spaces between the original notes of a piece. Indeed, these ornamental tones become numerically greater than the original, basic notes, and a frequency count including them would likely obscure the more essential notes of the original melody. It is thus necessary to eliminate the ornamental tones before taking a frequency count. (This reasoning was also used in the article on *Chung-yŏngsan*; see p. 121).

As is clear from the musical examples at the end of this article, the *kŏmun'go* part has, over the course of time, accumulated far less embellishment than the vocal part. For this reason, the *kŏmun'go* part is the better source for reduction to basic melody notes. The examples show the piece *Ujo Ch'osudaeyŏp* from an historical source, the modern *kŏmun'go* part, the modern vocal melody and my hypothetical reduction of the melody to basic notes.

Below the hypothetical melody line in the musical examples are numbers giving a running frequency count of melodic pitches (the first a^b is 1, the second a^b is 2, etc.). This is summarized in Chart 1.

(Chart 1)

Frequency Count

	F	A^b	B^b	c	e^b	f	a^b	b^b	c'	$e^{b\prime}$
First Vocal Section	0	0	1	1	2	5	5	1	0	1
Second Vocal Section	0	0	1	1	2	2	3	2	0	1
Third Vocal Section	0	0	4	1	1	4	4	2	0	1
Fourth Vocal Section	0	0	1	0	0	2	3	1	0	1
Fifth Vocal Section	2	2	4	1	4	3	0	0	0	0
Totals	2	2	11	4	9	16	15	6	0	4

The frequency totals for the use of pitches in the five sung sections show that the most common pitch overall is *f*, followed in order by a^b and

B^b. Rather than make immediate conclusions, we shall return to this information later.

2. Cadential tones:

Chart 2 shows the initial pitches of each section of the vocal part and the one or more pitches associated with the closing syllables of each section.

Chart 2

Section:	1	2	3	Int.	4	5	Post.
First Note:	a^b	$e^{b\prime}$	b^b	B^b	$e^{b\prime}$	f	a^b
Closing:	e^b	e^b-c-B^b	A^b-B^b	B^b	a^b-f-c-B^b	B^b-A^b-F	e^b

In determining the tonic pitch, the initial notes are less important than the final notes. Although ritual music imported from China uses the same pitch to begin and end, native Korean music places greater modal significance on the closing pitch; the initial pitch is flexible and variable. For example, *sijo* of descending melodic contour 지름時調 (see the article below on *sijo*) is a kind of variation on the standard *sijo* 平時調 : its first line (of three) is sung a sixth higher than the standard, but the middle and final lines are at the standard pitch level. Similarly, if we compare the modern *kagok* pieces *Ujo Ch'osudaeyŏp* and *Ŏllak,* the initial pitches of each vocal section are different, but, as shown in Chart 3, the cadential tones coincide.

(Chart 3)

Section:	1	2	3	4	5
Ch'osu:	e^b	e^b-c-B^b	B^b	a^b-f-c-B^b	B^b-A^b-F
Ollak:	a^b-f-e^b	f-c-B^b	B^b	f-c-B^b	B^b-A^b-F

When text is considered, however, the identification of cadential tones is not entirely obvious. As shown in the musical examples, section 1 of the vocal part comes to the pitch e^b on the last syllable of text, and, like the level tone *p'ing sheng* 平聲 in the Chinese language, it spreads out before stopping. On the other hand, Section 5 links the final syllable of text with a note which, like the Chinese entering tone *ju sheng* 入聲 , is brief and comes to a sudden halt. In these two sections, at least, there is essentially a single pitch associated with the closing syllable of text; the other sections are more problematical. The closing phrases of Sections 2 and 4, for example, have several pitches setting the final syllable of each text (see Chart 2). In such cases we shall simply choose the last of the pitches.

Thus, the cadential tone of section 1 is e^b, that of Sections 2, 3, and 4 is B^b, and that of section 5 is *F*. By this reasoning, the closing note of the final vocal section is *F,* possibly suggesting that *F* is the tonic pitch.

3. Determination of the tonic pitch:

The tonic note may be deduced from a combination of the three criteria discussed above: *ujo* being historically a *do*-mode (as distinct from the *re*-mode *kyemyŏnjo*), frequency of pitch occurrence, and cadential pitches. None of the five pitches used in *Ch'osudaeyŏp* satisfies all three conditions in an obvious way, and it is necessary to determine which criterion is most essential.

a) The pitch *f,* as shown in Chart 1, occurs most frequently. However, in vocal Sections 2 and 4, *f* appears only as an ornamental tone and this makes it an unlikely candidate for tonic. Section 5 does in fact conclude with the pitch *F*; but if it is the tonic, then modern *ujo* cannot be a *do*-mode. Indeed, with the given tonal supply, it would have to be a *re*-mode, which is *kyemyŏnjo*.

(Chart 4)

Half Steps:	X	X	X	X	X	X	X	X	X	X
re-mode:	*re*		*fa*		*sol*		*la*		*do*	
	E^b		F		A^b		B^b		c	
do-mode:	*do*	*re*		*fa*		*sol*		*la*		

b) The pitch a^b is second in frequency, but it is completely absent in the interlude; it never occurs as a cadential tone, and would imply a *fa*-mode for *ujo* (see Chart 4).

c) The pitch B^b occurs with nearly the same frequency as e^b, and these two pitches dominate the interlude. B^b is not the final cadential note of the piece, but there are instances in Korean music, such as in *sijo*, when the melody closes by dropping to a secondary ("dominant") tone rather than on the tonic. Thus the closing pitch F could be considered the "dominant" of B^b, and B^b would still be a candidate for tonic. However, having B^b as tonic would produce a *sol*-mode (see Chart 4).

d) The pitch c is the most infrequent, occurring basically as a passing tone from e^b to B^b in downward melodic motion and as an upper auxiliary tone for B^b. It is never a cadential tone and would produce a *la*-mode with the given tonal supply.

e) The pitch e^b is commensurate with B^b in frequency; together with B^b, it figures strongly in the interlude. It is the only pitch which can produce a *do*-mode with the given tonal supply. On the *kŏmun'go*, it is the pitch of II.4, the traditional tonic of *ujo*, whereas B^b is the pitch of III.5, the traditional tonic of *p'yŏngjo* (see preceding article). Further, except for the final vocal section, each section cadences on either e^b or its "dominant," B^b; this is also true of the instrumental interlude (closing on B^b) and the postlude (e^b dominating the melody and concluding the piece).

In sum, e^b is by far the best candidate for tonic note, since it occurs with fair frequency, is the only pitch which can make a *do*-mode with the available tonal supply, and (except for section 5) all chief divisions of the piece conclude on e^b or its dominant, B^b.

4. Tuning of the *kŏmun'go*:

A remarkable moment in *Ch'osudaeyŏp* occurs at the closing of the fifth vocal section: the vocal line (see musical examples) concludes abruptly on F, but the *kŏmun'go* continues by playing, in succession, the open strings IV, I, V, and VI. In modern tuning, these four are, respectively, B^b, E^b, B^b, and the B'^b an octave below the others. The modern tuning is fixed, being the same for both *ujo* and *kyemyŏnjo*.

Formerly, however, there were differing tunings for the *kŏmun'go*. This has already been demonstrated in the preceding article (see Chart 1, on page 48), and is thoroughly substantiated by historical sources such as *Yanggŭm sinbo*, *Akhak Kwebŏm*, and *An Sang kŭmbo*. The *ujo* tuning of the instrument was originally different from the modern tuning in that string VI was tuned to E^b, not B^b.

If the modern playing technique (open IV, I, V, and VI strings) is applied to the original tuning, then the closing phrase becomes $B^b - E^b - B^b - E^b$, and the piece ends on E^b, the pitch we have already determined as the tonic in modern *ujo*. This provides even further evidence for the choice of E^b as tonic.

5. Final cadence:

The preceding discussion shows that the vocal part concludes on the pitch F and that the *kŏmun'go* continuation traditionally finished on the tonic E^b. A look into historical sources suggests that E^b is the more representative ending note.

In sources such as the *Taeak hubo*, preserving music of the Sejo period (1455-1468), the final cadential phrases of pieces are almost uniformly the same: a gradual descent from the tonic pitch near the middle of the tessitura by scale degrees to a finish on the tonic pitch an octave lower. In *ujo*, for example, this would be the progression $e^b - c - B^b - A^b - F - E^b$.

The transcription in the musical examples reveals that the last two staves of the vocal part follow essentially this same outline even in modern *Ch'osudaeyŏp*, with the exception, of course, that the final E^b, which is too low to be sung, is left out. The *kŏmun'go* now provides an open VI string (B^b) after the vocal ending; this technique, in old tuning, would yield the concluding E^b. Thus, the traditional cadential formula is essentially still present in modern *kagok*, and the closing note is clearly seen as E^b, not the final F of the vocal part.

CONCLUSIONS

Modern *kagok* in *ujo* uses a pentatonic tonal supply: E^b, F, A^b, B^b, and c. The tonic pitch is E^b and from the standpoint of the Five Chinese Modes, *ujo* clearly is a *do*-mode. There is no essential difference between this and the older usage revealed in historical sources. *Ujo* differs from *p'yŏngjo* in having its tonic on e^b rather than B^b, and from *kyemyŏnjo* in being a *do*-mode, not a *re*-mode. If the strings of the modern *kŏmun'go* were retuned to the traditional tuning, but played with the current technique, even the closing cadential phrase would be like the cadential phrases in historical sources.

Although various alterations and embellishments have been introduced over the course of time, it is clear that modern *kagok* belongs to the
same genealogy as the old music preserved in sources such as the *Taeak
hubo*. The vocal ornamentations in *kagok* are like flower blossoms placed
on the withered melodic stalks of the old historical sources. To some
extent, we can recreate the ancient performances, and *kagok* is thus an
invaluable, unique surviving form of vocal music, essential for studies in
more ancient types of Korean music.

Ujo Ch'osudaeyŏp

KYEMYŎNJO
IN MODERN *KAGOK*

INTRODUCTION

The preceding article examined *ujo*, in its historical development down to its present use in the vocal genre *kagok*. The present article attempts a similar treatment of the other term used to describe modern *kagok*, *kyemyŏnjo*.

The current *kagok* repertory in *kyemyŏnjo*, for male singers, is as follows:

1. *Ch'osudaeyŏp* 初數大葉
2. *Isudaeyŏp* 二數大葉
3. *Chunggŏ* 中擧
4. *P'yŏnggŏ* 平擧
5. *Tugŏ* 頭擧
6. *Samsudaeyŏp* 三數大葉
7. *Soyong* 搔聳
8. *Ŏllong* 言弄
9. *P'yŏngnong* 平弄
10. *Kyerak* 界樂
11. *P'yŏn* 編
12. *Ŏllp'yŏn* 言編
13. *T'aep'yŏngga* 太平歌

As in the preceding article, we shall focus primarily upon *Ch'osudaeyŏp*.

The term *kyemyŏnjo* 界面調 appears in the *Akhak kwebŏm* 樂學軌範 (1493) and the *Yanggŭm sinbo* 梁琴新譜 (1610), but its present content appears to be quite different. That is, it now uses essentially three tones (e^b, a^b, and b^b) and lacks the important minor third. In the early sources, *kyemyŏnjo* was pentatonic (*re-fa-sol-la-do*) and had a minor third between the first two tones. It was chiefly by means of this interval that *kyemyŏnjo* was distinguished from *p'yŏngjo* or *ujo* (see Chart 8 on page 54). We shall investigate whether the present and past forms of *kyemyŏnjo* are fundamentally different or whether *kyemyŏnjo* has developed over time and is in origin the same as the old form.

TONAL SUPPLY OF MODERN KYEMYŎNJO

Chart 1 shows the pitches used in *Kyemyŏn ch'osudaeyŏp* and their frequency, based on scores kept at the National Institute of Classical Music.

(Chart 1)

		A^b	B^b	c	d^b	e^b	f	a^b	b^b	c'	$e^{b'}$
First	Vocal	1	6	4	0	7	3	5	11	4	1
Section	*Kŏmun'go*	0	2	0	0	4	0	8	14	0	7
Second	Vocal	1	3	2	0	4	0	6	5	1	2
Section	*Kŏmun'go*	0	4	0	0	3	0	6	14	2	2
Third	Vocal	2	11	2	0	12	4	9	4	0	2
Section	*Kŏmun'go*	1	13	1	1	12	0	4	4	0	0
Fourth	Vocal	(Same as Second Section)									
Section	*Kŏmun'go*										
Fifth	Vocal	6	13	6	0	10	3	6	2	0	0
Section	*Kŏmun'go*	4	15	1	1	8	0	4	3	0	0

Of the six pitches which occur, three (e^b, a^b, and b^b) appear by far the most frequently. If this were considered a hexatonic scale, it would be a very curious circumstance, since Korean music is basically pentatonic (see discussion under *Oŭm yakpo*, page 28) and should contain no half-steps. The three rare notes are examined below:

A. The pitch f:

The pitch f is the only pitch occuring between e^b and a^b, and appears only in the vocal part. Even in the vocal part, f is used merely as part of a vibrato on e^b and is thus not significant. (In Example 5 at the end of this article, see Section 1, beat 4, and Section 3, beats 1 and 2.)

B. The pitch c:

The pitch c occurs four times in the *kŏmun'go* part: in Section 2, beats 7-8, the motion is c-B^b-c-B^b, like a vibrato; and in Section 3, beat 20, and Section 5, beat 20, the progression is B^b-c-d^b-e^b and c occurs as a mere passing tone (for more on this, see C. below). In the vocal part, c appears mostly just with B^b or A^b, as part of a vibrato (Section 1, beats 9-10 and 17-18).

C. The pitch d^b:

The pitch d^b does not occur in the vocal part and only twice in the *kŏmun'go* part (Section 3, beat 20, and Section 5, beat 20). Actually, not all the *kŏmun'go* scores at the National Institute of Classical Music contain the d^b. In those that do, both instances occur in the progression B^b-c-d^b-e^b, and a special instrumental technique is called for: the e^b string is released by the left hand, causing a decrease in tension and lowering of the pitch. At this moment, the string is plucked, and the pitch d^b is produced; the string is pushed forward, causing tension, and the pitch moves up to e^b, the next pitch. Thus, the d^b in the *kŏmun'go* part is simply a kind of passing tone from B^b to e^b. Also, there are other instances when a motion from B^b to e^b does not use a d^b.

A great *kŏmun'go* player, the late Cho I-sun 趙彝淳 , clung fast to the *kŏmun'go* melodies of the past; on the other hand, a great *kagok* singer, the late Ha Kyu-il 河圭一 , advocated changing the *kŏmun'go* lines to follow the song lines. This shows that the *kŏmun'go* part is more conservative than the vocal part. Further, compared to the vocal part, the *kŏmun'go* pitches are precise. The *kŏmun'go* part, then, is more settled than the vocal part and is closer to old music. When there are differences between the vocal and *kŏmun'go* parts in modern *kagok*, the *kŏmun'go* part is more reliable.

At any rate, modern *Kyemyŏn ch'osudaeyŏp*, as in the chart above, uses six pitches; strictly speaking, this is not characteristic of native Korean music. The *f* is absent in the *kŏmun'go* part, the *d*ᵇ is absent in the vocal part, and the rare *c* is used only as an auxiliary tone. These three, then, are suspicious.

KYE-CH'OYŎP *IN THE* YUYEJI

The nineteenth-century *Yuyeji* 遊藝志 (for details, see above, page 60) contains a piece called *Kye-ch'oyŏp* (abbreviation of *Kyemyŏn ch'osu-daeyŏp*). We shall investigate whether or not the three problem pitches (*f*, *c*, and *d*ᵇ) occur in it.

For easy comparison, all the *kŏmun'go* strings and frets which appear in the *Yuyeji* tablature are shown next to their modern equivalents:

III.5 *B*ᵇ
III.6 *c*
III.7 *d*ᵇ
 II.4 *e*ᵇ
 II.6 *g*ᵇ
 II.7 *a*ᵇ
 II.8 *b*ᵇ
 II.9 *c'*
 II.10 *d*ᵇ '

1. The *f* absent in the modern *kŏmun'go* part is also absent here. However, *g*ᵇ (II.6), which is absent in the modern piece, is present and therefore attracts our attention. Occurrences of this pitch are as follows (see Example 5):

Section 1: beat 4
Section 2: beats 17, 19
Section 3: beats 9, 15, 23, 27
Section 5: beats 1, 2, 5, 14, 25, 27

2. In the modern *kŏmun'go* part, the pitch *c* appears in Section 2, beats 7-8; it appears in the corresponding place in *Kye-ch'oyŏp* (II.9). However, the *c* in the modern Section 3, beat 20, and Section 5, beat 20, does not appear in the corresponding portions of *Kye-ch'oyŏp*; *B*ᵇ (III.5) is used instead. III.6 (*c*) does occur once more in *Kye-ch'oyŏp* (Section 3,

beat 32), but comparison with the other scores (see Example 5) suggests this is just an error for II.4 (e^b).

3. Although the pitch d^b occurs only twice in modern *Kyemyŏn ch'osudaeyŏp*, it appears many times in *Kye-ch'oyŏp*:

Section 1: beats 17, 19
Section 2: beats 1, 3, 21*
Section 3: beats 25, 29*
Section 5: beats 10, 27* 32

The instances marked with an asterisk are occurrences of d^b (III.7) in passing tone situations, from e^b to B^b. These correspond to the situation in the modern *kŏmun'go* part, which is e^b-e^b-B^b: while the notation prescribes no d^b, in actual performances the second e^b is played by the lateral push of III.7 (increasing tension and raising pitch); when the string is released, the pitch d^b does, in fact, sound. In any event, g^b (II.6) and d^b (III.7) do appear in *Kye-ch'oyŏp*, and in this point the *Yuyeji* differs from modern practice.

RELATION BETWEEN P'YONGJO (UJO) AND KYEMYŎNJO

As explained in the preceding articles, *kyemyŏnjo* originally corresponded to the *re*-mode of the Five Chinese Modes and *p'yŏngjo* corresponded to the *do*-mode. In the *Yanggŭm sinbo*, the *do*-mode occurs in two keys: "*p'yŏngjo*," on B^b, and "*ujo*," on e^b. Similarly, *kyemyŏnjo*, or *re*-mode, appeared in two keys: "*p'yŏngjo kyemyŏnjo*," on B^b, and "*ujo kyemyŏnjo*," on e^b (on these, see Chart 8, page 54).

A passage in a 17th-century *kŏmun'go* book, *Paegunam kŭmbo* 白雲庵琴譜 , explains the difference between *ujo* and *ujo kyemyŏnjo* as follows: "*Ujo* begins on II.4 (e^b). *Ujo kyemyŏnjo* substitutes II.6 (g^b) for II.5 (f), III.7 (d^b) for III.6 (c), and II.10 (d^b) for II.9 (c)" (page 8). In other words, both start on the same note; we can tell from the frets whether it is *ujo* or *ujo kyemyŏnjo*. More generally speaking, this is the basic difference between *p'yŏngjo* and *kyemyŏnjo*; a piece can be played in either mode simply by making the appropriate fret changes. Some examples follow:

1. In the *Yanggŭm sinbo*, the piece *Pukchŏn* 北殿 is in *p'yŏngjo*. A comment under the title says, "By changing frets and nothing else, this piece can be played in *p'yŏngjo kyemyŏnjo*, *ujo kyemyŏnjo*, or *ujo*" (page 5a). Also, the piece *Chungdaeyŏp* 中大葉 is transposable and is recorded in four versions: *p'yŏngjo*, *ujo*, *ujo kyemyŏnjo*, and *p'yŏngjo kyemyŏnjo*.

2. In the 16th-century *Siyong hyangak-po* 時用鄉樂譜, a footnote to the piece *Chŏngsŏk-ka* 鄭石歌 says, "in either *p'yŏngjo* or *kyemyŏnjo*" (page 23a).

3. In the eighteenth-century *Sogak wŏnbo* 俗樂源譜 (Chapter 6), the piece *Tokkyŏng* 篤敬 is simply a conversion into *kyemyŏnjo* of the piece *Kimyŏng* 基命, which is in *p'yŏngjo*. As shown in Example 1, f and c in *Kimyŏng* have been changed into g^b and d^b, respectively, in *Tokkyŏng* (transposed notes have been marked with a small circle).

These and other examples show there was formerly the practice of performing a piece in multiple keys and modes. Since *Chungdaeyŏp* was performed in several versions, it is reasonable to examine whether *Kyemyŏn ch'osudaeyŏp*, our modern piece under consideration, is somehow an altered version of *Ujo ch'osudaeyŏp*, the piece studied in the preceding article.

First, however, we should check to see if modern *Kyemyŏn ch'osudaeyŏp* agrees with *Kye-ch'oyŏp* in the *Yuyeji*. Example 5 includes a transcription of both.

1. The *kŏmun'go* part of modern *Kyemyŏn ch'osudaeyŏp*, like *U-ch'oyŏp* of the *Yuyeji* (see example in preceding article), lacks the note g^b used in *Kye-ch'oyŏp*. Example 2 shows a conspicuous sample for comparison (Section 2, beats 17-24): *Kye-ch'oyŏp* formulaically changes the II.5 (f) of *U-ch'oyŏp* to II.6 (g^b); and modern *Kyemyŏn ch'osudaeyŏp* changes the II.5 (f) of *Ujo ch'osudaeyŏp* to II.6, but the resultant pitch is a^b rather than g^b.

2. In modern *Kyemyŏn ch'osudaeyŏp*, d^b occurs less frequently than c; in *Kye-ch'oyŏp*, on the other hand, d^b is the more frequent pitch. This sheds light on modern *Ujo ch'osudaeyŏp*: in the *kŏmun'go* part of *Ujo ch'osudaeyŏp*, the c (III.6) occurs rarely (Section 2, beat 20; Section 3, beats 23 and 28; and Section 5, beat 12) and only as a passing tone between e^b and B^b. In *U-ch'oyŏp*, c similarly appears as a passing tone. In Example 2, the e^b-c-B^b progression in *Ujo ch'osudaeyŏp* corresponds to e^b-e^b-B^b in *Kyemyŏn ch'osudaeyŏp*; d^b does not obviously occur in the

latter, but the first e^b is played on II.4 and the second on a III.7 stretched (normally d^b, but e^b when tightened), so that when the tension is released, the d^b pitch comes out. In *U-ch'oyŏp*, the progression II.4 (e^b) — III.6 (c) — III.5 (B^b), as shown in Example 2, is formulaically altered to II.4 (e^b) — III.7 (d^b) — III.5 (B^b) in *Kye-ch'oyŏp*, the c being altered to d^b.

At any rate, it can be observed that the *Yuyeji's Kye-ch'oyŏp* is more genuine than the irregular *Kyemyŏn ch'osudaeyŏp* of today: the g^b that corresponds to the f of *ujo* has risen higher to a^b in the modern piece. Because of this, the a^b originally in *kyemyŏnjo* has itself risen to b^b. Furthermore, in the modern case, the d^b which corresponds to c in *ujo* is much weaker than in *Kye-ch'oyŏp* and has a questionable existence.

As a result, modern *Kyemyŏn ch'osudaeyŏp* essentially displays a tritonic scale (e^b, a^b, and b^b), giving an impression like children's songs or *sijo*. Chart 2 summarizes the above discussion in tabular form.

(Chart 2)

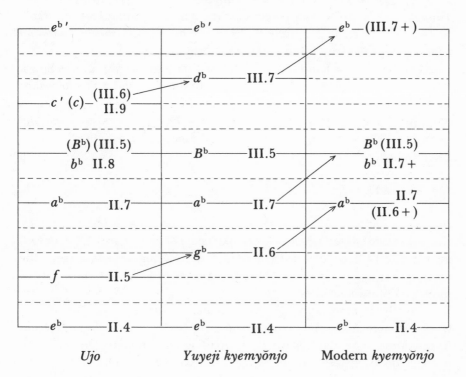

Ujo Yuyeji kyemyŏnjo Modern kyemyŏnjo

THE MODERN TONIC NOTE

The above discussion shows that modern *kyemyŏnjo* is in the same category as *kyemyŏnjo* in the *Yuyeji*. The next question to be investigated is whether it has B^b as tonic, like old *p'yŏngjo kyemyŏnjo,* or if it has e^b as tonic, like old *ujo kyemyŏnjo.* The preceding discussions have actually made it clear that *kyemyŏnjo* in the *Yuyeji* is like old *ujo kyemyŏnjo* and has e^b as tonic. Instead of re-examining those materials here, we shall take another approach and juxtapose *Kye-ch'oyŏp* of the *Yuyeji* with two pieces from the late seventeenth-century *Kŭmbo sinjŭng karyŏng* 琴譜新 證歌令 : *Ujo Kyemyŏnjo sudaeyŏp* (No. 1) and *P'yŏngjo kyemyŏnjo sudaeyŏp.* This is done in Example 3, which gives Section 5.

Both the *Yuyeji* and *Kŭmbo sinjŭng karyŏng* lack horizontal lines defining rhythm in these pieces. However, by referring to the *kŏmun'go* part of modern *Kyemyŏn ch'osudaeyŏp,* rhythm can be supplied for *Kye-ch'oyŏp;* similarly, reference to *Chungdaeyŏp* (*ujo kyemyŏnjo*) in the *Yanggŭm sinbo* can supply rhythm for the *Kŭmbo sinjŭng karyŏng.* Only Section 5 is given in Example 3, because the *Kŭmbo sinjŭng karyŏng* contains only Sections 4 and 5.

On the basis of Example 3, it is clear that *Kye-ch'oyŏp* in the *Yuyeji* is much closer to *Ujo kyemyŏnjo sudaeyŏp* of the *Kŭmbo sinjŭng karyŏng;* in other words, *kyemyŏnjo* in the *Yuyeji* is old *ujo kyemyŏnjo.* Since modern *Kyemyŏn ch'osudaeyŏp* is like *Kye-ch'oyŏp,* it also is old *ujo kyemyŏnjo.* Consequently, the tonic note of modern *kyemyŏnjo* is II.4 (e^b).

CADENTIAL FORMULA

As mentioned with reference to *ujo* in the preceding article (page 77), the old music preserved in sources like the *Taeak hubo* 大樂後譜 (1759) almost always concludes with a phrase descending scalewise from the tonic note to an octave below. This may also be investigated in the case of modern *Kyemyŏn ch'osudaeyŏp.*

Ideally, in *ujo kyemyŏnjo* the cadential form would be e^b-d^b-B^b-A^b-G^b-E^b. Modern *Kyemyŏn ch'osudaeyŏp* gives the e^b on beat 25 of Section 5; this is the same place as the corresponding note in *Chungdaeyŏp* (both *ujo* and *ujo kyemyŏnjo*) in the *Yanggŭm sinbo* (see examples in the article

"Modes in Early Korean Sources," above). Example 4 compares modern *Kyemyŏn ch'osudaeyŏp, Ujo ch'osudaeyŏp,* and *Kye-ch'oyŏp* in the *Yuyeji,* Section 5, beats 25-40.

In Example 4, the e^b-e^b-B^b of *Kyemyŏn ch'osudaeyŏp* corresponds to e^b-d^b-B^b in the *Yuyeji,* which is quite similar in rhythm and shape to *Ujo ch'osudaeyŏp.* The following B^b-B'^b is simple prolongation; while the *kŏmun'go* has this, the vocal line also has a decorated B^b.

The next pitch for *Kyemyŏn ch'osudaeyŏp* in the *kŏmun'go* part is another B^b, while *Ujo ch'osudaeyŏp* and *Kye-ch'oyŏp* have A^b. According to the *Yanggŭm sinbo (ujo kyemyŏnjo)* and *Kŭmbo sinjŭng karyŏng,* which are earlier than the *Yuyeji,* the next three beats are all B^b. Thus, the corresponding notes in the *Kye-ch'oyŏp* and modern *Kyemyŏn ch'osudaeyŏp* may be seen as mere decorations of the B^b pitch.

In the next several beats, the A^b of *Ujo ch'osudaeyŏp* should correspond to an A^b in *Kyemyŏn ch'osudaeyŏp,* but the latter still reads B^b. In the *Yuyeji* and *Kŭmbo sinjŭng karyŏng* (Example 3), the pitch in *kyemyŏnjo* is indeed A^b, just as in *ujo.* In the *Kŭmbo sinjŭng karyŏng,* in fact, there are only two pitches for this passage, B^b and A^b; this is also true of *Chungdaeyŏp (ujo kyemyŏnjo)* in the *Yanggŭm sinbo.* Accordingly, these several beats, which are B^b in modern *Kyemyŏn ch'osudaeyŏp,* were originally A^b, and correspond to the A^b in the basic cadential phrase.

Assuming that *kyemyŏnjo* is an alteration of *ujo,* the pitch corresponding to F in *ujo* is G^b in *kyemyŏnjo.* As we have already seen, in modern *Kyemyŏn ch'osudaeyŏp* this has moved up to A^b. In the *Yuyeji,* this A^b is produced by lateral push of III.3 (basically G^b), rather than using III.4, the basic A^b. The *Kŭmbo sinjŭng karyŏng,* significantly, also uses III.3, but without lateral push, so that the pitch is the expected G^b. Accordingly, the A^b of modern *Kyemyŏn ch'osudaeyŏp* is in fact a modification of the original G^b and corresponds to the G^b of the cadential form.

The final pitch in modern *Kyemyŏn ch'osudaeyŏp* is that of the open VI string, as it is in the earlier sources. However, VI is tuned to B^b in modern tuning; in the *Yuyeji* and earlier sources, it was tuned to E^b. Thus, *Kyemyŏn ch'osudaeyŏp*'s final open VI, B^b, corresponds to the open VI, E^b, of the earlier sources and the E^b of the basic cadential phrase.

Chart 3 summarizes the above discussion in tabular form.

(Chart 3)

Beat:	25	26	27	33	38	Last
Kŭmbo sinjŭng karyŏng	e^b	d^b	B^b	A^b	$G^b\text{-}A^b$	E^b
Yuyeji	e^b	d^b	B^b	A^b	A^b	E^b
Kyemyŏn ch'osudaeyŏp	e^b	e^b	B^b	B^b	A^b	B^b
Basic cadential phrase	e^b	d^b	B^b	A^b	G^b	E^b

CONCLUSIONS

Modern *Kyemyŏn ch'osudaeyŏp,* which has the basic tonal supply e^b, a^b, and b^b, appears to have no connection with old *ujo kyemyŏnjo,* which had the pentatonic e^b-g^b-a^b-b^b-d'^b. We have shown that the modern *kyemyŏnjo* is actually a derivative from old *ujo kyemyŏnjo*: g^b has moved to a^b, a^b to b^b, and d^b has mostly disappeared. Intermediate steps in the transformation may be seen in the seventeenth-century *Kŭmbo sinjŭng karyŏng* and the nineteenth-century *Yuyeji.* Accordingly, the two modes presently preserved are the descendants of the old *ujo* and *ujo kyemyŏnjo*; *p'yŏngjo* and *p'yŏngjo kyemyŏnjo* have vanished.

One factor in the disappearance of *p'yŏngjo kyemyŏnjo* might be that it was difficult to perform. For the piece in the *Yanggŭm sinbo,* this observation is made: "This piece has very difficult finger techniques and is not easy to teach. Therefore, I have recorded it at the very end of the *taeyŏp* section" (page 15b).

Modern *Kyemyŏn ch'osudaeyŏp* both have e^b as tonic, and, despite great modifications, both can be shown to have fundamentally the old descending scalewise cadential· formula. For more explorations with *kyemyŏnjo,* see the articles *"Yŏngsan hoesang"* and *"Sujech'ŏn."*

Example 1:

Example 2:

Example 3:

Example 4:

Example 5:

Abbreviations used in the transcriptions:

Ujo. Ch.   : *Ujo Ch'osudaeyŏp*
voc. pt.   : vocal part
Kye. Ch.   : *Kyemyŏn Ch'osudaeyŏp*
Kŏm. pt.   : *kŏmun'go* part
Yuy. Kye.   : *Yuyeji Kyech'oyŏp*

Section 4 is the same as Section 2

YŎNGSAN HOESANG:
A COMPARISON OF THE
MODERN PIECE AND THE VERSION
NOTATED IN THE *TAEAK HUBO* (1759)

INTRODUCTION

The piece of aristocratic chamber music entitled, *Yŏngsan hoesang* 靈山會相 exists today in two primary versions: the "string instruments" version (called *Kŏmun'go hoesang* 거문고會相 or *Chul-p'ungnyu* 줄風流 , and the "wind instruments" version (called *Samhyŏn yŏngsan hoesang* 三絃靈山會相 or *Tae-p'ungnyu* 대風流). The "string instruments" version, which we will be considering in this article, consists of the following nine movements:

1. *Sang-yŏngsan* 上靈山
2. *Chung-yŏngsan* 中靈山
3. *Chan-yŏngsan* 잔靈山
4. *Karak tŏri* 加樂除只
5. *Samhyŏn todŭri* 三絃도드리
6. *Hahyŏn todŭri* 下絃도드리
7. *Yŏmbul* 念佛
8. *T'aryŏng* 打令
9. *Kunak* 軍樂

(The "wind instruments" version has almost the same set of movements, but eliminates the "*Hahyŏn todŭri*.") There are commonly four additional movements performed after "*Kunak*:"

10. *Chan todŭri* 細還入

11. *Kyemyŏn karak todŭri*   界面加樂還入
12. *Yangch'ŏng*   兩清還入
13. *Ujo karak todŭri*   羽調加樂還入

The last three items (#11-13) are collectively known as *Ch'ŏnnyŏn manse* 千年萬歲 and are frequently performed as an independent three-movement piece. Dr. Chang Sa-hun 張師勛 has shown that the three appended movements derive from the famous court orchestral piece *Pohŏja* 步虛子 (*Kugak non'go* 國樂論攷 (1966), pp. 3-48).

The present article examines only the first movement, "*Sang-yŏngsan*," of the string instrument version; the second movement, "*Chung-yŏngsan*," is in fact a variant of the first movement and will be considered in some detail in the following article (p. 121).

As it has survived today, *Yŏngsan hoesang* is a purely instrumental suite with the movements listed above. If my memory serves, there was an explanation of a "program" for *Yongsan hoesang* in a book called Sidan 詩壇 published about thirty years ago: "*Sang-yŏngsan*" depicted Buddha preaching on *Yŏngch'wi* 靈鷲 mountain; for "*Chung-yŏngsan*" my memory fails; but "*Se-yŏngsan*" described Buddha finishing the sermon and going down the moutain. The source of this explanation, of course, was not recorded, but doubtless the need was created by the absence of a sung text which would have shed light on the meaning of the music.

Although *Yŏngsan hoesang* is now purely instrumental, there is a text given for it in several written sources on Korean music. For example, the famous musical treatise *Akhak kwebŏm* 樂學軌範 (1943) and a primary source of fifteenth-century music, the *Taeak hubo* 大樂後譜 (1759), clearly state the text as "*Yŏngsan hoesang pulbosal*" 靈山會相佛菩薩. The *Taeak hubo*, indeed, includes the text with the music in a metrical notation (*Chŏnggan-po;* see p. 39).

In this article we shall examine the relationship between modern *Yŏngsan hoesang* and the version notated in the *Taek hubo*, which gives only a single movement, corresponding to modern "*Sang-yŏngsan*." In so doing, we shall have an opportunity to investigate whether or not the original text could be attached to the modern version, and examine the question of modes in both versions.

The modern *Yŏngsan hoesang* has survived in a mode which is called *kyemyŏnjo* 界面調. Since the *Taeak hubo* notates music from the period of King Sejo 世祖 (ruled 1455-1468), we must examine whether the present mode coresponds to the explanation of *kyemyŏnjo* in the *Annals of King Sejo* (*Sejo sillok* 世祖實録). The *Annals* present *kyemyŏnjo* as corresponding to the *ujo* 羽調 of the five Chinese modes, that is, to the Western *re*-mode (*re-fa-sol-la-do*).

DESCIPHERING THE MODE OF YŎNGSAN HOESANG IN THE TAEAK HUBO: UJO KYEMYŎNGJO

The *Taeak hubo*, in fact, contains two versions of the melody of *Yongsan hoesang,* notated in adjacent columns. In similar notational situations in the *Annals of King Sejong* (*Sejong sillok* 世宗實録 ; (he ruled 1418-1450) and the *An Sang kŭmbo* 安瑺琴譜 (1572), the right column gives the string instrument part and the left presents the wind instrument part. The same clearly holds true for the *Taeak hubo,* since the left column has at one point the indication "舉吹", meaning "lift and blow." Thus, the right column can only be the string line, and it is this part which we will compare with the modern version as preserved at the National Classical Music Institute.

The score of *Yŏngsan hoesang* given in the *Taeak hubo* is as follows: (See p. 106).

This notation system, *Chŏnggan-po* combined with *Oŭm yakpo* (see p. 28), clearly shows the basic outline of the melody, but without an indication of mode, it is ambiguous as to the precise intervals involved. That is, for example, unless it is known whether the piece is in *p'yŏngjo* 平調 or *kyemyŏnjo* 界面調 , it is impossible to determine whether the interval between 宮 and 上一 is a major second or a minor third. Furthermore, the actual pitch of the central tone (or "tonic"), 宮 is uncertain.

Luckily, there are other written sources which provide clues for solving this modal problem. The *Kŭmbo sinjŭng karyŏng* 琴譜新證假令 (1680?) notates only a single column of *Yŏngsan hoesang,* in *kŏmun'go* tablature (see p. 107):

Our attention is drawn to the notes 方六 and 大七 , that is, 2nd string, 6th fret (g^b) and 3rd string, 7th fret ($d^{b'}$): the only mode which includes both these notes is *ujo kyemyŏnjo,* defined as a *re*-mode (one of

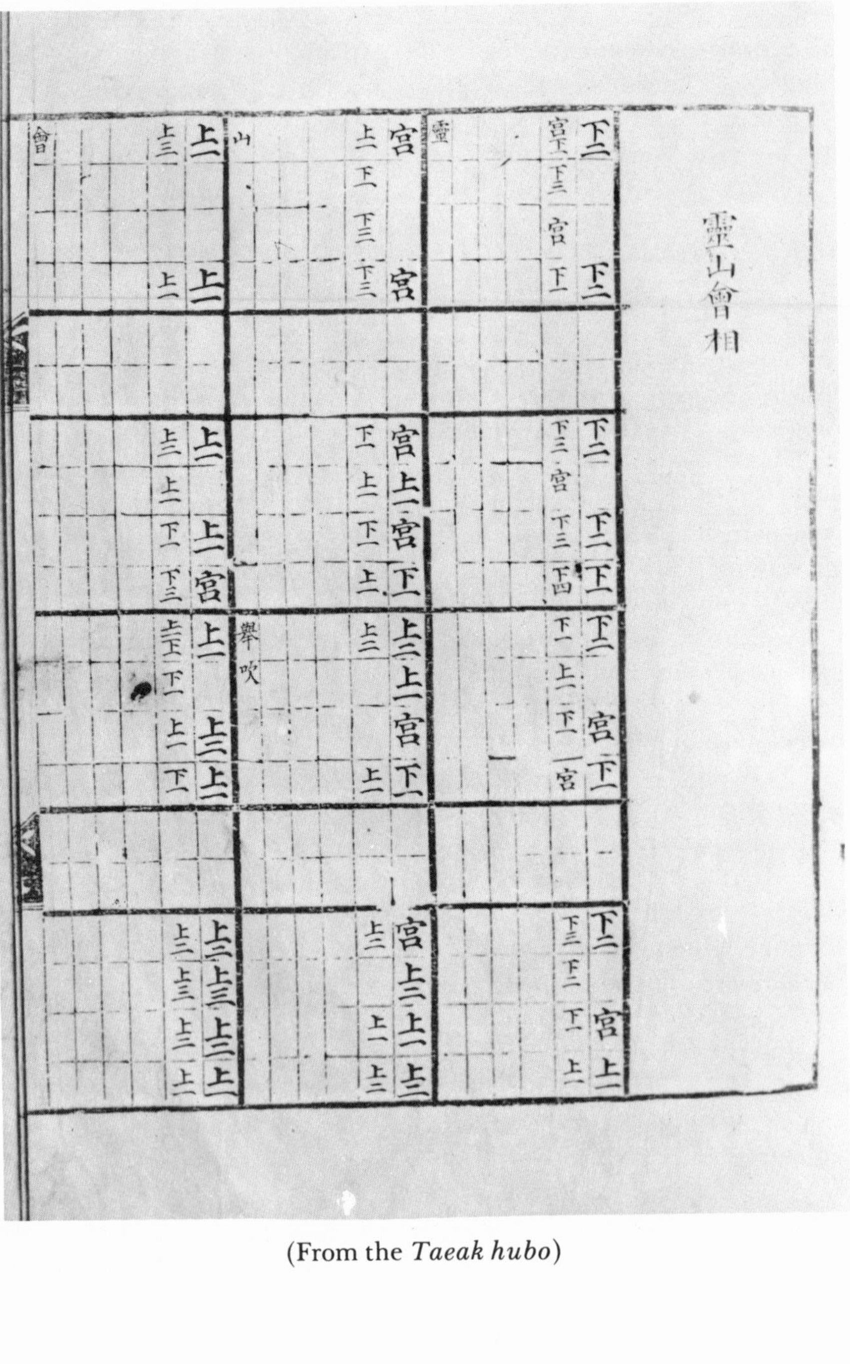

(From the *Taeak hubo*)

靈山會上

上一作相

(From the Kŭmbo sinjŭng karyŏng)

the five Chinese modes) with central tone on e^b (2nd string, 4th fret). This is due to the fact that of the four modes (*p'yŏngjo, ujo, p'yŏngjo kyemyŏnjo,* and *ujo kyemyŏnjo*), the note d^b is present only in the latter two; and of the latter two modes, only one, *ujo kyemyŏnjo,* contains the note g^b. Chart 8 on p. 54 compares the four modes just mentioned.

A clear statement of this is to be found in a manuscript in my private collection, the *Paegunam kŭmbo* 白雲庵琴譜 (ca. 1650), which says, "Convert *ujo* into *ujo kyemyŏnjo* by substituting 方六 (g^b) for 方五 (*f*) and 大七 (d^b) for 大六 (*c'*)." Since the *Yŏngsan hoesang* in the *Kŭmbo sinjŭng karyŏng* contains both g^b and $d^{b''}$, this is further proof that it is in the mode *ujo kyemyŏnjo.* For chronological reasons, the *Yŏngsan hoesang* in the *Taeak hubo* must also belong to *ujo kyemyŏnjo,* which means that its central tone is e^b.

Even further support for this choice of mode is afforded by the 17th century manuscript *Isu samsan chaebon kŭmbo* 二水三山齋本琴譜 . The *Yŏngsan hoesang* in the manuscript containes the text "*Yŏngsan hoesang pulbosal*" and begins with 大五 (B^b); both these features are shared with the abovementioned *Kŭmbo sinjŭng karyŏng.* The following textual comment appears in the manscript article: "*Yŏngsan hoesang* is in *ujo kyemyŏnjo* and is repeated from the beginning."

Consequently, since the central tone 宮 in the *Taeak hubo* is e^b, we may associate 大七 (d^b) with 下一 , and 方六 (g^b) with 上一 . If the beginning of the *Taeak hubo* version is transcribed on this basis, the result is virtually identical to the single column of *Yŏngsan hoesang* given by the *Kŭmbo sinjŭng karyŏng* (see Example 1a and b). A full transcription of the *Taeak hubo* version is given in Example 2a.

COMPARISON OF THE MODERN VERSION WITH THE TAEAK HUBO

A. Rhythm and meter:

One line (*haeng* 行) of 20 squares of the *Taeak hubo* version of *Yŏngsan hoesang* is easily seen to correspond to two lines (40 squares) of the modern *kŏmun'go* notation used by the National Classical Music Institute. The correlation is shown in Example 2a and 2c. This sort of relationship, one line of old notation corresponding to two in a modern version, may also be observed in two versions of the piece *Yŭmillak* 與民樂, in the *Sogak wŏnbo* 俗樂源譜 (eighteenth century) and the modern version.

From a first glance at Example 2, it is evident that the modern version is rhythmically more active; this is an example of the normal phenomenon of notes being added and rhythms quickened over the course of time. A closer look reveals that 10 beats (half notes) in the *Taeak hubo* are divided into a meter of $3 + 3 + 4$, whereas the modern version is divided $3 + 2 + 3 + 2$. That is, three beats (beats 4, 5, and 6) of the *Taeak hubo* have become compressed, in the modern version, into two beats (beats 4 and 5); and conversely, beat 10 in the *Taeak hubo* has become expanded into two beats (beats 9 and 10) in the modern version. This metrical relationship is consistent throughout. Another example of this sort of metrical relationship can be found by comparing the modern version of *Pŏho'ja* with the version notated in the *Sogak wŏnbo*.

B. Melody:

The two versions have basically the same melodic structure, but they differ considerably in the sections of Example 2 marked B, C, D and E, F. Nevertheless, as Example 2 reveals, in the places where B, C, D and E, F are repeated in the *Taeak hubo,* virtually the same repetition occurs in the modern version. This assures us that both versions belong to the same genealogy. The only difference to be observed is that in the modern version, E is repeated in a slightly varied form, E '.

Yŏngsan hoesang also appears in a different source which is chronologically intermediate between the *Taeak hubo* and the modern version: the *Yuyeji* 遊藝志 , by Sŏ Yu-gu 徐有榘 (1764-1845). The transcription in Example 2b shows that it is also melodically intermediate: in sections A, B, and C, it closely resembles the modern version, and in sections D, E, and F, it closely resembles the *Taeak hubo*. The *Yuyeji* thus further helps to clarify the relationship between the other two versions.

C. Alternation of notes over the course of time:

1) The下—pitch: the 10th beat of the first line of *Yongsan hoesang*

in the *Taeak hubo* has the pitch 下一, that is, d^b in *ujo kyemyŏnjo*. The corresponding notes in the modern version and Yuyeji however, is e^b. The reading of the *Kŭmbo sinjŭng karyŏng* agrees with the *Taeak hubo* in the pitch d^b.

2) The 上一 pitch: the 20th beat of the first line in the *Taeak hubo* has the pitch 上一, or g^b in *ujo kyemyŏnjo*. The corresponding note in the modern version and *Yuyeji* is a^b. Again, the *Kŭmbo sinjŭng karyŏng* agrees with the *Taeak hubo*. Other instances of this occurrence are: a) line 2, beat 12; b) line 3, beats 1 and 7; c) line 5, beat 11; and d) line 7. beats 1 and 10.

3) The 上二 pitch: the 11th beat of the second line in the *Taeak hubo* is 上二, or a^b in *ujo kyemyŏnjo*. The modern version and *Yuyeji* have b^b. Other examples of this are: a) line 2, beats 18 and 20; b) line 4, beat 11; c) line 5, beats 1 through 10; and d) line 7, beat 4.

Combining the above three observations, we see that the notes d^b, g^b, and a^b in the *Taeak hubo* have become altered over the course of time into, respectively, e^b, a^b, and b^b. In other words, the pentatonic scale of the *Taeak hubo* has become supplanted by an essentially tritonic scale:

Taeak hubo:	e^b	g^b	a^b	b^b	$d^{b\,\prime}$
Modern:	e^b		a^b	b^b	

This particular phenomenon can also be observed in the aristocratic chamber music with vocalist, *kagok* 歌曲 . For example, the piece *Kyemyŏn ch'osudaeyŏp* 界面初數大葉 (in *kyemyŏnjo*) is nothing more than such an alteration of *Ujo ch'osudaeyŏp* (in *ujo*). The *ujo* scale is:

$$e^b \quad f \quad a^b \quad b^b \quad c\,' \qquad (do\text{-mode})$$

When turned into *kyemyŏnjo,* this should become:

$$e^b \quad g^b \quad a^b \quad b^b \quad d^b \qquad (re\text{-mode})$$

But in modern *Kyemyŏn ch'osudaeyŏp,* as in the *Yŏngsan hoesang* case, the tones g^b and a^b have, respectively, become raised to a^b and b^b. This is shown schematically in Chart 2 on p. 000.

Thus, intervallic alterations have accumulated over the centuries separating the *Taeak hubo* and modern versions of *Yŏngsan hoesang,* but fundamentally they are still the same piece.

D. The extra two lines of the *Yuyeji* and modern versions:

The last comparative matter to be examined is that, as shown in Example 2, the score of *Yŏngsan hoesang* in the *Taeak hubo* consists of only seven lines, whereas the *Yuyeji* and modern versions both extend for two further lines. Investigating those extra two lines carefully, we note the following points:

1) In the modern version, beats 16 through 20 of line 8 are the same as section A in the corresponding portion of line 1. Further, beats 1 through 10 of line 9 clearly relate to sections B and C in the corresponding position in line 2. The same observations hold true for the *Yuyeji* version, but the *Yuyeji* version extends for five beats beyond the modern version. Those extra five beats are virtually the same as section D in the corresponding segment of line 2.

2) Despite the correspondences just noted, the first 16 beats of line 8 of the *Yuyeji* and modern versions are melodically distinct from the corresponding segments of line 1.

At this point we recall the quotation from the *Isu samsan chaebon kŭmbo* mentioned above: "*Yŏngsan hoesang*. . . is repeated from the beginning." For this reason, we have shown in Example 2a a repeat in the *Taeak hubo* version, beginning at line 8. But simple repetition would create a musically uninteresting situation, and there is evidence in favor of looking for a varied repetition. The *Yuyeji* describes a varied repetition for "*Samhyon todūri*" (the fifth movement of modern *Yŏngsan hoesang*), noting that simple repetition is too boring. Taking this as a clue, I have discovered that "*Chung-yŏngsan*" (the second movement of *Yŏngsan hoesang*) is, in fact, a variation of "*Sang-yŏngsan*," the movement we have been discussing. A detailed exposition of the variation technique is the subject of the following article on "*Chung-yŏngsan*" (p. 121).

In any event, it can be safely said that the extra two lines of the *Yuyeji* and modern versions are essentially "repeats from the beginning." To foreshadow some results from the "*Chung-yŏngsan*" article, it may be observed here that the mysterious first 15 beats of line 8 of the *Yuyeji* and modern versions are varied transpositions at the upper fourth of line 1.

CONCLUSIONS

A. The *Yŏngsan hoesang* recorded in the *Taeak hubo* has a text which has been lost in the modern instrumental version. As shown in Example 2, the text could be superimposed on the modern version by using one syllable per line, on the first beat. From the eighth line on, there would be no text.

B. The *Yŏngsan hoesang* of the *Taeak hubo* has e^b as its central tone and is in the mode *ujo kyemyŏnjo*, which is a *re*-mode. The modern *Yŏngsan hoesang* is in a so-called *kyemyŏnjo*, which we have shown to be a variant of the *ujo kyemyŏnjo* of the *Taeak hubo*. In the modern repertory is another version of *Yŏngsan hoesang*, called *P'yŏngjo hoesang* 平調會相, which can also be shown, by the same reasoning, to be in a variant form of *p'yŏngjo kyemyŏnjo*.

POSTSCRIPT

Yŏngsan hoesang is the only surviving example in Korea of purely instrumental performance of Buddhist music, but others existed in the past. The *Akhak kwebŏm*, for example, mentions three other such pieces: *Mit'ach'an* 彌陀讚, *Ponsach'an* 本師讚, and *Kwanŭmch'an* 觀音讚. Originally, according to the *Akhak kwebŏm*, the musicians and *kisaeng* (female entertainers) walked in a circle, singing "*Yŏngsan hoesang pulbosal*" in chorus; this makes it clear that *Yŏngsan hoesang* was not used to accompany dancing. Further, Sŏng Hyŏn 成俔(1439-1504) explains in his essay collection, *Yongje ch'onghwa* 慵齊叢活, that *Yŏngsan hoesang*, like *Kwanŭmch'an*, was originally Buddhist music. Later, in the time of King Chungjong 中宗 (ruled 1506-1544), the text of *Yŏngsan hoesang* was changed to *Sumannyŏn* 壽萬年, and thus was secularized. Today, of course, the text has been lost altogether.

As we have seen above, the *Yŏngsan hoesang* (i.e. modern "*Sang-yŏngsan*") of the *Taeak hubo* and *Akhak kwebŏm* was a vocal piece, but by the time of the *Yuyeji* (mid-19th century) it had been trans-formed into a purely instrumental piece. Having lost its supportive text, "*Sang-yŏngsan*" came to be divided into four or five sections; that is, it is in four sections in the *Yuyeji* and modern versions, but some sources consider the concluding passage from beat 10 of line 8 to be a fifth section. This division into sections, as is clear from its irregular spacing in Example 2 (circled numbers), was not originally dependent upon text placement. Also, as shown below, the sections of the *Yuyeji* and the modern versions do not coincide:

	1	II	III	IV
Yuyeji	35 beats	45 beats	30 beats	65 beats
Modern version	30 beats	40 beats	40 beats	60 beats

While the cadential phrase of each section in the *Yuyeji* has a different form, those in the modern version are all quite similar. In other words, when *Yŏngsan hoesang* lost the formal support of a text, it gradually gained a new formal support based upon consistent cadential phrases.

One unusual characteristic of *Yŏngsan hoesang* as recorded in the *Taeak hubo* is that it is written in lines of twenty squares (beats); the other seven pieces recorded in volume VI of the *Taeak hubo* are all written in lines of sixteen squares. Also, the other pieces all conclude with the same cadential pattern, 宮, 下一, 下二, 下三, 下四, 下五; only *Yŏngsan hoesang* differs. It is difficult to say whether or not these two distinguishing features are due to an origin in Buddhist music.

We have seen in this article how the *Yŏngsan hoesang* versions of the *Taeak hubo, Yuyeji,* and the present day clearly belong to the same genealogy, despite small alterations accruing through time. But there is also a version of *Yŏngsan hoesang* recorded in the *Sogak wŏnbo* which appears to be completely different from the other versions. It resembles the *Taeak hubo* version in only two ways: it is written in lines of twenty squares and is in the mode *ujo kyemyŏnjo,* the central tone being e^b. Beyond this, whatever relation it might bear to the other versions remains a mystery. For reference, the *Sogak wŏnbo* version is given below:

靈山會相

Example 1

Example 2

"CHUNG-YŎNGSAN" AS A VARIATION OF "SANG-YŎNGSAN"

INTRODUCTION

As played today, the second movement of the instrumental suite *Yŏngsan hoesang* 靈山會相 , *"Chung-yŏngsan"* 中靈山 , consists of five sections (*chang* 章). Dr. Chang Sa-hun 張師勛 , in his book *Kugak non'go* 國樂論攷 (1966; p. 183), has presented the opinion that the fifth section of *"Chung-yŏngsan"* should actually be considered the first section of the third movement of the suite, *"Se-yŏngsan"* 細靈山 . His opinion is supported by the late nineteenth-century source *Samjuk kŭmbo* 三竹琴譜 , which was discovered after his postulate had been published; in that source, the fifth section of *"Chung-yŏngsan"* is in fact notated as the first section of *"Se-yŏngsan."* This sheds considerable light on the relationship between *"Chung-yŏngsan"* and *"Se-yŏngsan,"* but as yet the relationship between *"Chung-yŏngsan"* and the first movement, *"Sang-yŏngsan"* 上靈山 , has not received an adequate explanation.

Both *"Chung-yŏngsan"* and *"Se-yŏngsan"* are basically performed on the seventh fret of the six-string *kŏmun'go* 玄琴 , which makes them easy to compare. But *"Sang-yŏngsan"* is played primarily on the fourth fret (a fourth below) and, in addition, there are differences in the *kanŭm* 間音 ("in-between," ornamental tones), making the comparison of *"Sang-yŏngsan"* and *"Chung-yŏngsan"* more difficult.

The comparison in the present article is founded primarily on the modern *kŏmun'go* part, which is most basic, but occasional references will be made to the *kayagŭm* 伽倻琴 (twelve-string zither) and *p'iri* 觱篥 (oboe) parts. The source for the modern version is Volume I of the

transcription series *Han'guk umak* 韓國音樂 , published by the National
Classical Music Institute in 1969. In addition, it is productive, in search-
ing for unornamented basic melodies, to consult older written sources
such as the *Taeak hubo* 大樂後譜 (1759), *Yuyeji* 游藝志 , by Sŏ Yu-gu
徐有榘 (1764-1845), *Kurach'ŏlsa kŭmbo* 歐邏鐵絲琴譜 by Yi Kyu-gyŏng
李圭景 (1788-?), *Aksŏ chŏnghae* 樂書正解 (1932) by Yi Ki-t'ae 李起兒 ,
Hakp'o kŭmbo 學圃琴譜 (ca. 1910-15), and the abovementioned *Samjuk
kŭmbo* (late 19th century).

For simplicity, we have changed the dotted quarter notes in the
National Calssical Music Institute transcription to plain quarters and
have dropped the complicated key signature to facilitate comparison
with the older sources (the original scale of e^b f a^b b^b $d^b{}'$ becomes
written simply as e f a b d').

The National Classical Music Institute score has here been altered
in one further way: one line (*kak* 刻) contains 20 beats (*pak* 拍), divided
into a meter of four groups (*kun* 群) arranged as 6 + 4 + 4 + 6 beats.
In this article, the meter has been changed to 6 + 4 + 6 + 4. The reason
is that the *hŭng* 흥 note (pitch *E*, played on the open 1st string of the
kŏmun'go), which functions as an indicator of continuation, often
occurs on the 15th beat (e.g. "*Sang-yŏngsan*," Section II, line 2; and
Section III, line 2; "*Chung-yŏngsan*," Section I, line 4; and Section II,
line 4), and it is functionally better to have this note come at the end of
the third group than on the lead-off beat (*ch'ŏnmŏri* 첫머리) of the
fourth group. Similarly, the *hŭng* normally occurs not at the beginning
of the second group, but at the end of the first group (e.g. "*Sang-
yŏngsan*," Section I, line 3; Section II, lines 1 and 2; and Section III,
line 1). A precedent for this interpretation is the transcription of
Yŏngsan hoesang in traditional notation in the book *Aksŏ chŏnghae*
(1932) by Yi Ki-t'ae.

For convenience in the discussion below, we will abbreviate references in this fashion: *Sang* and *Chung* for "*Sang-yŏngsan*" and "*Chung-
yŏngsan*," Roman numerals for sections (*chang*), Arabic numerals for
lines (*kak*), and lower case letters in parentheses for the four groups
(*kun*) in a line. Thus, "*Sang-yŏngsan*," Section II, line 2, third group
would be written *Sang* II.2 (c). The transcriptions in Examples 1
through 14 are arranged so that each example contains a single line of
20 beats, the 14 lines in succession making up a complete transcription

of the music under discussion and including reference transcriptions from old musical sources and where appropriate, instruments other than *kŏmun'go* in the modern version. Since the type of analysis presented here is rather unusual in studies of Korean music, it will initially be presented in careful detail and later less completely as it becomes more familiar and natural.

COMPARISON OF SECTIONS AND LINES OF SANG AND CHUNG

If we compare modern *Sang* and *Chung* in the obvious manner, relating *Sang* I to *Chung* I, and so on, the result is as in Chart 1:

(Chart 1)

	Sang	*Chung*
Section I	3 lines	4 lines
II	4	4
III	4	3
IV	6	3
V	/	4
Total	17 lines	18 lines

It is clear from Chart 1 that the correspondence between *Sang* and *Chung*, assuming one exists, is not simple. In the preceding article on *Sang* it was observed that the *Taeak hubo* score corresponded to only the first 14 lines of modern *Sang*, that is, to the length of the text "*Yŏngsan hoesang pulbosal*" 靈山會相佛菩薩 , with two lines per syllable. In that article (p. 111), it was suggested that the remaining three lines in modern *Sang* could be interpreted as a varied repeat from the beginning, transposed up a fourth; we will fill in the details of that suggestion here. (Note that since two lines of modern *Sang* correspond to one line in the *Taeak hubo*, the word "line" in the preceding article refers to a length twice that of "line" in the present article).

At this point, several of the older sources of *Yŏngsan hoesang* provide clues for solving the problem:

1) The *Hakp'o kŭmbo,* a book which probably dates between 1910 and 1915, notates *Sang* in five Sections, taking the modern Section IV of six lines as two, Sections IV and V, of four and two lines respectively.

2) The abovementioned *Aksŏ chŏnghae* (1932) similarly divides modern *Sang* IV into two sections, IV and V, but of equal length: three lines each.

3) In the *Samjuk kŭmbo* (late 19th century), as mentioned above, *Chung* V is notated as "*Se-yongsan*" I.

If, as suggested by the *Samjuk kŭmbo* example, "*Sang* V" (i.e. modern *Sang* IV. 4-6) is considered to be *Chung* I, uniformity results as in Chart 2:

(Chart 2)

	"Original" *Sang* Form	"Original" *Chung* Form
Section I	3 lines	3 lines (modern *Sang* IV.4-6)
II	4	4 (modern *Chung* I)
III	4	4 (modern *Chung* II)
IV	3	3 (modern *Chung* III)
Total	14 lines	14 lines

The seven lines of *Chung* IV and V shown in Chart 1, but eliminated from Chart 2, will be discussed later. More immediately, we must investigate whether there are musical correspondences between these two proposed "original" forms, thereby confirming whether or not this construction is valid. Examples 1 through 14 show *Sang* and *Chung* juxtaposed according to this proposed scheme, to facilitate comparison in the discussions that follow. We will continue to refer to *Chung* by its modern section numbers.

I. CONSPICUOUS CORRESPONDENCES BETWEEN SANG AND CHUNG

A. Closing lines of *Sang* II and *Chung* I (Example 7), and closing lines of *Sang* III and *Chung* II (Example 11):

Here we must introduce the concept of ornamental, "in-between" notes, *kanŭm* 間音 : these are extra notes which have been added to *Yŏngsan hoesang* in the natural accrual of extra notes and quicker rhythms which occurs with the passage of time. *Kanŭm* are contrasted with "fundamental" notes, *wŏnjŏm* 元點 , which are the basic structural notes of the melody, often manifested in older notated sources such as the *Taeak hubo*. The further back one reaches in time, the fewer *kanŭm* he encounters.

1) *Sang* II.4(a): referring to Example 7, we see that the modern *kŏmun'go* part (to which we will henceforth refer simply as the "modern" version, unless otherwise specified) is *E a.a.(E)*. The final note, *E* (*hŭng*), serves the purpose of prolonging the preceding note *a*. For similar cases, see Example 9: *Yuyeji, Sang* III.2(a) and (c). This interpretation is supported by the fact that in all three cases, the un-ornamented *Taeak hubo* version does not give the *E*. Thus we consider the final *E* to be a *kanŭm* (shown by parentheses) and the *wŏnjŏm* of *Sang* II.4(a) to be *a*.

Chung I.4(a): here the modern version is *a.(ba).(ee)*, in which the *ba* is just an auxiliary ornamentation and the *ee* corresponds in function to the *E* (*hŭng*) in *Sang* II.4(a). Hence the *wŏnjŏm* is simply *a*. Example 15.A summarizes in graphic form the several variations of *hŭng* that occur: the present cases are shown in the first two lines under A-1. Further, the modern *kayagŭm* part of *Chung* I.4(a), *a.(ab).d'b*, has the same *wŏnjŏm*, *a*: the *ab* is transitory (see Example 15.C-1: 15.B through D summarize the occurrence of *kanŭm* in *Sang* and *Chung*) and the *d'b* corresponds to the *hŭng* note, *E*, of *Sang* II.4(a) (see Example 15.A-2). In the *kŏmun'go* part, the reason the *kanŭm* go downward, *ba*, is that they are followed by another downward melodic motion, to *e*; in the *kayagŭm* score, conversely, the rise to *d'* requires that the *kanŭm* be *ab* rather than *ba*.

In sum, the *wŏnjŏm* of both *Sang* II.4(a) and *Chung* I.4(a) is *a;* the two melodic lines differ only in *kanŭm*.

2) *Sang* II.4(b): in the modern *p'iri* part, *Sang* II.4(b)-(d) and *Chung* I.4(b)-(d) are virtually identical, clearly supporting the proposed correspondence of *Sang* II and *Chung* I. The modern *kŏmun'go* version of *Sang* II.4(b) is *e.(BA)*. This *BA* motion is special, occurring only in the closing lines of each section of *Sang*. The corresponding *Yuyeji* part

is *e.B,* indicating the *A* is a *kanŭm.* Further, since the *Taeak hubo* has only *e,* we know the *B* is also a *kanŭm,* leaving *e* as the *wŏnjŏm.*

Chung I.4(b): the modern *kŏmun'go* part has *a.(eB),* of which the *eB* is *kanŭm,* by the same reasoning as above (see Example 15.B-5). Similarly, the *ba* in the modern *kayagŭm* part, *Yuyeji,* and *Kurach'ŏlsa kŭmbo* is always *kanŭm.* (Example 15.B-2)

Thus, the *wŏnjŏm* of *Sang* II.4(b) is *e;* in *Chung* I.4(b), the modern *kŏmun'go* part is a fourth higher, *a,* and in the modern *kayagŭm* part the note is an octave higher, *e'.* These *wŏnjŏm* are shown in Example 16, which is a running comparison of the *wŏnjŏm* melodies of *Sang* and *Chung,* in the proposed alignment.

3) *Sang* II.4(c)-(d): in the modern version, these groups are the same as the corresponding groups in the closing line of Section III (i.e. *Sang* III.4(c)-(d)) (Example 11). The *Yuyeji* part is also the same in Section II, but in Section III it is identical with the modern version (*kŏmun'go*) of *Chung,* both Sections I and II. This implies that the closing phrases of *Sang* II and III and of *Chung* I and II all belong to the same derivation. The closing phrase of both *Sang* II and III (i.e. 4(c)-(d)) is *e.a.(Be)/a.(Be),* of which the *Be* are *kanŭm.* This leaves the *wŏnjŏm* as *e.a/a* (Example 16).

Chung I and II, 4(c)-(d): the modern version is *e.a.E/a.a,* identical to *Sang* III.4(c)-(d) in the *Yuyeji* transcription. The *wŏnjŏm* here are clearly *e.a/a* by the usual reasoning, and this is as the same as the *wŏnjŏm* just mentioned for *Sang.*

It may be observed here that the notes *E* (*hŭng*) in *Chung* and *Be* in *Sang* are *kanŭm* serving to prolong the basic *wŏnjŏm* (see Example 15.A-3). This manner of variation occurs frequently.

Summarizing #1) to 3): based on the modern *kŏmun'go* version and *wŏnjŏm,* the closing line of *Chung* I is altered from that of *Sang* II by only one note (the *p'iri* part, however, coincides) (Example 16). That small discrepancy is certainly insufficient to disturb the clear fact that *Sang* II.4 and *Chung* I.4 correspond. Also, since *Chung* I and II have their closing lines as the fourth line, they would more likely correspond to *Sang* II and III, which also have their closing lines as the fourth line, rather than to *Sang* I, which has its closing line as the third line.

B. *Sang* III.2 and *Chung* II.2 (Example 9):

First of all, the corresponding line of the *Taeak hubo* uses only a single note, *a*, and for *Sang*, *Yuyeji* has *b* running overwhelmingly through the whole line. The modern *Sang* part has fewer *b*'s than *Yuyeji*, but *b* is still preponderant. In *Sang* III.2(b), *b.(eb)*, the *eb* is thus considered *kanŭm* by comparison with *Yuyeji* (Example 15.C-3). *Sang* III.2(d), *b.(Be)*, by similar comparison to *Yuyeji* and also from the comments above in the paragraphs on closing lines (I.A) (Example 15.C-2), has *wŏnjŏm b*. The *wŏnjŏm* of the modern version, then, is *b*, throughout the line. (Example 16)

1) *Chung* II.2(a): the modern reading is *(b).e'.(ab)*. The first tone, *b*, corresponds to the first *E* in *Sang*, being a preparatory tone for the *e'* a fourth higher; there are many examples of this sort of melodic movement (listed in Example 15.D). The *ab* is also *kanŭm*, as referred to above in the section on closing lines (see Example 15.C-1). *Sang* (a) and (c) are identical; in *Chung* (a) and (c), the *ab* in (a) becomes *E* (*hŭng*) in (c), further supporting the interpretation of both as *kanŭm*. At any rate, the *wŏnjŏm* is *e'* in *Chung* II.2(a).

2) *Chung* II.2(b): the modern reading is *(f').e'*. The *e'* is evidently the more fundamental tone, because of comparison with *Sang* (especially in the *Yuyeji* (b) and (d)), which has only the note *b*. In the *Chung* case, (b) and (d) are melodically different, *f'.e'* versus *e'.d'b*, but they have the common tone *e'*. Furthermore, the modern *kŏmun'go* version of *Sang* IV.1(d) (Example 12) similarly has *f.fe*, while the corresponding *Yuyeji* and modern *kayagŭm* parts have only *e* (see Example 15.B-1). Another such case occurs in *Sang* IV.4(a) (Example 1). The conclusion is that the *f'* in *Chung* II.2(b) is a *kanŭm*.

3) *Chung* II.2(c): in this group, the *b* of *(b).e'.(E)* functions as it did in (a), described above. The *wŏnjŏm* again is *e'*.

4) *Chung* II.2(d): *e'.(d'b)*. *d'b* is *kanŭm*, like *hŭng E*; the *wŏnjŏm* is *e'*, as suggested above in the section on closing lines (see Example 15.A-2).

In sum, from the standpoint of *wŏnjŏm*, *Sang* III.2 has *b* running all the way through, and *Chung* II.2 has *e'*, a fourth higher, all the way through (Example 16). The interval of a fourth arises from the fact that *Sang* is basically played on the *kŏmun'go* 4th fret and *Chung* mostly on the 7th fret. Thus we can consider this line of *Chung* to be a transposition up a fourth of the corresponding *Sang* line. The long, drawn-out *b* of this *Sang* line is also the climax of *Sang*. All of these features are closely in accord with the older notations of the *Taeak hubo* and *Yuyeji*, and the correspondence cannot be doubted.

C. *Sang* I.1 and *Sang* IV.4 (= "original" *Chung* I.1) (Example 1):

From this point on, the technical explanation is abbreviated, and results will be presented on the basis of reasoning similar to what has preceded.

The first 16 beats (quarter notes) of *Sang* IV.4 have the fundamental note *e* running throughout. The first 16 beats of *Sang* I.1 similarly emphasize *B* (Example 16). This means these lines are another case of transposition by a fourth, showing that indeed *Sang* I.1 corresponds not to modern *Chung* I, but to modern *Sang* IV.4 which we have suggested (Chart 2) should be the beginning of the "original" *Chung*. This is quite similar to the documented case in the *Samjuk kŭmbo* concerning "*Chung-yŏngsan*" and "*Se-yŏngsan*."

D. *Sang* II.2 and *Chung* I.2 (Example 5):

In terms of *wŏnjŏm*, the first 16 beats of both *Sang* and *Chung* have only one note, *a*, although their *kanŭm* differ (Example 16). It is curious that the two are not a fourth apart, since this is not a closing line of a section; but perhaps by avoiding the *d'* in *Chung* it gives greater emphasis to the climax on *e'* coming up in *Chung* II.2. In *Sang* II.2(d), the *wŏnjŏm* is *e*; in *Chung* I.2(d), it is *e'*, so there is an octave alteration.

Summarizing A through D, it is clear that the correspondence between *Sang* and *Chung* proposed in Chart 2 is valid. In Chart 3 below, the conspicuous musical correspondences pointed out in A through D are summarized and indicated by dotted enclosures ⌐‾‾‾⌐; so far, the similar portions amount to five lines.

(Chart 3)

	1	2	3	4
Sang I	a b c d	a b c d	a b c d	
Sang IV. 4-6	a b c d	a b c d	a b c d	
Sang II	a b c d	a b c d	a b c d	a b c d
Chung I	a b c d	a b c d	a b c d	a b c d
Sang III	a b c d	a b c d	a b c d	a b c d
Chung II	a b c d	a b c d	a b c d	a b c d
Sang IV. 1-3	a b c d	a b c d	a b c d	
Chung III	a b c d	a b c d	a b c d	

II. TIMES OF COMPLETE AGREEMENT BETWEEN SANG *AND* CHUNG

A. *Sang* I.2(c)-(d) and *Sang* IV.5(c)-(d) (Example 2):

In the modern *kŏmun'go* part, these two are identical. In (c), *eB* is *kanŭm* (Example 15.B-5), leaving *B.e* as *wŏnjŏm* (Example 16); and in (d), *eb* is *kanŭm*, leaving *a* as *wŏnjŏm* (Example 16). This corresponds to the reading of the *Taeak hubo*.

B. *Sang* I.3 and *Sang* IV.6 (Example 3):

These two lines are identical. The *wŏnjŏm*, *a.e.ea.a*, are clear from preceding discussions (I.A) (Example 16).

C. *Sang* II.1(a)-(b) and *Chung* I.1(a)-(b) (Example 4):

In *Chung* (a), the *wŏnjŏm* is *d'*, and in *Sang* (a), the *wŏnjŏm* is *b.a*; thus, *Chung* is a fourth higher than the *a* in *Sang* (Example 16). It is hard to explain why the *p'iri* parts of *Sang* and *Chung* are on the same pitch level, but their similarity and correspondence is quite clear.

In *Sang* (b), the *wŏnjŏm* is *a*; in *Chung* (b), it is *e'*. But a fourth above *a* would be *d'*, not *e'*. There are several other examples of this occurrence, to be examined below.

D. *Sang* II.3(c)-(d) and *Chung* I.3(c)-(d) (Example 6):

In the *kŏmun'go* part, *Sang* (c) has *wŏnjŏm B.e* (see above, II.A), as does *Chung* (c), an octave higher. In this case, the *kayagŭm* parts of *Sang* and *Chung* are identical. *Sang* (d) has the *wŏnjŏm a* (Example 15.C-3), and *Chung* (d) has *wŏnjŏm d'* (Example 15.B-5). It is clear that these parts correspond, although *Sang* (c) is an octave below the older sources and *Chung* (d) is a fourth above *Sang* (d).

E. *Sang* III.1(a)-(b) and *Chung* II.1(a)-(b) (Example 8):

Chung (a) has the *wŏnjŏm e* , quite similar to the situation in *Chung* I.1(a) where the *wŏnjŏm* is *d'* (Example 4; see paragraph C above). Further, it is clear from a comparison of Examples 4 and 8, both modern and older versions, that there is a close resemblance between *Sang* II.1(a) and III.1(a), as well as between *Chung* I.1(a) and II.1(a). This holds true despite the fact that *Chung* has *wŏnjŏm e'* in one case and *d'* in the other; also, this is by no means a unique example of inexact transposition. Other examples include the next group, *Chung* II.1(b) (Example 8), where the modern *kŏmun'go* version gives *d'* while *kurach'ŏlsa kŭmbo* presents *e'*, and similar cases in *Chung* III.1(b) (Example 12) and *Chung* III.3(a) (Example 14). At any rate, the correspondence of *Sang* II and *Chung* I is clear from the *kayagŭm* parts which are virtually identical. *Sang* (b) and *Chung* (b) certainly have the same *wŏnjŏm, a* (*kanŭm* are as in Example 15.B-5).

G. *Sang* IV.1(c)-(d) and *Chung* III.1(c)-(d) (Example 12):

In the *Kurach'ŏlsa kŭmbo*, *Sang* and *Chung* are virtually identical. The modern *kŏmun'go* parts are also quite similar (Example 15.A-2). The *kŏmun'go* part for *Sang* (c) has the *wŏnjŏm b*, while the *Yuyeji* and modern *kayagŭm* parts have *a*. The *p'iri* part comes and goes between *a* and *b*. This sort of occurrence appears elsewhere, as in Example 13, and is evidently something that happens only over the interval of a major second and only with the notes *e* and *f(#)*, *a* and *b*, and *d'* and *e* . In *Sang* (d) and *Chung* (d), the *kayagŭm* has *wŏnjŏm e*, while the *kŏmun'go* has *f* in one case and *e* in the other.

H. *Sang* IV.2(a)-(b) and *Chung* III.2(a)-(b) (Example 13):

Again, these are identical in the *Kurach'ŏlsa kŭmbo* and very similar in the modern *kayagŭm* and *p'iri* parts. The *kŏmun'go* part of *Sang* (a) has *wŏnjŏm a.e,* as in the *Taeak hubo* and *Yuyeji;* however, the *kayagŭm* part has *wŏnjŏm a.b,* perhaps because the ensuing leap to *e'* is more reasonable from *b* than from *e.* The modern *kŏmun'go* part of *Sang* (b) is like the *Taeak hubo* and *Yuyeji,* while the *kayagŭm* is a fourth higher.

It appears that here the modern *kŏmun'go* part in (a)-(b) is near to the original form, having a close resemblance to the old sources, while the *kayagŭm* has transposed its version up a fourth in group (b). Thus, the *kayagŭm* has already varied the original form in *Sang* and repeats the variation in *Chung;* the *kŏmun'go,* however, has the original form in *Sang* and the varied form in *Chung.*

I. *Sang* IV.2(c)-(d) and *Chung* III.2(c)-(d) (Example 13):

In *Sang* (c) and *Chung* (c), the *kayagŭm* parts are identical and the *kŏmun'go* parts clearly related. In *Sang* (d), the *wŏnjŏm* is *a* (Example 15.C-3) and in *Chung* (d) it is *e',* a fifth higher. This transposition by a fifth has already been observed, and groups (a) through (c), in any case, have a clear relationship.

Chart 4 summarizes all the points of correspondence discussed so far. The portions discussed in II.A through J are shown by solid-line enclosures ☐ .

(Chart 4)

	1	2	3	4
Sang I	a b c d	a b c d	a b c d	
Sang IV.4-6	a b c d	a b c d	a b c d	
Sang II	a b c d	a b c d	a b c d	a b c d
Chung I	a b c d	a b c d	a b c d	a b c d
Sang III	a b c d	a b c d	a b c d	a b c d
Chung II	a b c d	a b c d	a b c d	a b c d
Sang IV.1-3	a b c d	a b c d	a b c d	
Sang III	a b c d	a b c d	a b c d	

III. OTHER OBSCURELY CORRESPONDING SEGMENTS
OF SANG *AND* CHUNG

By reasoning similar to that in the preceding discussion, we can postulate correspondences between several other bits of *Sang* and *Chung*. Lest too much attention to detail obscure our primary goals of demonstrating the primary correspondence between *Sang* and *Chung* and the process of variation which has occurred, we will simply show these remaining correspondences in Chart 5, notated with brackets ⌐⌐ . The reader may examine these segments on his own if he so desires, as the necessary information and summaries are given in the musical examples.

(Chart 5)

	1	2	3	4
Sang I	a b c d	a b c d	a b c d	
Sang IV. 4-6	a b c d	a b c d	a b c d	
Sang II	a b c d	a b c d	a b c d	a b c d
Chung I	a b c d	a b c d	a b c d	a b c d
Sang III	a b c d	a b c d	a b c d	a b c d
Chung II	a b c d	a b c d	a b c d	a b c d
Sang IV. 1-3	a b c d	a b c d	a b c d	
Chung III	a b c d	a b c d	a b c d	

CONCLUSIONS

The relationship, or correspondence of sections, between "*Sang-yŏngsan*" and "*Chung-yŏngsan*" is not trivial and requires looking deeper than the form of the movements as delineated by modern performance. It is interesting that even though performers have forgotten the actual formal relationship between "*Sang-yŏngsan*" and "*Chung-yŏngsan*," their performance of the music itself still manifests the relationship clearly when a few adjustments of form have been made. In this article we have shown that the correspondence exists throughout, in both metrical lengths and musical content. It is also interesting to note that, as shown in Chart 5, the correspondences revealed by our examination between *Sang* II and *Chung* I and between *Sang* III and *Chung* II run almost parallel.

For the most part, the modern *kŏmun'go* melody is most basic and best reveals the relationships in question; however, there are times when the *kayagŭm* or *p'iri* more clearly demonstrates the relationships (e.g. Example 13). The remaining segments, outlined in III above, can often be deduced to be corresponding by the reasoning demonstrated earlier; raising and lowering of notes by a major second is a frequent occurrence.

As we have shown, the last three lines of *Sang* IV should be considered the beginning of *Chung*; these three lines constitute a bridge to the rather faster tempo of *Chung* and are what is now called a *toljang* 回章 . As notated in the *Taeak hubo*, "Sang-yŏngsan" extends only as far as *Sang* IV.3 in the modern version, the same place that we now take to be the original beginning of "*Chung-yŏngsan*."

As mentioned in the introduction, Dr. Chang Sa-hun has suggested that the "original" "*Chung-yŏngsan*" corresponds to what in the modern piece is *Chung* I-IV. But our study has shown that it is more accurate to say that the "original" "*Chung-yŏngsan*" extended from modern *Sang* IV.4 through *Chung* III. This is shown in Chart 6:

In other words, the original form had the same number of sections and lines for each of "*Sang-yongsan*," "*Chung-yongsan*," and "*Se-yongsan*."

In the process of variation from *Sang* to *Chung*, the following points are significant: for the most part, *Chung* is a fourth higher than *Sang*, but the closing lines of each section are back at the original pitch level. This is related to the fact that *Chung* is played mostly on the 7th fret of the *kŏmun'go*, a fourth higher than the 4th fret used in *Sang*. This technical matter also results in the confusion of the pitches e and f, a and b, and d' and e', so that there are frequent instances when *Chung* is a fifth higher than *Sang*, rather than a fourth.

Modern *Sang* departs in many ways from the old sources, and *Chung* is yet a further variation. There are several cases, however, where there appears to be no relationship between modern *Sang* and *Chung* until both are compared with the old sources.

The present article is a first effort in this type of study of variation in Korean music, and much remains to be further studied. For example, an interesting modal case is when *ujo* 羽調 changes to *p'yŏngjo* 平調 in the piece *Chungdaeyŏp* 中大葉 recorded in the source *Yanggŭm sinbo* 梁琴新譜 (1610). It is necessary further to clarify the characteristics of variation technique in Korean music.

(Chart 6)

	MODERN FORM			"ORIGINAL" FORM	
	Section	Lines		Section	Lines
"Sang-yŏng-san"	I	3	"Sang-yŏng san"	I	3
	II	4		II	4
	III	4		III	4
	IV	6		IV	3
"Chung yŏng-san"			"Chung-yŏng-san"	I	3
	I	4		II	4
	II	4		III	4
	III	3		IV	3
	IV	3	"Se-yŏng-san"	I	3
	V	4		II	4
"Se-yŏng-san"	I	4		III	4
	II	3		IV	3
	III	3	"Karak tŏri"	I	3
	IV	4		II	4
"Karak tŏri"	I	4		III	4
	II	3			
	III	3			

Example 1:

Sang I. 1

and *Sang* IV. 4

Example 2:
Sang I. 2
and *Sang* IV. 5

Example 3
Sang I. 3
and *Sang* IV. 6

Example 4:
Sang II. 1
and *Chung* I. 1

Example 5:
Sang II.2
and *Chung* I. 2

Example 6:
Sang II. 3
and *Chung* I. 3

Example 7:
Sang II. 4
and *Chung* I. 4

Example 8:
Sang III.1
and *Chung* II. 1

Example 9:
Sang III. 2
and *Chung* II. 2

Example 10:
Sang III. 3
and *Chung* II. 3

Example 11:
Sang III.4
and *Chung* II. 4

Example 12:
Sang IV. 1
and *Chung* III. 1

Example 13:
Sang IV. 2
and *Chung* III. 2

Example 14:
Sang IV.' 3
and *Chung* III. 3

Example 15.A:
Variants of *Hŭng*
(marked with bracket   )

Abbreviations:
7 : Example 7
11 : Example 11
S : *"Sang-yŏngsan"*
C : *"Chung-yŏngsan*

Example 15. B:
Types of *Kanŭm* (1)
(marked with bracket)

Example 15.C:
Types of *Kanŭm* (2)

Example 15.D:
Types of *Kanŭm* (3)

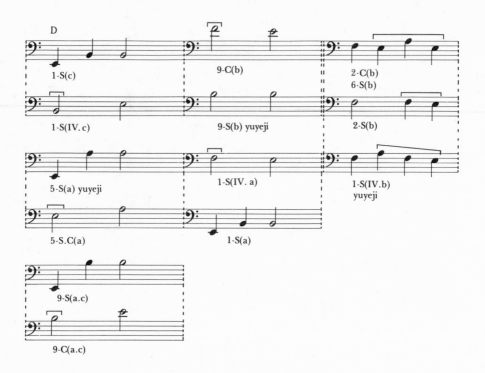

Example 16:
Comparision of *Wŏnjŏm* melodies

Abbreviations:

⌐ : Variant of *Sang*

x : Not a fourth higher than *Sang*

( ) : Not *kŏmun'go* part

APPRECIATION OF *SIJO*

INTRODUCTION

Although the written musical transcription appears quite simple, there is little which is subject to more dispute than a musical performance of the poetic form *sijo* 時調 . It is said that in *sijo* singing there is no *myŏng ch'ang*, singer whose fame is well-established: every time when *sijo* were performed on the radio, they were unfavorably criticized. This makes it difficult to define the qualities which make *sijo* famous.

Some hate listening to the high falsetto voice used in *sijo* melody sung in the capital region of Korea (*Kyŏngp'an sijo* 京관時調). There are others who condemn the *sijo* of *Ch'ungch'ŏng* 忠清 province (*Naep'o sijo* 內浦時調) as popular *tan'ga* 短歌 style. Another disparagingly refers to the *sijo* of Cholla 全羅 province. There are those who say that the best *sijo* are those in the determined and deep *sijo* style of *Kyŏngsang* 慶尚 province; on the other hand, some find this style too stiff and prefer hearing a mixed style with features of both capital and *Kyŏngsang sijo*. In short, appraisals of *sijo* differ strongly for every geographical region.

Given this situation, one might well ask how *sijo* has become the most frequently sung form of traditional vocal music. That is, how can we define the standards of good *sijo* singing? What produces the characteristic elegance of *sijo*? More fundamentally, what, in broad outline, constitutes a *sijo*? How is its character different from other types of Korean vocal music such as *kagok* 歌曲 (see page 71), *kasa* 歌詞 (long narrative songs), and songs in the slow *chinyangjo* 진양조 rhythmic pattern (see page 182)? The present article addresses questions such as these.

Although there are three main types of *sijo* melody (standard, *p'yŏng sijo*; descending melodic contour, *chirŭm sijo*; and reciting style, *sasŏl sijo*), we shall be primarily concerned here with only the standard *sijo*. Further, a fuller examination would include the important textual factors in the musical setting of *sijo* (the grammatical structure of the poem and pitch characteristics of particular words are both reflected in the music), but only purely musical matters are discussed here.

BASIC CHARACTERISTICS OF THE SIJO

First of all, the *sijo* has a very slow tempo. A *sijo* performance is made up of three musical sections, corresponding to the three lines comprising the poetic form; the time required is between two and a half and three minutes. The first and second sections each consist of thirty-four "beats" (*pak* 拍), subdivided metrically into $5 + 8 + 8 + 5 + 8$. The concluding section has twenty-six beats, divided $5 + 8 + 5 + 8$. Altogether, then, there are 94 beats, each of which lasts roughly two seconds, corresponding to a metronome setting of 30 to 35. Not only is each beat thus quite slow-paced, but also most sung pitches are sustained over several beats (see musical example).

   In such a slow tempo, it is difficult to get a sense of any regular rhythm. This might be compared to the rhythm of water dripping from a faucet into a washbasin: if the drops occur only about once each second (M.M. 60), it is very hard to get any feeling of a rhythm. If the rate of fall is more rapid, making strong and weak sounds, like a drop every half second (M.M. 120), it is quite easy to detect the regular pulse of the rhythm. It is difficult to specify the limits within which it is easy to get a real feeling for rhythmic pulse; roughly speaking, though, it seems to be M.M. 40 up to M.M. 208. Since the *sijo* beats proceed at M.M. 30 to 35, they are below the lower limits within which regular rhythm is easily perceived. Indeed, when a tempo is this slow, it is a moot question whether or not one can really say the piece has a regular rhythm. *Sijo* are not alone in this matter; *kagok* is much the same, typically having a tempo of approximately M.M. 30.

   While *kagok* is in one of two modes, *ujo* or *kyemyŏnjo* (see page 71), *sijo* has only a single mode. Mr. Hong Wŏn-gi 洪元基 , a famous *sijo* performer, reports that the singer Ch'oe Sang-uk 崔相旭 performed *sijo* in both *ujo* and *kyemyŏnjo*, but the author has had no opportunity to verify this. One frequently encounters terms such as *kyemyŏn-ch'ŏng* 界面청 , *ujo-ch'ŏng* 羽調청 , and *p'yongjo-ch'ŏng* 平調청 in connection with *sijo* performance, but these are merely used to indicate the starting pitch, in the event there is an instrumental accompaniment on the *tanso* 短簫 (vertical flute) or *taegŭm* 大芩 (transverse flute). Specifically, *kyemyŏn-ch'ŏng* indicates the starting pitch a^b, *p'yŏngjo-ch'ŏng* is $e^{b'}$, *ujo-ch'ŏng* is e^b, and *ŏl'ch'ŏng* 얼청 is $d^{b'}$.

If ornamental tones are excluded, the *sijo* scale consists primarily of three pitches: a^b, e^b, and B^b (in the case of *kyemyŏn-ch'ŏng*). This is examined in more detail in the next section, on basic and varied forms of *sijo*; in the attached musical example, the melody is transposed up a half-step for clarity. In other words, the basic scale is tritonic; there is much melodic movement by fourth, and the melodic compass rarely exceeds an octave. The melody has minimal rise and fall; compared to *kagok* or *kasa*, *sijo* melody is simple.

In sum, the tempo of *sijo* is very slow, and one could almost say there is no regular rhythm. There are no changes of mode, and the melody is extremely simple. Music is often considered to have three basic elements: rhythm, melody, and harmony. *Sijo*, of course, lacks harmony in the usual sense; its rhythm is open to some doubt; and its melody is quite simple. What, then, are the important constituents of *sijo* performance?

Long ago, when I was in college preparatory school, I went one day to a grove of pine trees and lay down alone on the ground. I had not meditated for long before my imagination was filled with wild fancies; to this day I remember clearly the impression made by the sound of the wind blowing through the pines, like a heavenly music. Blowing in the pine grove over my head, the wind rushed by in a crescendo, followed by a descrescendo as the wind died away; after straining, the pine needles shook back in a kind of tremolo, giving a very settling sound. The delicate variations in sound made by the pine trees varied with the force of the wind blowing in and passing out.

The long, drawn-out sounds of the wind blowing through the pine grove could hardly be said to have melody or rhythm; what gave the sense of beauty could only be the dynamics, that is, the changes in power. Like the wind in the pines, *sijo* has no harmony, little rhythm, and a simple melody; the sense of pleasure in hearing *sijo* is aroused by the variations in dynamics. Dynamic change is the most vital element in *sijo* performance and produces its elegance. There is, of course, no music in which dynamics play no part, but dynamics are practically everything in *sijo*. When a tone lasts from four to ten seconds, the music would be lifeless were dynamics absent, and; *sijo* is largely made up of such long tones. Since *sijo* has a simpler melody than *kagok,* dynamics are correspondingly more important.

The performance of *sijo*, with its long-held tones and few turns of melody, varies more with the dynamic inclinations of an individual performer than performance of music with greater melodic complexity. This brings to mind writing Chinese characters with a brush: the simplest character, —("one"), consists of a single, long horizontal stroke. The amount of force used on the brush varies widely with every writer, and the resulting calligraphies are very individual. Such individuality is less common in characters which have a large number of strokes; it is more difficult to set a fixed standard for the simplest characters.

In summary, the *sijo* lacks harmony, has unclear rhythm, and uses an extremely simple melody. It is no exaggeration to say that its most characteristic and essential musical feature is its use of dynamics.

BASIC FORM AND VARIED FORM IN THE SIJO

As already mentioned, there are many differences in *sijo* according to the region and even the individual singer. Here the discussion centers on the style of singing in the capital region, and many references will be made to the musical example, a standard *sijo* transcribed by Dr. Chang Sa-hun 張師勛 . Unfortunately, transcriptions of the various regional styles are not available, and the author has had no opportunity to examine the regional variants on the basis of phonograph recordings; it is necessary to rely upon memory of performances heard in the past and discussions with persons in the field.

In the first section of the *sijo* (see musical example), there is a determined push from the first to second beats, with a strong crescendo, all on the pitch *a*. In the third beat, the sound diminishes and the voice begins to vibrate, still on *a*. In the fourth beat, the voice seems to break and drops a fourth to the pitch *e*. The technique of singing beats 1 to 3 is the same in both capital and regional styles and gives a sense of determination; this feeling may be recognized by comparison with beats 22 to 24, having a similar tonal structure, but different feeling. In beat 3, the strength of the voice in the vibrato gradually diminishes, and, almost like reverberation, the sound seems to continue of its own strength; but absolutely nothing is done at random in this vibrato. When the tone is strong, there is no room for vibrato; as the tone weakens, the vibrato comes into play. This is like the abovementioned music of the wind in the pine grove and is perfectly natural. Beats 1 to 2 are strained, and in beat 3, there is no sudden lapse into relaxation; from the standpoint of text and tone strength, the voice seems to bump lightly into beat 4; that is, it snaps downward and flows forward in a relaxed fashion. This phenomenon occurs only in this particular passage and gives it a special flavor (compare beats 14 to 21).

This technique of increasing and decreasing the force of the voice, that is, dynamics, is the lifeblood and elegance of *sijo*. When one is learning *sijo*, the beats and melody are simple and easy, presenting no difficulties; the demanding part is the dynamic structure, and one's mastery depends on the depth of his knowledge of this aspect, which is gained through experience. For the opening five beats, the various styles of *sijo* are similar, so that this passage may be considered part of the basic form of the *sijo*. In the styles of Ch'ungch'ŏng and Chŏlla provinces, however, this passage is somewhat different, having the melodic motion $e—a$; these may be considered variant forms.

This opening *sijo* passage might be compared with the opening phrase of a piece of *kagok* such as *Ujo ch'osudaeyŏp* 羽調初數大葉 (see the musical example on page 79). Both are very slow, with a beat having a time value about M.M. 30; as a result, both have a grave feeling. However, the melodic structure of the *sijo* is simpler and gives an effect of swelling and determination; since the *kagok* melody has many ornamental notes, its effect is of greater length, mildness, and disjointedness.

In beat 6 of the musical example in this article, the melody moves from b to a; in the transcription done by the *Sijo yŏn'gu-hoe* 時調研究會, however, this is given as merely a to a. The reason for the difference is that the first tone is sung more strongly than the second, giving the impression that the first pitch is somewhat higher. Similar cases are to be found in beats 14 and 74. Corresponding instances are also to be found in certain folksongs such as *Pagyŏn p'okp'o* 朴淵瀑布 . It seems, therefore, that such tones are not performed as independent, individual sounds; it is reasonable to suggest that they should not be considered part of the fundamental tonal supply of *sijo,* which is thus only three pitches (*a, e,* and *B* in the attached musical example). According to Mr. Ch'oe Sang-uk, beat 6 may also be performed with the melodic motion *e'-a.*

In beat 8, the melody drops a fourth, *a-e;* similar melodic movement occurs in beats 18, 47, and 78. In the cases of beats 8 and 47, the melody immediately leaps back up to *a* in the next beat, giving the effect of an undulation. The singer's breath is not broken, and two syllables of text are sung in the same breath on the same pitch, *a* ("*ta ul*" and "*ga pak*"); this technique effects a distinct beginning sound for the second syllable of text. In beats 18 and 78, the singing technique is known as "reversing voice;" the drop to *e* serves the purpose of reinforcing the effect of the preceding, long-held *a,* without dying away. The reason is that after the *e,* the continuation is with an even lower pitch, *B,* and the *e* must be sung with comparative strength.

In beat 9, the *a* is sung with a solid sound and rises to *b*ᵇ; the *b*ᵇ is not sung with a stronger voice than the *a,* but rather more weakly. Without a breath, the singer returns to *a;* this sort of auxiliary progression from a pitch to a neighboring tone and back is called "pushing" (*minda* 민다). Two similar examples occur in beats 53 to 56 and beats 59 to 61. In all these cases, the pitch which is "pushed," *b*ᵇ, is not given a new syllable of text; since it is sung more weakly than the preceding pitch and the melody returns afterward to the same pitch, making a slight convexity, the *b*ᵇ is an ornamental pitch, not one of the fundamental ones. In performance it lends a extending effect.

From beat 14 to beat 22, the sweeping melody is weighty and kinetic; after beat 22, it becomes lighter and more static, providing a nice contrast. Beat 22 ("*ssuda*") begins with heavy vibrato on *e* ("*ssu*") and then lightly springs up to *a* ("*da*"); similar occurrences are found in beats 26-27, 59, and 82, and may be contrasted with the melodic motion at the very beginning of the *sijo.*

The *b*ᵇ appearing at beat 38, near the beginning of the second section, is a special feature of *sijo* melody in the capital region, being avoided by singers in regional styles. Since this is the case, it is preferable to view this note as a variant rather than as part of the basic *sijo* melodic form. In addition to the scheme shown in the musical example, there are several additional ways to perform the passage from beat 39 to beat 42: some sing this without a breath before beat 40, some sing beat 40 with an *e* to a melodic progression, and some sing the continuation after beat 40 with a descrescendo rather than a crescendo.

The *e'* in beat 43 is sung falsetto, this being another special feature of *sijo* in the capital area; a similar example occurs in beat 70. A new syllable of text is not given to the *e'*; it is sung more weakly than the preceding notes; and the melody returns to the preceding pitch, making an arch form. This indicates that the *e'* is just an ornamental tone, not part of the fundamental *sijo* melodic form.

The passage from beats 49 to 52, and from 56 to 58 are, for novices, awkward to sing and are also difficult for the listener. These passages are considered to "drag on," and the performer's scheme of vocal strength, that is, dynamics, is hard to comprehend quickly.

The first note of the last section (beat 69) is shown in the example as *b*, but there are also performers who just sing *a*. As explained in the similar case above (beat 6), because this tone is sung with great force, it sounds as if the pitch is higher. Also, it is quite reasonable to have the next interval, up to the falsetto *e'*, be a fifth.

The final cadence of the *sijo* has the melodic line *a* to *e*. For listeners accustomed to Western music, this does not give the effect of a complete close, and it is easy to get the impression that the melody has just been chopped off in the middle. However, as has been shown several times in this volume, full cadential figures in traditional Korean music involve falling melodic lines (see, for example, the article "*Ujo* in Modern *Kagok*"). Half cadences, on the other hand, use rising figures, as in the *e-a* at the end of the first section, or the *a-B-e* at the end of the second section of the *sijo*. Similarly, in *kagok* the third vocal section ends with a rising figure, A^b-B^b, and the final (fifth) section concludes with a falling line, A^b-F (see page 77). The Western term "cadence" comes from the Latin *cadere*, meaning "to fall"; this reminds us that in the cadences of ancient Western music, as in *sijo*, the voice drops downward.

In sum, we could say that the simpler melodic passages, which have few ornamental notes, are part of the fundamental melodic form of *sijo*, and that the more complex passages with comparatively many ornamental notes are melodic variants. The *sijo* style of Kyŏngsang province, which largely limits the melody to the three basic pitches (*B*, *e*, and *a*), thus has the most fundamental melodic form of *sijo*; the other regional styles and the capital style are variants. However, the question of which style is the best must be answered according to individual taste.

CONCLUSIONS

The tempo of a *sijo* is very slow, and it is hardly an exaggeration to say that it has no recognizable rhythm; the melody is also extremely simple. The striking feature of the *sijo* is that dynamics play a remarkably important role. The slow tempo and weak sense of rhythm give rise to a weighty and leisurely effect. Because the melody is quite simple, and ornamental tones are comparatively few, a *sijo* performance has an air of determination. It is especially due to the simplicity of melody that the subtle use of dynamics can play a disproportionately significant part, lending a sense of profundity and elegance. *Sijo* is truly the music of scholars.

Standard *Sijo*
(Capital Region)

Transcribed by
Dr. Chang Sa-hun

Special Notational Symbols:

〜〜〜 smooth vibrato

○- - - falsetto

♪ note of uncertain pitch

SUJECH'ŎN: MODE AND FORM

INTRODUCTION

One of the most beloved pieces of court music preserved in Korea is *Sujech'ŏn* 壽齊天, also known as *Pitkarak Chŏngŭp* 빗가락井邑 or simply *Chongŭp*. The instrumentation is the standard "wind" orchestration known as *samhyŏn yukkak* 三絃六角 : *tangjŏk* 唐笛, small transverse bamboo flute; *taegŭm* 大笒, large transverse flute; *p'iri* 觱篥, cylindrical bamboo oboe; *changgo* 杖鼓, hourglass drum; *chwago* 座鼓, barrel drum; *haegŭm* 奚琴, two-string fiddle; and *ajaeng* 牙箏, seven-string zither bowed with a rosined stick. Although the last two instruments are bowed strings, they are included in the "wind" orchestra because of their sustaining ability.

The *Taeak hubo* 大樂後譜 of 1759 contains a piece called *Chongŭp*, but as yet no relationship has been established between it and the present *Sujech'ŏn*. In any event, it is necessary to examine the modern piece in some detail before attempting to discover possible relationships with the old version. The present analysis is based upon the transcription in Volume I (1969) of the series *Han'guk ŭmak* 韓國音樂 published by the National Classical Music Institute, and on a tape recording made by the Korean Broadcasting System.

Modern *Sujech'ŏn* is in four sections: the first three sections each have six occurrences of the *changdan* 長短 , or rhythmic pattern (expressed in the drums), and the last section has only two *changdan*. References to the music will be made by section and *changdan* numbers.

TONAL SUPPLY

Based on the line of the most important melodic instrument, *p'iri*, *Sujech'ŏn* essentially uses four tones: *c* (namnyŏ 南呂). *f* (*t'aeju* 太簇), *g* (kosŏn 姑洗), and *b*^{b} (*imjong* 林鐘). There are, as would be expected, other pitches used, but they are rare.

The first of these rare pitches is *e*^{b} (*hwangjong* 黃鐘), which appears in *changdan* 6 of both Sections I and II, and in *changdan* 2 of Section IV. In each case, it serves to create a variant of a previously heard melodic line, functioning rather like a passing note between *c* and *f*. On the *p'iri*, the technique to produce the pitch *e*^{b} is special and uses the hole for *f*. Except for the unusual appearance of *e*^{b}, *changdan* 6 of Section I is almost similar to *changdan* 1 of the same section.

The other extra pitch is *a*^{b} (*chungnyŏ* 仲呂), which appears only in *changdan* 3 and 4 of Section III, and only in the *p'iri* part: while the *taegŭm*, *ajaeng*, and *haegŭm* hold the note *b*^{b}, the *p'iri* drops from *b*^{b} down to *a*^{b} and then back up, so that it really serves only as an auxiliary tone. Since the *a*^{b} pitch is produced through the *b*^{b} hole of the *p'iri*, the result is a remarkable shading of the *b*^{b} tone.

For these reasons, *e*^{b} and *a*^{b} should not be considered components of the basic tonal supply, and only the four pitches *c*, *f*, *g*, and *b*^{b} are basic.

THE "TONIC" PITCH

The tonal supply of four basic pitches suggests an analogy with the mode *kyemyŏnjo* 界面調 as used in *kagok* 歌曲 (see page 86). This in turn suggests that the chief pitch is *c*. There are no notes used between *c* and *f*, with the abovementioned exception of the three unusual occurrences of *e*^{b}; this corresponds to the lack of notes between *e*^{b} and *a*^{b} in the case of *kagok*. When the melody in *Sujech'ŏn* moves from *g* down to *f*, the pitch gradually and delicately wavers downward; instances of this are limited to the *f* and *g* a fourth higher than the chief pitch *c*, not occurring in other octaves. *Kagok* displays a similar melodic characteristic and octave limitation.

These two points mean that the central tone, or "tonic," is *c* and that the mode of *Sujech'ŏn* is *kyemyŏnjo*. The comparison with *kyemyŏn kagok* is summarized in the following chart:

Sujech'ŏn	c		f	g	b^b
Kagok	e^b		a^b	b^b	d^b '

If we were to take b^b, instead of c, as tonic, several problems would arise. The scale B^b c e^b f g with b^b as tonic is not *kyemyŏnjo*, but *p'yŏngjo* 平調 . But if we take *Sujech'ŏn* to be in *p'yŏngjo*, as the comparison with *ujo kagok* 羽調歌曲 would suggest (see page 72), the tone a fourth above B^b, that is e^b, would have to be a wavering tone such as was described above. However, the hard fact is that the wavering tone in *Sujech'ŏn* is g, not e^b, so *p'yŏngjo* cannot be a viable alternative.

Overall, then, *Sujech'ŏn* is in *kyemyŏnjo* with the tonic pitch c, the scale being c (e^b) f g (a^b) b^b.

RHYTHMIC PATTERNS (CHANGDAN)

The *changdan* and tempo of *Sujech'ŏn* resemble those of the pieces *Nŭrin yŏmillak* 느린與民樂 , "*Kin-yŏngsan*" 긴靈山 in *Samhyŏn yŏngsan hoesang* 三絃靈山會相 , and the *kagok Isudaeyŏp* 二數大葉 . That is, the *changgo changdan* starts not with simultaneous striking of both ends of the drum, but with a stroke on the "stick side" (right) of the drum, which is soon followed by a stroke on the "drum side" (left). In slow Korean court music, the basis for a tempo seems to be the interval of time within this succession of stick side and drum side. In some music using string instruments, the corresponding event seems to be a particular standard progression of notes and rhythm played on the *kŏmun'go* 玄琴 and known as "*ssŭl-kidung*" 쓸기등 (♩ ♫ ♩.)

The *changgo* pattern in *Yŏmillak* and *Samhyŏn yŏngsan hoesang* is consistent from beginning to end: stick side, drum side, stick side, drum side, and both sides together plus a roll of the stick. The basic *Sujech'ŏn* pattern has the same succession of strokes, with this approximate rhythm (upward stems indicate stick side, downward stems the drum side):

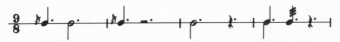

However, *Sujech'ŏn* is not entirely consistent: *changdan* 3 of both Sections I and II and *changdan* 2 of Section III have an abbreviated pattern:

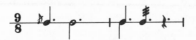

In *Yŏmillak,* 6 + 4 + 4 + 6 beats comprise one *changdan.* In *Sujech'ŏn,* according to the *Han'guk ŭmak* transcription, the first *changdan* of Section I contains 3 + 3 + 3 + 3 beats, after which the basic *changdan* are all 6 + 3 + 3 + 3 beats. Each of these *changdan* is followed by three empty beats for the drums. However, the tape recording shows that in fact the timings are very irregular in a *changdan; changdan* 1 of Section I, for example, has these timings for the four groups of "beats": 11″ + 10″ + 4″ + 9″ (see chart below), which is quite different from the transcription (3 + 3 + 3 + 3 beats). *Changdan* 2 of Section I is similarly irregular: 15″ + 8″ + 9″ + 10″. Lengths of all the *changdan* are shown in the following chart.

Changdan	1	2	3	4	5	6	Total
Section I	42″	52″	25″	55″	48″	1′30″	5′12″
II	30″	50″	24″	54″	42″	1′27″	4′47″
III	50″	30″	37″	34″	24″	1′21″	4′16″
IV	33″	27″					1′00″

These two features of *Sujech'ŏn,* irregular *changdan* lengths and non-uniform beat structure, show that it cannot be considered to have fixed *changdan.* It seems as if the music needs to expand and contract according to the speed of a ritual procession. Similar features are to be found in the music performed at the Royal Ancestral Shrine (*Chong-myo* 宗廟).

RHYTHM

As suggested by the preceding paragraphs, the tempo of *Sujech'ŏn* is extremely slow; indeed, each note is drawn out so long that it is practically impossible to feel the rhythm, and one could even say the piece is entirely free-rhythmed.

Generally speaking, each *changdan* contains essentially five melodic notes; exceptionally, the first *changdan* of both sections I and II have four notes, not five. Each note is quite long and, at a cursory listening, would seem to take about the same amount of time. In the *Han'guk ŭmak* transcription, each of the basic five notes is given three beats; that is, they are notated isochronically. But if we carefully examine the actual performance, the precise timings (in seconds) are as follows:

Changdan	1	2	3	4	5	6
	10.9	9.3	8.3	9.5	9.5	9.1
	—	5.4	7.0	4.5	6.4	2.0
Section I	10.6	9.5		9.2	9.0	7.1
	3.5	9.5		9.8	7.5	5.9
	9.3	11.0		10.0	9.8	11.5
	7.9	9.6	8.8	8.5	7.0	11.4
	—	5.1	8.5	4.5	6.4	
Section II	6.0	8.5		8.9	8.2	7.1
	7.0	9.2		8.9	6.5	5.3
	—	7.0		7.6	7.2	11.1
	6.5	11.7	6.5	4.9	5.9	9.2
	5.8	8.5	6.9	6.6	4.0	2.0
Section III	8.6		3.7	3.5	3.0	4.6
	9.8		3.1	3.6	4.4	4.3
	7.8		8.4	7.4	6.0	10.7
	7.5	6.5				
	7.2	4.0				
Section IV	5.6	7.4				
	5.7	9.0				
	6.7					

Thus, on the average, a *changdan*'s first note lasts 9.3 seconds and the second note is shorter, 5.4 seconds, so that the basic notes are not isochronic.

FORM

Modern *Sujech'ŏn,* as already mentioned, is in four sections. At the ends of Section I, II, and III are passages, called *yonŭm* 連音 , without drum accompaniment; these are much longer than the similar, brief passages which normally occur at the end of each *changdan.* Sections I, II, and III each have six *changdan*; exceptionally, Section IV has only two. In addition to the similarity in number of *changdan* in Sections I, II, and III, there are similarities in the music itself, detailed below:

A. Section I:

1. *Changdan* 1 starts with melodic motion from *c* up a fourth to *f*; these two pitches fill the opening *changdan* from beginning to end. At the end of the *changdan,* the *p'iri* plays *f* and *g* in a slow vibrato, so although *g* appears, it cannot be considered a basic constituent note. This melodic shape is denoted A (see chart below).

2. *Changdan* 2 is quite different; it opens with a short melodic phrase b^b *g* b^b *c'*. The *c'* is the most important note, as clearly demonstrated by the fact that all instruments except the *p'iri* start directly on *c'*. From this *c'*, the basic melody reaches a climax on $e^{b'}$, and then proceeds to *g, f,* and *c.* This melodic shape is denoted B.

3. *Changdan* 3 opens with the same melodic phrase as *Changdan* 2, but proceeds to *f* rather than rising to $e^{b'}$. The melodic shape of this abbreviated *changdan* is denoted C.

4. *Changdan* 4 is simply a repetition of *changdan* 2 (B).

5. *Changdan* 5 opens with a new melodic shape: a long note on *c* is followed by *g,* which wavers down to the important pitch *f.* This special characteristic of *g* was described above in the paragraphs on the "tonic" pitch. (D).

6. *Changdan* 6 opens with a phrase moving from *c* to *f,* via e^b, and ends on *c* rather than on the *f.* Although there are differences of detail from *changdan* 1, this *changdan* opens with essentially the same

melodic motion and uses the same two notes throughout. Thus, it may be considered a variant of *changdan* 1 (A').

B. Section II:

1. *Changdan* 1 opens with a long-held *c,* followed by *g,* which then wavers down to *f.* This succession of tones is quite similar to *changdan* 5 of Section I. (D').

2. *Changdan* 2 through 6 are repetitions of corresponding *changdan* in Section I.

C. Section III:

1. *Changdan* 1, like *changdan* 1 of Section II, resembles *changdan* 5 of Section I (D), but the *c'* that occurs with the "drum side" stroke is an octave higher than the corresponding note in D. Thus, it may be called D".

2. *Changdan* 2, the abbreviated one, is almost identical to the second half of *changdan* 1 of this section, as well as very similar to *changdan* 3 of Section I. (*C'*).

3. *Changdan* 3, if examined carefully, may be taken as a transposition (up a fourth) of *changdan* 2 of Section I. However, this version eliminates the opening melodic flourish, and the *e*^{b} of the earlier version is not changed. The reason that this single pitch remains the same is very likely that Korean instruments (not just the *p'iri*) cannot produce the required *a*^{b}' a fourth above *e*^{b}'; the upper limit of the *p'iri* is *f'*. The transposition is summarized in the following table. (B').

Section III, *changdan* 3:	/	*e*^{b}'	(not *a*^{b}')	*c'*	*b*^{b}	*f*
Section I, *changdan* 2:	*c'*	*e*^{b}'		*g*	*f*	*c*

4. *Changdan* 4 is a repetition of *changdan* 3. It should be noted that in Section I, *changdan* 2 is repeated in *changdan* 4, whereas here the repetition is immediate.

5. *Changdan* 5 is a transposition (up a fourth) of *changdan* 5 in Section I, as follows:

Section III, *changdan* 5:	*f*	*c'*	*b*^{b}
Section I, *changdan* 5:	*c*	*g*	*f*

The unusual thing to note in this *changdan* is that unlike elsewhere in *Sujech'ŏn*, the *taegŭm* and *tangjŏk* play fewer notes than the *p'iri*, using only the two pitches *c"* and *b*^{b}*'*. (D''')

    6. *Changdan* 6 is a transposition (up a fourth) of *changdan* 6 in Section I. But the *e*^{b} of the earlier *changdan* is not transposed to *a*^{b}, but comes out as *g;* this is likely due, as above, to technical restrictions of the instrument. Otherwise, as shown below, the transposition is not problematic:

Section III, *changdan* 6:	*g*	*b*^{b}	*f*	*b*^{b}	*f*
Section I, *changdan* 6:	*e*^{b}	*f*	*c*	*f*	*c*

The following chart summarizes the formal discussions preceding:

Section	I	II	III
Changdan 1	A	D '	D "
2	B	B	C '
3	C	C	B '
4	B	B	B '
5	D	D	D " '
6	A '	A '	A "

    This discussion makes it clear that, broadly speaking, Section I is repeated in Section II and transposed up a fourth in Section III. (For another example of such transposition, see the article on *Chung-yŏngsan,* page 121).

CONCLUSIONS

Sujech'ŏn has a basic tonal supply of four pitches: *c, f, g,* and *b*^{b}; if the very infrequent *e*^{b} and *a*^{b} are included, the total is six. The *e*^{b} and *a*^{b} are primarily used to provide highly effective shading. Each note is majestically extended, but the notes are not pure: each note attends upon the preceding and following notes and is pliant rather than unyielding.

The slow Section I is repeated in Section II; both of these sections yield an impression like a vast ocean. The upward transposition by a fourth in Section III, together with the *taegŭm* and *tangjŏk* drawing out their high single notes, offers a colossal transformation.

The technical descriptions in this article are inadequate to describe the extraordinary qualities of *Sujech'ŏn*. It seems as if *Sujech'ŏn* departs this earthly existence and reaches high into the sky like a gleaming mountain in a spring scene.

Sujech'ŏn

YUKCHABAEGI:
A KOREAN FOLK SONG

Few studies on Korean music are available in any Western language. Dr. Keh Chung Sik's *Die koreanische Musik*[1] is the only monograph on Korean music written by a Korean scholar in a Western language. Of the seventeen songs and instrumental pieces he analyzes, *Yukchabaegi* 六字백이 (*Nuk za bäki* in his romanization) and its faster companion, *Chajin Yukchabaegi* 자진六字백이 , are representative folk songs of Korea's southern provinces. Dr. Keh's analysis of *Yukchabaegi* will here be studied in depth, and then my own views will be given.

TEXT OF THE SONG

The song text, which cannot be clearly understood from the phonograph record used by Dr. Keh,[2] is as follows:
1. Sarami salmyŏnŭn/myŏt paengnyŏnina saldŭran marinya?/
     (When one lives, how many hundred years does one live?)
   Chugŏme tŭrŏsŏ/taejangbu innŭnya?/
     (In death, does it make any difference to be a hero?)
   Sarasŏ/saengjŏne/kakki mamdaero nol/kŏna e./
     (While we are alive we may as well enjoy what we like.)
2. Chadŭn chimbang/tŭrŏ kalje/
     (As she went into her bedroom,)

---

1. Dr. Keh's study of *Yukchabaegi* can be found in his *Die koreanische Musik* (Heitz and Co.; Leipzig, Strassburg, and Zürich, 1935), pp. 63-56; his transcription is on pages 10-11 of the Appendix.
2. The record referred to is the Columbia Viva-Tonal Recording 40063-A (20707).

Hyangdanege/puttŭlnyŏ/
  (Helped by Hyangdan,)
Iri pit'ŭl/chŏri pit'ŭl/chŏngsin ŏpsi tŭrŏwasŏ/
  (Tottering to and fro, losing herself, she entered.)
Pangsŏgŭl/puyŏ chapko/
  (And hugging the cushion,)
Pangsŏng tonggok/unnŭn moyangŭn/
  (She burst into tears.)
Saramŭi/injŏngŭron/ch'ama polsu chŏnhyŏ ŏp/kona. e./
  (With a human heart one cannot bear to look at this.)

The first stanza, the theme of which is frequently encountered, is the standard text of *Yukchabaegi*. The second stanza, which is nearly twice as long as the first, is borrowed from a *p'ansori* (dramatic song), *Ch'un-hyang ka* 春香歌 (The Story of Ch'un-hyang). As is the case with many folk songs, these stanzas have no continuity. It is obvious from this that the music of *Yukchabaegi* on this record must be divided into two parts.[3] It goes without saying that there are many other texts for this folk song. More than ten, for example, are contained in the song book *Sin'gu chapka* 新舊雜歌 (New and Old Songs).

THE SCALE

As Dr. Keh points out,[4] there are four main tones used in *Yukchabaegi*: *A, d, e,* and *f*. When *Yukchabaegi* is sung by either two men or two women, it is usually preceded by a short, pattern phrase with meaningless syllables ("*Sanhajiro kuna*") (Example 1).[5] This short introductory phrase pattern is sung in duet, followed by the song proper,

3. Contrary to Dr. Keh's contention that it is in three parts. See "The Form" below.
4. "Die Gebrauchstöne lassen über den Mollcharakter keinen Zweifel: d, e, f, und a, sind Haupttöne. Die halbtonlose Pentatonik ist hier aufgegeben. Ausser diesen vier Tönen kommen als Ausnahme noch ges und as vor, jedoch nur in umspielender Funktion." (p. 64).
5. As transcribed by Mr. Han Man-yong; his complete transcription is appended as Example 4. Example 1 shows this pattern phrase and compares it with the final phrases of the two stanzas.

which is sung solo. Thus, this short phrase might be said to set the stage for the solo song.

(Example 1)

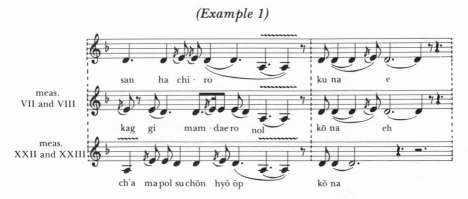

meas.
VII and VIII

meas.
XXII and XXIII

The introductory phrase clearly reveals the central tone *d,* which is neither rendered in vibrato like the note *A* (marked with a wavy line), nor does it tend to slide down like the note *f* (Example 4, measure V).[6] It spreads out straight through. The strong vibrato on the note *A* gives an effect of restlessness, like the fluttering of wings, in preparation for reaching the central tone *d,* sometimes via *e.* Between *A* and *d,* no other tone is used. The interval between *e* and *d* is actually a little smaller than a whole tone and slightly larger than a half tone.[7] This interval between *e* and *d* does not produce such an effeminate effect as that between *f* and *e.*[8] The note *f,* when it is sustained, glides down in a *descresendo* to *e* (the notes are marked "gl"), as in measures II, V, and XX. In these cases, the first note, *f,* has text, whereas the following note, *e,* has none. When such a phrase ends on *e* rather than on the central tone *d,* it creates musical tension, because it makes the listener anticipate the central tone *d,* but does not fully satisfy him. This pattern is often found in *p'ansori,* which frequently expresses a pathetic mood.[9]

6. The Arabic numbers refer to the measures in Dr. Keh's transcription and the Roman numerals to those in Mr. Han Man-yong's transcription.

7. See measure VII and XIX in Example 4.

8. The nature of *e* is described in the following section.

9. For examples, see *Minsok akpo* 民俗樂譜, Vol I, p. 38, staff 5; p. 42, staff 5; p. 66, staff 6; etc.

The tone pattern *d-f-e,* sung *legato,* is characteristic of the music of southern Korea. The note *f* acts like a short appoggiatura to *e*. Dr. Keh sometimes gives this pattern in its full form, as in measures 13 and 15 (notes marked by "fl") and sometimes drops the note *f*, which is so short that it may be missed (for example, the notes marked by "ms" in measures 6 and 16). When only the first note of the pattern has text, the following two notes *f* and *e* are like a *Nachschlag,* and the very short note *f* is even more easily missed. It is to be observed that when this pattern ends with *e* rather than the central tone *d,* an event which occurs at the end of a phrase (or rhythmic pattern), it gives the impression of a half cadence (see measures III, VI, X, and XI).

The exceptional tones g^b and a^b, to which Dr. Keh has referred, appear only in measures 2 and 3 of his transcription. However, these parts are transcribed differently by Mr. Han Man-yong, who left these exceptional tones out completely (Example 4). I prefer Mr. Han's transcription to Dr. Keh's, for the following reasons: first, in the music of southern Korea the appoggiatura is stressed more than the main tone. Let us examine, for example, the appoggiatura to the tone *f*. The dynamics can be easily understood by studying the performance of this pattern on the *kayagŭm* 伽倻琴 (twelve-string zither). The player presses the string down strongly with his left hand to the left of a high bridge and at the same time plucks the string with his right hand; this produces the tone *a*. Then his left hand releases the string relatively slowly, until the tone *a* glides down to *f*, while his right hand is idle. This technique produces the tone *a* in *sforzando* and then *f* in *diminuendo*. In this way, the appoggiatura is an important means of stressing tones in Korean music.

It would, however, be meaningless to apply the appoggiatura to the unstressed word *myon,* as Dr. Keh has done (measure 1). The appoggiatura from *a* to *f* should be, and actually is, on the note for the stressed syllable *sal*. Generally, words ending in the consonants k, p, and t (for example, *paek*[10] in measure II, *chuk* in measure III, *kak* in measure VII, *put* in measure XII, and *chap* in measure XVII) start from a higher pitch and are pronounced more energetically than words ending in the consonants l, m, and n. Therefore, for the word ending

10. *Paek,* when followed by n, is changed into *paeng,* as in measure II.

in k, *paek,* the larger interval of a third (*a-f*) is more suited and poignant than the smaller interval of a second (*a*b-*g*b) (measure 3). Thus, *a*b should be replaced by *a*. Incidentally, just as the third is stronger than the second, the fourth is even more energetic than the third. For example, the fourth (*a-e*) in measures III, XII, and XVIII (notes marked by "ˀ") is very strongly accentuated. However, the notes *a-f-e* are sung in *glissando,* not separately, resulting in apparently undetermined pitches. This results in different transcriptions, even by the same person! Let us imagine *f-e, g-e, a-e,* and *b-e* respectively, sung quickly in *glissando* with the first note stressed. Their definite pitch can hardly be determined.

THE FORM

As mentioned before, *Yukchabaegi* on this record contains two stanzas. Musically, too, the song is divided into two parts, rather than into three.[11] As Dr. Keh has noticed, the music for the last line of the first stanza (measures 8 to 13) is mostly the same as that for the last line of the second stanza (measures 23 to 27). The melody of the last line corresponds to the chorus of many folk songs worldwide, and adheres to a constant pattern. The preceding lines, the music of which varies, correspond to the solo part of folk songs; the music for these lines is improvised by the solo singer. As the first part of each stanza of the song varies substantially, the form of *Yukchabaegi* cannot be simply called strophic. Suffice it to say that *Yukchabaegi* on this record is divided into two rather than into three parts: part 1 (measures I to IV and measures V to VIII) and part 2 (measures IX to XIX and measures XX to XXIII).

11. Formal ist eine Gliederung in 3 Abschnitte festzustellen:
    1. Abschnitt Takt 1 bis 7;
    2. Abschnitt Takt 8 bis 18.
    3. Abschnitt Takt 19 bis 27.
Melodisch und rhythmisch entsprechende Takte sind 8 bis 12, 23 bis 27 (abgesehen von der Variante in Takt 10 und 25) (p. 64).

THE RHYTHMIC PATTERN

The rhythmic pattern used in *Yukchabaegi* is called *chinyangjo* (slow music). One occurrence of the rhythmic pattern, which consists of six beats, requires about eight seconds. Twenty-three measures, or rhythmic patterns, are contained on this ten-inch record, which runs for about three minutes. Four to six beats are sung in one breath.

(Example 2)

The basic rhythmic pattern, played on the *changgo* 杖鼓 (hourglass-shaped drum), is shown in Example 2. The drum pattern begins with striking both sides of the drum together and concludes with striking the right side of the drum (see the fifth and sixth beats in Example 2). This basic pattern is not repeated mechanically, unlike most dance music and classical music, which need a constant rhythm to keep time. The drum pattern is varied according to the music it accompanies, and thus this simple percussion instrument much enhances the effect of the music.

At the very beginning, the drum player usually waits for the singer to give the tempo in the first four beats; while the singer rests for the final two beats of the rhythmic pattern, the drum player comes in, filling the hiatus with drum strokes (see measures I and X). On this particular record not every first beat of the measures is given, but almost always only that of every other rhythmic pattern. On the other hand, throughout the song the fifth and sixth beats, the last two beats of one basic rhythmic pattern, are strongly supported by the drum (except in measure XI where only the fifth beat is given, the sixth being silent). As mentioned above, the text of the second part is borrowed from *p'ansori,* and the musical style of the first four measures comes from the same source. In *p'ansori* the singer usually pauses at the fifth and the sixth beats of measures 1, 2, and 4 in each group of four measures. In the third measure, the so-called *puch'inŭnde,* the singing goes on to the following measure without pause, and the drum player gives only a single strong stroke on the fifth beat, as in measure XI.

This basic drum pattern is very reserved, in order to permit the words of the song to be clearly understood. However, in measures V, XI, and XX, where one vocal tone is sustained, the drum beats are increased to give additional support to the sustained single tone. This is completely at the discretion of the drum player and, therefore, not written down. The drum player, in fact, not only beats the drum but also often exclaims "*chot'a!*" ("good"), normally at the end of the rhythmic pattern (see measures I, IV, IX, X, XII, XV and XIX). The last syllable of "*chot'a*" is so accented that at times the first syllable is inaudible. Sometimes the drum player sharply shouts the monosyllable "*ŭ*" (measures VII and XVIII). This shout encourages the singer. A professional woman singer once told me that when an amateur drum player accompanies her song with too exact a beat and without shouting, she feels as if her sense of time were being tested and her song cannot unfold freely.

In short, *Yukchabaegi* is definitely bound to the basic rhythmic pattern. Without knowing this, the listener would interpret its free variation as "ungebundener Vortrag."[12]

Even the parts in recitative style strictly keep the beat. This style is called in Korean *chusŭnda* (literally, "to pick up"). It means that a great many words have to be knit into the same framework of the song normally used for fewer words. This is done by subdividing one beat into notes of smaller time value, but of the same pitch. For example, measure II is crammed with eleven syllables, almost all of which are set to the single note *f*: *Myŏt paengnyŏnina saldŭran marinya?* In contrast to the recitative style, where the music has many words set to notes of small time value, there are also more songlike moments with notes of longer value; these are defined in Chinese as "words long-drawn-out" (*ko yung-yen* 歌永言). Whether or not *Yukchabaegi* varies between recitative style and song style, it remains definitely in the rhythmic pattern *chinyangjo*, consisting of six beats.

---

12. "Der freirezitierende melodische Stil und der ungebundene Vortrag lassen eine exakte rhythmische Aufzeichnung nicht zu, zumal hier Sprech- und Gesangsrhythmus selbständig einander gegenüberstehen." (p. 64).

DOTTED NOTES AND TRIPLETS

Dr. Keh's transcription shows many dotted eighth notes[13] which are preceded or followed by a sixteenth note (as in measures 6, 11, 18, 20, and 21). Dr. Keh transcribed the ninth beat of his measure 18 as a dotted eighth followed by a sixteenth, but in measure 26 he represented the first beat as two eighths.

These two parts should have the same rhythm. These two ways of representing the same rhythm suggest that a dotted eighth is in fact too long and a sixteenth is too short. Especially in music which is as slow as this song, the difference between the dotted eighth and the sixteenth is larger than in fast music. Indeed, the proportion of six to two in slow tempo is mathematically the same as that of three to one in fast tempo, but for the listener there is a definite difference. In measure II, one beat is divided into a triplet set to three syllables (*nyŏnina*). Moreover, in the drum part one beat is mostly divided into three (quarter and eighth, or *vice versa*). This rhythm is very common in Korean music, whereas the dotted rhythm is rare.

Of the two transcriptions of the music set to the words "*chŏngsin ŏpsi*" (measure XV and 18), the jerky dotted rhythm is less suited to the text "losing herself" than the smooth triplet rhythm.

THE CONTRAST

Measure 19 provides a rhythmic contrast to the preceding measures.[14] The note *a* in measure XVI is not broken by taking a breath, as opposed to the note *f* in measures V and XX. It does not glide down in *descrescendo* at its end, but keeps on straight to the end of the measure, restressed by the appoggiatura in its middle.

13. "Vorherrschend sind punktierte Achtel, deren Leidenschaftlichkeit und Unruhe noch durch die 32 stel Melismen (Takt 9 u. 24) verstärkt, dem Stück seinen eigentümlichen Charakter geben." (p. 64).

14. "Einen rhythmischen Kontrast bildet auch der 19. Takt, dessen lang gahaltener Ton in dem ganzen Stück nur einmalig ist und besonders wirksam hervortritt, weil er unmittelbar vor dem melodischen Höhepunkt steht." (p. 64).

Measure 19 provides not only rhythmic contrast, but also pitch contrast. The preceding measures range from *A* to *f,* but in measure 19 the pitch is raised to *a,* which in the following measure goes up to *f'.* It is to be noted that this rising tone pattern occurs at the beginnings of the measures. Another performance of *Yukchabaegi* transcribed by Mr. Han Man-yong opens with this very tone pattern, and in the *Chajin Yukchabaegi* transcribed by Dr. Keh, the second phrases of stanza 2 (measure 19) and of stanza 3 (measure 35) begin with this tone pattern.

THE RANGE OF THE MELODY

The range of the melody, an octave and a sixth, is clear beyond doubt.[15]

PHRASING AND BREATH PAUSES

Dr. Keh draws a bar line each time a breath is taken. This causes the irregularity of bar length characterizing his transcription. The bar length ranges from three beats (measure 10) to 12 beats (measure 16). It is almost impossible, however, to sing twelve beats in a single breath, because twelve beats of *Yukchabaegi* would take more than sixteen seconds; actually, at the end of the sixth beat of measure 16, a breath is taken so lightly that it is almost unnoticeable.

Each phrase in the text coincides with the rhythmic pattern. In the text of *Yukchabaegi,* as given earlier in this article, each slanting line indicates the end of one rhythmic pattern. However, the musical phrasing, that is, the music of one rhythmic pattern, does not always coincide with the breathing pause.[16] A rhythmic pattern is often broken by taking a breath at the end of the fourth beat (as in measures II, V, and XX). It is frequently the case that the music of one rhythmic pattern simply ends after the fourth beat, which is followed by rests (measures I, IV, VIII, IX, X, XII, and XV).

15. "Der Umfang der Melodie reicht von *a* bis *f²*. Melodisch wichtige Töne sind *d¹* und *f¹* u. a."(p. 64).

16. "Die Phrasierung schliesst sich eng an die Worte an, derart, dass das Ende eines Phrasierungsbogens gleichzeitig die Atempause bezeichnet." (p. 64-65).

The reason why the musical phrase does not necessarily coincide with breathing is that the music is very slow. One musical phrase of six beats lasts more than eight seconds and can hardly be sung in one breath. On the other hand, when a phrase is halted at the end of the fourth beat, the first part of the phrase takes five to six seconds, and is easily managed in. a single breath. *Yukchabaegi* shows that in slow Korean music the musical phrasing and breathing pauses do not always coincide.

MELODIC CLIMAX AND ITS RESOLUTION

Dr. Keh's analysis shows sensitivity to the music and is beautifully written.[17] In measure 20 the melody goes from a to f', which is sung in falsetto. This high, but thin and soft, tone is partly responsible for the falsetto's pathetic effect. This high tone f' quivers, then touches briefly down to e' and drops to e by the end of the measure. This represents the climax, which is softened by the following two measures.

MELISMAS

The exact transcription of melismas (such as in measures VI and XXI) is very difficult.[18] Accents are not marked, and the notes that are transcribed are almost as non-organic as sand. Taking into consideration the corresponding part of another performance *Yukchabaegi* (Example 3), the melismas of measure VI, *f-a-f-a-f* and *f-a-f-a-e*, may be simplified to *f-a-f* and *f-a-e*, respectively; these may be further reduced to simply *f* and *f-e*. The basic melody merely moves from *f* to *d*

17. "Takt 20 und 21 mit der leidenschaftlich zu f^2 aufsteigenden kleinen Sexte und den anschliessenden schluchzend zur Tiefe a führenden Achteln und Sechzehnteln sind als melodischer Höhepunkt zu bezeichnnen." (p. 65).

18. "Besonders ins Ohr fallend ist die melismatische Stelle in Takt 9 und 24. Sie bildet in ihrem schmerzlichen Ausdruck ein Gegenstück zu Takt 20 und 21 und wirkt in Takt 24 besonders intensiv. Die vielen Vorschläge sind für das Lied charakteristisch; sie malen den Zustand seelischer Erschütterung, die ihren Höhepunkt in den erwähnten Stellen (Takt 9 und 24 und 20/21) findet." (p. 65).

through *e*; it is elaborated here to provide contrast to the preceding sustained note *f*.

(Example 3)

from
meas VIII

Saeng

from
another
Yukchapaegi

nok su ka

CONCLUSIONS

This folk song, with its very slow tempo, in non-strophic lyrical and recitative styles mixed with long-sustained notes, and with the drum accompaniment freely varying the basic rhythmic pattern, is so subtle as to be unintelligible to the listener who hears it for the first time. But its emotional power will inevitably move him even if he has no idea of its formal structure. This subtle folk song, as rendered by one of the best singers of *p'ansori*, Miss Yi Hwa-jung-son, is more than a simple folk song; it certainly approaches art song.

Example 4.

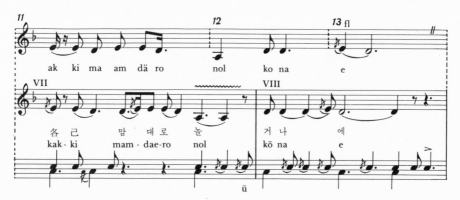

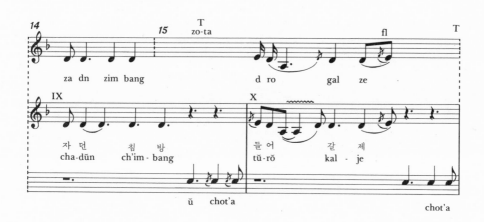

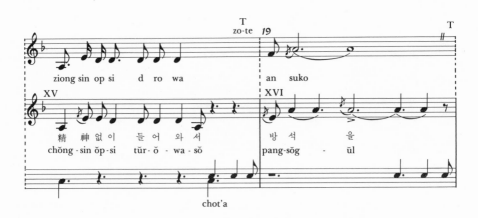

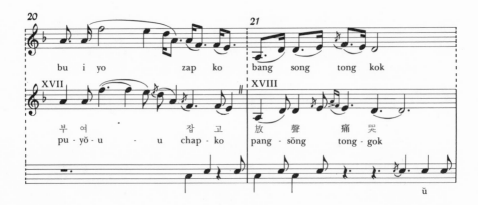

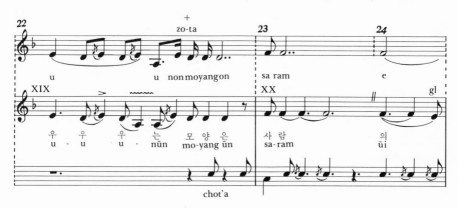

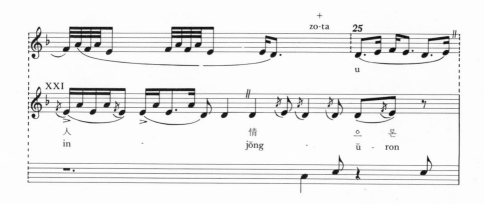

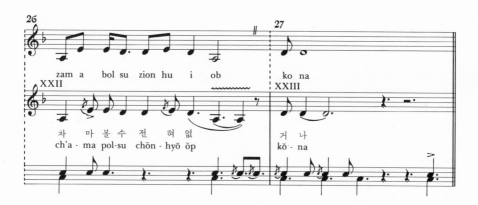

CREATIVE ACTIVITY IN
TRADITIONAL KOREAN MUSIC

INTRODUCTION

This article investigates the question of whether compositional activity in Korean music before the introduction of Western music was like the (Western) type of compositional process now practiced in modern Korea. Unfortunately, there are few musical sources which pertain to periods earlier than the Yi dynasty (1392-1910), and comments here are consequently largely confined to deductions about the Yi period. Three main areas are examined: parody technique in court songs of the early Yi period, variation and transposition in chamber music, and improvisation in folk music. Frequent reference is made to other articles in this volume, and comments on the role of these traditional methods of composition in the contemporary musical scene are appended.

EARLY YI DYNASTY COURT SONGS

In an entry for 1393 in the *T'aejo sillok* 太祖實錄 (4.3a-4a), it is stated that the famous official Chŏng To-jŏn 鄭道傳 (?-1398) compiled three song texts as an offering to the king: *Monggŭmch'ŏk* 夢金尺 , *Suborok* 受寶籙 , and *Yuborok* 維寶籙. The king ordered the musicians to practice (*isŭp* 肄習) these songs. In 1424, the official Pyŏn Kye-ryang 卞季良 presented the king with a new song text; the king ordered it sent to the *Kwansŭp togam* 慣習都監 , a governmental music office, to be added to the court music repertory and performed at banquet ceremonies (*Sejong sillok* 世宗實錄 26.30a). In both these cases, the author of the text is clearly specified, but nothing is said about the composition of musical settings except that the texts were given to musicians for performance purposes. Were new pieces of music composed for these texts?

A. Compositional activity in Early Yi:

In the early Yi period, there were many vocal pieces and few purely instrumental ones. Further, music seems to have been a mere attachment to the poetic texts. According to Chŏng To-jŏn, music is borrowed for the purpose of transmitting to later generations a song extolling the achievements of a king (*T'aejo sillik* 4.2b). A similar example is afforded by the *Kyunyŏ-chŏn* 均如傳 of 1075, a biography of a Buddhist priest: in order to spread Buddhism far and wide, they used popular music called *sanae* 詞腦 . It was reported in 1431 that two pieces of music, *Chach'ŏngjo* 紫青調 and *Wŏnhŭnggok* 元興曲 , had not disappeared, due to their texts (*Sejong sillok* 54.4b).

The essential point here is that the text was more important than the music; the music was merely a conveyance for the text. Authors of texts, like Chŏng To-jŏn and Pyŏn Kye-ryang, are named, but the identity of composers remains unknown; it is not definitely certain, for example, what person in the *Kwansŭp togam* was responsible for the musical setting of Pyŏn Kye-ryang's text.

There is, however, a suggestive passage from 1418: "The king [Sejong] said to Pyŏn Kye-ryang, 'You are good at writing song texts; my father praised you highly.' To Maeng Sa-song 孟思誠 he said, 'You are the Director of the *Kwansŭp togam* and have taught the musicians new texts and combined the texts with melodies (*hap ŏ yuljo* 合於律調); my father was very pleased'" (*Sejong sillok* 2.14a). It is uncertain whether "combined the texts with music" resembles musical composition in the modern sense, but it does appear that the Director of the *Kwansŭp togam,* in some manner, planned the music for new song texts. On the other hand, in the section on musicians' examinations in the statutes of 1865, *Taejŏn hoet'ong* 大典會通 , there is no examination for musical composition; this indicates that there was no instruction in composition for musicians. Accordingly, it seems likely that the composers were not merely few, but non-existent. Further, contemporary notational systems were inadequate for writing down compositions.

In sum, it may be deduced that in the early Yi period there was no such musical activity as composition in the modern sense.

B. Sample pieces of music:

In this section, the origins of several early pieces of music are investigated.

1. *Kŭnch'ŏnjŏng* 覲天庭

A text associated with this title was presented to the Korean king in 1402 by the official Ha Yun 河崙 (*T'aejong sillok* 太宗實録 3.31b). In 1447, it was stated that music associated with this title belonged to a type of Korean military music called *koch'wi* 鼓吹 (*Sejong sillok* 138.1a): "The *koch'wi* music of our nation has the following set of titles: *Suborok, Monggŭmch'ŏk, Kŭnch'ŏnjŏng*, and *Sumyŏngmyŏng* 受明命 ." Already in 1432, however, it had been proposed to use *Kŭnch'ŏnjŏng* in banquet music, that is, to set the same text to ritual music, *a-ak* 雅樂 (*Sejong sillok* 55.23b). The music of *a-ak* was Chinese in origin, not Korean; in the treatise *Akhak kwebŏm* 樂學軌範 (2.28ab) of 1493, indeed, the text of *Kŭnch'ŏnjŏng* is set to a piece from the *I-li ching-chuan t'ung-chieh* 儀禮經傳通解 of the Sung dynasty Chinese philosopher Chu Hsi 朱熹 (1130-1200).

It thus appears that the text of *Kŭnch'ŏnjŏng*, written by Ha Yun, was originally set to a piece of Korean *koch'wi*; later, the same text was set to a piece of ritual music of Chinese origin. This implies that a piece of music was not specially composed for the *Kunch'onjong* text, but rather pre-existing pieces were borrowed for the purpose.

The poetic text of *Kŭnch'ŏnjŏng* has a very strict structure: five stanzas, each consisting of four lines of four syllables each. Thus, each stanza has sixteen syllables. It has been mentioned that the music for the *a-ak* setting was borrowed from Chu Hsi, but the original Chu Hsi music and text had a somewhat different structure: the setting is syllabic, with a single stanza of six lines of four syllables each. Altogether, then, the Chu Hsi music has twenty-four notes. For setting the entire new *Kŭnch'ŏnjŏng* text, the Koreans had to repeat Chu Hsi's music, but they did so without attempting to make the musical repetitions coincide with the strophic structure of the text. Thus, the second verse of *Kŭnch'ŏnjŏng* begins before the music has been played through fully; the musical repetition begins halfway through the second verse of text, and so forth. Schematically:

Text lines:	x x x x	x x x x	x x x x	x x x x	x x x x
Text stanzas:	1	2	3	4	5
Music repetitions:	1	2		3	4

As this chart shows, the music concludes a third of the way through the final repetition.

This treatment of *Kŭnch'ŏnjŏng* is by no means an isolated occurrence, and several other examples could be cited.

2. *Hwanhwan'gok* 桓桓曲

Hwanhwan'gok was performed in the sacrificial rite at the ancestral shirne called *Munso-chŏn* 文昭殿 . The text is preserved in the *Akhak kwebŏm* (2.19b-20a), but a notated melody does not survive. According to a 1433 entry in the *Sejong sillok* (62.28b):

> Now in performing the new hymn texts for the *Munso-chŏn,* the first offering of wine uses the melody of [a piece of] *tangak* 唐樂[music of Chinese origin], *Chunggang yŏng* 中腔令; the second offering uses the melody of a piece of *hyangak* 鄉樂[native Korean music], *P'ungipsong* 風入松 . However, proper names for the hymn texts have not been assigned, and this goes contrary to our established system. I want you [the king] to proclaim honorary titles [for these hymn texts] in order to hand them down to future generations. For the first offering of wine to [the spirit of] King T'aejo, call the text '*Hwanhwan'gok*'; for the second offering, call it '*Yuhwanggok*' 維皇曲 .

The above passage makes it clear that both the title and text of *Hwanhwan'gok* were new in 1433; the music itself, however, was not composed for the occasion, but borrowed the melody of a piece of *tangak, Chunggang yong.*

3. *Yuhwanggok* 維皇曲 and *Yunghwa* 隆化

According to the above passage, the text of *Yuhwanggok* was newly written in 1433, but its musical setting was borrowed from a piece of Korean music called *P'ungipsong. P'ungipsong* was a piece of popular music from the Koryŏ dynasty (918-1392), and its text is recorded in the history of Koryŏ, *Koryŏ-sa* 高麗史 (71.39a-40a); both text and music of the Koryŏ song are given in the *Siyong hyangak-po* 時用鄉樂譜 (34a-43b), a book of notated music written down about 1500. The *Yuhwanggok* text is given in the *Akhak kwebŏm* (2.20a); music, without text, is given in the 1759 collection, *Taeak hubo* 大樂後譜 (Chapter 2). These show clearly that the new text was simply set to pre-existent music.

Yunghwa was one of eleven pieces comprising a suite named *Pot'aep'yŏng* 保太平 . Both the text and music of *Yunghwa* are recorded in the *Sejong sillok* (138.32b-33a) and *Sejo sillok* 世祖實錄 (48.23b-25a). *Pot'aep'yŏng* was attributed to Sejong, who "made the new music on the basis of *koch'wi* and *hyangak*" (*Sejong sillok* 138.1a). In other words, the text was new, but the music was borrowed from earlier pieces.

A comparison of *Yunghwa* (as recorded in the *Sejong sillok*) and *Yuhwanggok* (as recorded in the *Taeak hubo*) reveals that measures two through six (columns in the original notation) of the former are the same as measures five through fourteen of the latter. This shows that Sejong borrowed the music for *Yunghwa* from *hyangak*, rather than *koch'wi*, since it is the same as *Yuhwanggok*, which was taken from the Korean song *P'ungipsong*.

In sum, the texts of *Yuhwanggok* and *Yunghwa* were newly written in the time of King Sejong, but their musical settings were borrowed from a Koryŏ song, rather than composed anew.

4. *Chŏngdongbanggok* 靖東方曲

The title and text of *Chŏngdɔngbanggok* were written by Chŏng To-jŏn and presented to King T'aejo in 1393 (*T'aejo sillok* 4.4a). Comparison of this piece (as recorded in the *Taeak hubo*, Chapter 2) and the Koryŏ song *Sŏgyŏng pyŏlgok* 西京別曲 (as recorded in the *Siyong hyangak-po*, 14a-15a) shows that the former consists of six measures (columns) and the latter of eight. A closer examination shows that measures five through seven of *Sŏgyŏng pyŏlgok* are compressed and abbreviated to form measure five of *Chŏngdongbanggok*, and that otherwise the music is the same.

The preceding are only four of the many examples available, but the general conclusion is clear: when new texts were written, new music was not composed for them. Rather, pieces of music already in the repertory were either borrowed intact or adapted to fit the new texts.

This calls to mind the borrowing of pre-existent pieces in Western music of the Renaissance, often termed "parody technique."

C. Koreanization of Chinese music:

A technique related to the abovementioned system of borrowing from existing pieces is the conversion of pieces from one category of music to another. Most often, this meant conversion of pieces of *tangak* (entertainment music from China) into *hyangak* (native music); in other words, Koreanization. Such a change involved not only elusive matters of performance style, but also orchestration and musical form.

For example, as Dr. Chang Sa-hun 張師勛 has shown, the three movements often appended to the suite for chamber orchestra, *Yŏngsan hoesang* 靈山會相 , are all derived from the *tangak* piece *Pohŏja* 步虛子 (see page 104), which was originally a piece of Chinese *tz'u* music (see page 234).

A detailed discussion of this sort of transformation may be found in "Left and Right Music in Korea" in this volume (page 275).

VARIATION AND TRANSPOSITION

Although existing pieces of music were borrowed for the purpose of setting newly written texts in the early Yi dynasty, those pieces did not remain unaltered. One method of change, of course, is the conversion of instrumentation and form just described. In the course of time and propagation, the individual performance styles of performers and epochs were impressed upon antique traditional melodies. This sort of "variation" may easily be found in the differing regional versions of a folksong in any musical culture. Just as there are regional linguistic dialects, there are also musical dialects.

The primary manifestation of different musical dialects is the use of ornamental tones. In Korea, this is most easily found in instrumental music, for which we have written notations centuries old; comparison of earlier sources with later written materials and modern performance reveals the great extent to which the original melodies have become surrounded with a thick profusion of ornamental notes. The article

"'*Chung-yŏngsan*' as a Variation of '*Sang-yŏngsan*'" (page 121)
examines in detail the use of ornamental tones in a single piece.

Another possibility for variation is conversion between modes. In a
books of texts for *kagok* 歌曲 and *sijo* 時調, *Kagok wŏllyu* 歌曲源流 (nineteenth century), it is explicitly stated that music in the modes *ujo* or
kyemyŏnjo (see page 71) is not fixed, but can be converted from one
mode to the other. In addition to this sort of immediate conversion
between modes, there is the gradual alteration which occurs with the
passage of time, the modal character itself becoming slowly transformed; this subject is treated at length in the article "Modes in Early
Korean Sources" (page 62).

As explained in the abovementioned article on "*Chung-yŏngsan*,"
the second movement of the chamber suite *Yongsan hoesang* is
essentially a transposition at the fourth of the first movement, played in
a slightly faster tempo. Korean transposition differs from that in the
West, however, since certain parts of the music, especially ends of
sections, tend to remain at the original pitch level, even though the
remainder of the piece has been transposed.

This sort of transposition also occurs in the fifth, "*Samhyŏn todŭri*"
三絃도드리, and sixth, "*Hahyŏn todŭri*" 下絃도드리, movements of
Yŏngsan hoesang. "*Hahyŏn*" is a transposition of two sections of
"*Samhyŏn*." The early nineteenth-century *Yuyeji* 遊藝志 states the
reasoning as follows:

> If '*Samhyŏn*' is played over again, it is boring. Therefore, its second
> and third sections are played a fourth lower, the beginning and end of
> the original remaining unchanged.

In sum, the borrowing of pre-existent pieces by no means excludes
originality. New materials may enter as ornamental tones, changes of
mode, and transpositions.

IMPROVISATION

While the sorts of variation mentioned above might be compared with
the small forms of poetic verse, improvisatory music might be compared
to long prose stories. In Korea, improvisation is practiced primarily in

dramatic story-singing, *p'ansori* 판소리 , and the music, *nongak* 農樂 , of farmers' percussion bands. *P'ansori* may last for several hours and farmers' music for about half an hour; such long performances lend freedom to the performers' improvisation. Just as verse is easily memorized, the variations and transpositions described above, once established, tend to remain relatively unchaged for a long period; but just as long prose stories are difficult to commit to memory, improvisatory music changes every time it is performed.

An old *p'ansori* singer once confided to me, "These days, *p'ansori* is degraded to photographic music; each time a young singer performs *p'ansori* excerpts, they are exactly the same. One cannot expect the unexpected in such photographic music." This remark underscores the importance of improvisation in *p'ansori*.

The leader of a farmers' band was once stopped during his playing and asked to repeat a rhythmically complex passage he had played a few moments earlier. He was bewildered and could not identify the requested section; the marvelous passage had flashed through his mind and could not be restored. Thus, improvisatory music, which changes every time it is performed, might be considered the possible diverse creations on a mold.

Improvisation also bears a resemblance to a speech without a prepared script. Only when the person is inspired can his music or speech be rendered fluently, surprising and delighting his audience in a manner unachievable with "photographic music" or a written script. But when the music or text is not planned beforehand and the performer awaits his next inspiration, he must stop and reiterate some tonal patterns or thoughts until he finds the way to proceed; this problem of redundancy is absent in "photographic music" or a prepared script. Improvisatory music may seem to have an interminable length, either because the performer is carried away by inspiration or because he waits endlessly for a real inspiration.

Improvised music, then, has the great merits of spontaneity and fluency, but it also has the drawbacks of indeterminate length and undependable effect.

CONCLUSIONS

Although the court music tradition of the Yi dynasty involved comparatively little composition in the modern sense, that is, creation of entirely new pieces of music, the techniques analyzed in this article were creative activities of great potential. The system of variations on a model is far from exhausted and offers a potential means for further development of the Korean musical heritage. Certainly the creation of new music would attract more musicians than would the mere preservation of extant music. Needless to say, new pieces of music cannot always be expected to be masterpieces on a par with the immortal works of long standing, but one may certainly hope for the occasional creation of a new masterpiece.

Adapting improvisatory Korean music for radio, television, and the stage necessitates removal of the drawbacks mentioned earlier: indeterminate length and undependable effect. The modern environment requires that this music be carefully transcribed and reconstructed so as not to sacrifice its spontaneity and fluency. In the absence of its traditional environment, improvisatory music faces real problems of survival, and conscious adaptation is probably the only means of preserving its special character.

SSANGHWAJŎM
AND ITS SINICIZED VERSION

THE TEXTS OF SSANGHWAJŎM

Two notated versions of the music of *Ssanghwajŏm* 雙花店 (The Pastry Store) are extant today; these are in the *Taeak hubo* 大樂後譜 of 1759 (Chapter 6), which contains music performed in the period of King Sejo 世祖 (ruled 1455-1468), and the *Siyong hyangak-po* 時用鄉樂譜 , a collection of songs written down about 1500. Both these versions are texted; in addition, a text is recorded in a sixteenth-century text collection, *Akchang kasa* 樂章歌詞 . The texts in the *Taeak hubo* and *Akchang kasa* are written using the Korean script and are closely related; the *Siyong hyangak-po* text is in Chinese.

As given in the *Taeak hubo*, the text concerns the adventures of a girl and relates the amorous overtures of a Moslem, a priest, and a dragon in the village well. Each line of text corresponds to a single measure of music, that is, to a single column of music notated in *Chŏnggan-po* (on this, see page 39). The *Taeak hubo* text is as follows:

(Text 1)

1. 상화뎜에 상화사라
   가고신딘 휘휘아비
   내손목을 주여이다」
   이말숨이 이뎜밧긔
   나명들명 다로러니
   죠고맛감 삿기광대」
   네마리라 호리라 더러
   둥셩다로러 긔자리예

나도자라 가리라 위위」
다로러거디러거 다롱디
다로러 그잔듸굿치
덥거츠니 없다」

2. 삼장ᄉ애 블을혀라」
가고신듸 그덜샤쥐
내손목을 주여이다
이말ᄉ미 이덜밧끠
나명들명 삿기샹재
네말이라 호리라」
드레우믈의 믈을길라

3. 가고신듸 우물눙이
내 [손목을 주]여
[이]다.

The above text is arranged in three verses of diminishing length, separated by interludes. The first verse contains twelve lines, corresponding to twelve measures of music; the first interlude is two measures in length. The second verse has only six lines, and the second or "half" interlude has only one measure. The third verse has a mere three lines and is followed by a brief postlude.

The bracketed syllables in verse 3 are missing in the *Taeak hubo*, but can be supplied by comparison with corresponding passages in verses 1 and 2. The hourglass drum, *changgo* 杖鼓, repeats the same rhythmic pattern over and over; each appearance requires three measures (corresponding to three lines in the text above). The last line of each verse is accompanied by a standard cadential formula in which the melody drops scalewise from the tonic note to an octave below (on the significance of this formula, see page 77). Thus, even though each verse has a different length, each has a regular cadential phrase for its conclusion.

The text in the *Akchang kasa* has four, not three verses, and each is of the same length; nonsense syllables appear in each verse, so that each verse is longer than even the first verse of the *Taeak hubo* version. This raises the question of which is the older version, but that is the subject of a future article; for the moment, it is adequate to know that these two texts are very similar.

The text of *Ssanghwajŏm* in the *Siyong hyangak-po* is written in pure Chinese and is completely different in meaning from that of the *Taeak hubo*; it praises the achievements of the king:

(Text 2)

寶殿之傍　　雙花萬芳
來瑞我王　　馥馥其香
燁燁其光　　允矣其祥
於穆我王　　俾熾而昌
繼序不忘　　率由舊章
無怠無荒　　綱紀四方

Interlude (four measures)

君明臣良　　魚水一堂
儆戒靡遑　　庶事斯康
知氣滂洋　　嘉瑞以彰

Interlude (one measure)

嘉瑞以彰　　福履穰穰
地久天長　　聖壽無疆

The background of these texts deserves mention. In the music section of the *Koryŏ-sa* 高麗史 , there is recorded no *Ssanghwajŏm* as such; there are however, two songs, *Samjang* 三藏 and *Saryong* 蛇龍, the first of which has the same content as the second stanza of the *Taeak hubo* text (*Koryŏ-sa* 71.42a):

(Text 3)

Samjang (三藏)

三藏寺裏點燈手　有社主兮執吾手
徜此言兮出寺外　謂上座兮是汝語

Saryong (蛇龍)

有蛇含龍尾　　聞過太函岑
勘酌左兩心　　萬人各一語

In a comment following the texts, the *Koryo-sa* explains that the songs were written during the rule of King Ch'ungnyŏl 忠烈 (ruled 1274-1308), who was fond of banquet music; the songs were taught to entertainment girls, who performed them for the king.

During the rule of the Yi king Sŏngjong 成宗 (ruled 1469-1494), songs such as these were condemned as having lewd texts; three texts, including *Ssanghwajom*, were revised in 1490 (*Sŏngjong sillok* 成宗實錄 240.18b). It would appear that this 1490 revised version of *Ssanghwajŏm* is the one which is recorded in the *Siyong hyangak-po*.

In sum, the *Ssanghwajŏm* text reproduced in the *Taeak hubo* appears to be the original Koryŏ version, while that in the *Siyong hyangak-po* appears to be the rewritten version of the late fifteenth century.

THE MUSIC OF SSANGHWAJŎM

The two notated versions of *Ssanghwajŏm*, in the *Taeak hubo* and *Siyong hyangak-po*, have been transcribed and juxtaposed as Example 1. At first glance, the two melodies appear to be as different as the texts to which they are set. However, for the following reasons it is clear that the two pieces belong to the same genealogy:

1. Since there are, in corresponding places, two interludes and a postlude in each, the two versions have the same formal structure.

2. Measures 3-5 of the *Taeak hubo* version are repeated in 6-8 (marked "A" in Example 1); exactly the same thing occurs in measures 5-10 and 11-16 of the *Siyong hyangak-po* version. Similarly, measures 10-12 of the *Taeak hubo* ("C") are repeated in 18-20, corresponding to measures 19-24 and 35-40 of the *Siyong hyangak-po*. These relationships make it clear that each measure (column) of the *Taeak hubo* version corresponds to two measures (columns) of the *Siyong hyangak-po*. The only exceptions to this are measures 21 and 25 of the *Taeak hubo*, which correspond to measures 41 and 48-50 of the *Siyong hyangak-po*, respectively.

3. The sixth through eighth and fourteenth through sixteenth quarter notes of each measure of the *Taeak hubo* version are, without exception, expanded to eight quarter notes $(3 + 2 + 3)$ in the *Siyong*

hyangak-po version.

These three points show that the two versions belong to the same family tree; the chief differences are that the *Siyong hyangak-po* has been changed to a more regular rhythmic structure and from a neumatic to a nearly syllabic style.

SSANGHWAJŎM *AND THE ESSENTIAL ELEMENTS OF* HYANGAK

It has already been demonstrated that the *Siyong hyangak-po* version of *Ssanghwajŏm* is a textual and musical revision of the earlier version recorded in the *Taeak hubo*. Just as the text was changed from a lewd poem in Korean to a proper eulogy in Chinese, the music was evidently altered from native style to include Chinese characteristics.

1. The interludes and postlude of the *Taeak hubo* have been kept in the *Siyong hyangak-po*. However, such interludes and postlude are not to be found in the Chinese-style music, such as *Yasimsa* 夜深詞 and *Saengga yoryang* 笙歌寥亮 , also recorded in the *Siyong hyangak-po*. In other Korean pieces, such as *Pot'aep'yŏng* 保太平 and *Chŏngdaeŏp* 定大業 , which were converted from *hyangak* 鄉樂 (native Korean music) into Chinese-text songs, the interludes and postlude do not appear. Because of the existence of these instrumental interludes and postlude, the version of *Ssanghwajŏm* in the *Siyong hyangak-po* cannot be viewed as purely Chinese-style music.

2. Both the *Taeak hubo* and *Siyong hyangak-po* versions have the same standard cadential formula which drops scalewise from the tonic note to the note an octave lower. This sort of cadential phrase appears in the *Siyong hyangak-po* only in the *hyangak* pieces, and not in the Chinese-style pieces. It may be found in other examples of modified *hyangak,* such as *Pot'aep'yŏng* and *Chŏngdaeŏp*.

3. In the *Taeak hubo* version, the clapper *pak* 拍 is not used, while, as an instrument of Chinese origin, it is employed in the *Siyong hyangak-po* sinicized version. In the *Taeak hubo,* seven pieces of music employ the clapper and ten do not: both Chinese and Korean-style pieces use the clapper, but in those of Chinese origin, like *Pohŏja* 步虛子 , the clapper is played at the end of musical phrases and in

hyangak, like *Manjŏnch'un* 滿殿春 , it is played at the beginning of phrases. The same observation is true of pieces in the *Siyong hyangak-po.* Thus, the Chinese and Korean-style pieces are clearly differentiated by clapper use. Since the *Ssanghwajŏm* in the *Siyong hyangak-po* uses the clapper at the beginning of phrases, it is, from this standpoint, still in a *hyangak* style. Other sinicized pieces, like *Pot'aep'yŏng* and *Chŏng-daeŏp,* have moved the clapper to the end of phrases and thus are further from a *hyangak* style than is the *Ssanghwajŏm* in the *Siyong hyangak-po.*

4. The drum patterns in the *Taeak hubo* and *Siyong hyangak-po* versions of *Ssanghwajŏm* are different. Example 2 shows the *Taeak hubo* drum pattern (notes with upward stems are strokes with the stick held in the right hand, and notes with downward stems are strokes with the open left hand), which lasts three measures and is then repeated over and over without alteration. This particular drum pattern is not to be found in any other piece in the *Taeak hubo;* a special feature is the succession ♪ ♪ ♩ at the end of each measure, found only in *Ssang-hwajŏm.* Noteworthy also is the fact that a single pattern requires three measures (columns); this is half that of other *hyangak* pieces such as *Ch'wip'unghyŏng* 醉豊亭 and *Ch'ihwap'yŏng* 致和平 . Example 3 shows the drum pattern of *Ch'wip'unghyŏng* (*Sejong sillok* 世宗實錄 145.1b); this six-measure pattern is double the length of the three-measure pattern of *Ssanghwajŏm* in the *Taeak hubo,* but it is clear they are both patterns in the same genealogy and can be considered characteristic of *hyangak.*

The drum pattern of *Ssanghwajŏm* in the *Siyong hyangak-po,* shown in Example 4, is brief and different from either Example 2 or 3. This four-stroke pattern also appears in thirteen other pieces in the *Siyong hyangak-po;* since these pieces are *hyangak,* it appears that this is a pattern characteristic of *hyangak.* It does not appear in the Chinese-style pieces in the *Siyong hyangak-po,* nor is it found in the abovementioned sinicized pieces *Pot'aep'yŏng* and *Chŏngdaeŏp.*

Thus, even though the drum patterns of *Ssanghwajŏm* are different in the *Taeak hubo* and *Siyong hyangak-po,* they are both patterns characteristic of *hyangak,* not Chinese-style music.

5. The Chinese text in the *Siyong hyangak-po* version is set quite regularly, with one syllable in every half measure, coinciding with the

drum strokes. This is similar to the pieces of Chinese derivation, such as *Pohŏja*, which have one syllable of text at the beginning of each measure. In this way, the *Siyong hyangak-po* version gives the impression of being like Chinese music. However, other pieces of *hyangak* in the *Siyong hyangak-po*, like *Taeguk-sam* 大國三 ,have almost the same sort of regular text setting (one syllable per half measure), so that this type of text setting cannot be considered unique to Chinese-style music.

The piece *Taeguk-sam* is part of a trilogy: *Taeguk-il* 大國一 , *Taeguk-i* 大國二 , and *Taeguk-sam*. *Taeguk-il* corresponds to *man* 慢, that is, slow; *Taeguk-i* corresponds to *chung* 中, medium speed; and *Taeguk-sam* corresponds to *sak* 數, fast speed. This suggests, by analogy, that the *Ssanghwajŏm* in the *Siyong hyangak-po* might be a faster version of the earlier *Ssanghwajŏm* in the *Taeak hubo*.

6. It was noted above that the sixth through eighth and fourteenth through sixteenth quarter notes in each measure of *Ssanghwajŏm* in the *Taeak hubo* have been expanded to eight quarter notes $(3 + 2 + 3)$ in the *Siyong hyangak-po* version (see Example 1); one measure in the *Taeak hubo* has been expanded to two in the *Siyong hyangak-po*. The same occurrence may be found in *Chŏngdaeŏp* and *Pot'aep'yŏng*: in "*Hwat'ae*" 和泰, a movement of *Chŏngdaeŏp*, and "*Chŏngmyŏng*" 貞明 , a movement of *Pot'aep'yŏng*, the same succession of drum strokes is used. As shown in Example 5 (*Sejong sillok* 138.21a and 35b), "*Hwat'ae*" pattern uses one measure and is expanded to two measures in "*Chŏngmyŏng*." Thus, the square rhythm in the expanded version does not necessarily imply Chinese-style music.

CONCLUSIONS

The *Ssanghwajŏm* in the *Siyong hyangak-po* is both a musical and textual revision of the earlier *Ssanghwajŏm* recorded in the *Taeak hubo*. Though the text was changed from Korean to Chinese, the music was only slightly adapted in the direction of Chinese style; it retains many essential features of *hyangak*. There are, however, some other pieces of *hyangak*, like *Chŏngdaeŏp* and *Pot'aep'yŏng*, which have been converted into settings of pure Chinese texts, keeping some characteristics of Korean music while mixing in certain prominent features of Chinese music.

Example 1: Ssanghwajŏm

Example 2: Drum pattern in *Taeak hubo*

Ssanghwajŏm

Example 3: *Ch'wip'unghyang* drum pattern

Example 4: Drum pattern in *Siyong Hyangak-po*

Example 5: Patterns in "*Hwat'ae*" and "*Chŏngmyŏng*"

HYUMYŎNG AND
CH'ŎNGSAN PYŎLGOK

INTRODUCTION

Recorded in the *Sejong sillok* 世宗實錄 are four long suites, named *Chŏngdaeŏp* 定大業, *Pot'aep'yŏng* 保太平, *Palsang* 發祥, and *Pongnaeŭi* 鳳來儀. According to a prefatory note (138.1a), King Sejong 世宗 (ruled 1418-1450) prepared this "new music" on the basis of *koch'wi* 鼓吹 (military music) and *hyangak* 鄉樂 (native Korean music). The author has set himself the task of identifying which of the fifteen pieces in *Chŏngdaeŏp* and eleven pieces in *Pot'aep'yŏng* were based on *koch'wi* and which on *hyangak*.

In the article "Creative Activity in Traditional Korean Music" (page 196), it was pointed out that *Yunghwa* 隆化, a piece performed in *Pot'aep'yŏng*, and *Yuhwanggok* 維皇曲, a piece performed in certain sacrificial rites for royal ancestors, were both derived from the same Koryŏ song, *P'ungipsong* 風入松. Professor Chang Sa-hun 張師勛 has verified this identification through further research (*Kugak non'go* 國樂論攷 [1966], pp. 68-79), and he has also verified the following identifications: *Hwat'ae* 和泰 (later version, *Yŏnggwan* 永觀) in *Chŏngdaeŏp* is derived from a Koryŏ song, *Sŏgyŏng pyŏlgok* 西京別曲 (*Kugak non'go*, pp. 55-67); and *Sunŭng* 順應 (later version, *Hyŏkchŏng* 赫整) in *Chŏngdaeŏp* is from the song *Manjŏnch'un* 滿殿春 (*Kugak non'go*, pp. 80-118). In short, of the twenty-six pieces in *Chŏngdaeŏp* and *Pot'aep'yŏng*, only the sources of three (*Yunghwa, Hwat'ae,* and *Sunŭng*) have hitherto been identified.

While preparing a commentary to *Chŏngdaeŏp* and *Pot'aep'yŏng*, the author incidentally noticed that every second measure of the piece

*Hyumyŏng*休命 , from *Chŏngdaeŏp,* gave an impression of monotony, since each repeated the same melodic formula; this was a clue that *Hyumyŏng* might be derived from the song *Ch'ŏngsan pyŏlgok* 靑山別曲 , which similarly repeats a melodic formula. A connection between these two pieces is not mentioned at all in old written sources, but the characteristic repetition of a melodic formula in the notated sources led to the discovery of the relationship.

Ch'ŏngsan pyŏlgok, as recorded in the *Siyong hyangak-po* 時用鄕樂譜 (ca. 1500), consists of ten measures (columns of *Chŏnggan-po;* see page 39), each measure containing sixteen quarter notes (3-2-3 + 3-2-3). *Hyumyŏng,* as recorded in the *Sejong sillok,* consists of twelve such measures (six columns, each twice as long as a column in *Ch'ŏngsan pyŏlgok*). Length is not the only difference between the pieces; the starting notes are different. We shall compare the two pieces measure by measure, together with the pieces *Kyŏnggŭn chi kok* 敬勤之曲 No. 1, as recorded in the *Sejo sillok* 世祖實錄 , and *Napssiga* 納氏歌 , recorded in the *Siyong hyangak-po.* The latter piece is included because its connection with *Ch'ŏngsan pyŏlgok* has already been established by Professor Chang (*Kugak non'go,* pp. 49-54).

Hyumyŏng is in the mode *kyemyŏnjo* 界面調 (see page 62) with the tonic pitch *A. Kyŏnggŭn chi kok* No. 1 is prescribed as being in the *do*-mode on *G,* which is to say it is in the mode *p'yŏngjo* 平調 (see page 61). Both *Napssiga* and *Ch'ŏngsan pyŏlgok* are prescribed as *p'yŏngjo.* An annotation to the piece *Chŏngsŏkka* 鄭石歌 in the *Siyong hyangak-po* indicates that the piece could be performed either in *kyemyŏnjo* or *p'yŏngjo,* so it is not unreasonable to compare the *kyemyŏnjo* piece *Hyumyŏng* with the three other pieces in *p'yŏngjo.*

TEXTS

The text of *Hyumyŏng* is written in pure Chinese and consists of a single stanza made up of twelve lines of four syllables each. Rhyme is an important structural feature: the last syllables of the second and fourth lines rhyme; there are corresponding, but different rhymes between the sixth and eighth lines and between the tenth and twelfth lines. This rhyme scheme suggests a division of the text into three equal parts of four lines each. Each line of text is set to a single measure of music, so that the musical length, as already noted, is twelve measures. The text is as follows:

(Text 1)

休　命

我旂載回	帝命是順
誰其倡義	神斷獨運.
路載懽聲	三軍陶陶
既警既戒	孰犯秋毫.
沿途搏獸	我舒保作
大順以正	景命有僕

The full text of *Kyŏnggŭn chi kok* consists of nine stanzas with a consistent structure; we are concerned here with the setting of only the first stanza. Each stanza is made up of two parts: a verse and a refrain, the latter appearing identically in all nine stanzas. Each verse is fundamentally a four-line poem in Chinese, with five syllables per line; however, Korean particles and auxiliary verbs, written with the native alphabet, are added to each line. The refrain is essentially a single seven-syllable line of Chinese, with Korean particles and auxiliary verb attached.

In the musical setting, each full line of text in the verse is basically set to two measures of music. Normally, the five syllables of the Chinese line, together with attached Korean particles, are set to one measure of music; the Korean auxiliary verb concluding each full line is also set to one measure. The measure division is shown by virgules (/) in the text below. The only exception to this scheme is that the first two syllables of the fourth line of Chinese text are included in the sixth, not seventh measure. The seven syllables of the refrain are divided into two parts (4 + 3); each part, with its associated Korean particles or auxiliary verb, is set to two measures of music, as shown below. Altogether, then, the musical setting for the five-line text, like *Hyumyŏng*, requires twelve measures.

(Text 2)

敬勤之曲其一

皇天이 眷大東 / ᄒ샤
聖繼而神承이 / 어시늘
我后ㅣ今受之 / ᄒ시니, 王業
이 載中興이 / 샷다.
萬有千歲 / 를
享天福ᄒ / 죠셔

The text of *Napssiga* is similar in structure to that of *Kyŏnggŭn chi kok* No. 1, but it lacks a refrain. The *Siyong hyangak-po* gives a single stanza, basically a four-line poem in Chinese with five syllables per line; Korean particles and auxiliary verbs are added. As in *Kyŏnggŭn chi kok* No. 1, each full line is set to two measures of music, with the result that the musical length is eight measures; this is shorter than *Hyumyŏng* or *Kyŏnggŭn chi kok*.

(Text 3)

納氏歌

納氏恃雄强 / ᄒ야
入寇東北方 / ᄒ더니
縱傲誇以力 / ᄒ니
鋒銳라不可當이 / 로다

The text of *Ch'ŏngsan pyŏlgok*, unlike the others, is written almost exclusively in the Korean alphabet; the only exceptions are two occurrences of the characters 靑山 for *Ch'ŏngsan*. The *Siyong hyangak-po* gives only a single stanza of text and its musical setting, but the sixteenth-century text collection *Akchang kasa* 樂章歌詞 records eight stanzas. Comparison of these shows that each stanza naturally divides into three parts: the first two parts have two lines each and make up the verse; the third part is a single-line refrain of nonsense syllables: "Yalli yalli yalla yallisŏng yalla." Generally, each line is set to two measures of music; however, the last line of the verse (that is, line 4) is compressed into one measure, and the refrain is expanded to three measures. Altogether, the setting requires ten measures.

(Text 4)

青山別曲

1. 살어리 살어리 / 라쌰
   靑山의 살어리 / 라쌰.
2. 멀위랑 드래랑 / 빠먹고 따
   靑山의 살어리랏다.

Refrain 얄리 얄리 / 얄라 / 얄라셩 얄라.

From the standpoint of text, then, the song written in Korean with a nonsense-syllable refrain, *Ch'ŏngsan pyŏlgok,* is the original song. The two texts in Chinese with Korean particles and auxiliary verbs, *Kyŏnggŭn chi kok* No. 1 and *Napssiga,* bear similarities to each other; *Kyŏnggŭn chi kok,* however, has a refrain, which *Napssiga* lacks. These two texts are newer than *Ch'ŏngsan pyŏlgok,* but the most distant from *Ch'ŏngsan pyŏlgok* is *Hyumyŏng,* which is written entirely in Chinese.

THE MUSIC

As mentioned above, the four pieces under consideration vary in musical length: two are twelve measures, one is ten, and one is eight. In this section, we will examine the putative correlations measure by measure (see the musical example).

A. Measure one:

Ch'ŏngsan pyŏlgok, the original piece, begins on the note $f^\#$, that is, one scale degree below the tonic (the pentatonic *p'yŏngjo* scale here being transcribed as A-B-D-E-$F^\#$). *Hyumyŏng,* on the other hand, begins on the tonic, a. For the remainder of measure 1, the two pieces correspond very closely. As already pointed out, *Hyumyŏng* is in *kyemyŏnjo* (A-C-D-E-G), and the other three pieces are in *p'yŏngjo;* the difference between these is that B and $F^\#$ in *p'yŏngjo* correspond, respectively, to C and G in *kyemyŏnjo.* Thus, throughout this discussion these corresponding modal degrees will be considered equivalent. In measure 1, for example, all the b's in *Ch'ŏngsan pyŏlgok* correspond modally to c's in *Hyumyŏng*.

Napssiga and *Kyŏnggŭn chi kok*, like *Ch'ŏngsan pyŏlgok*, start on
f#; *Hyumyŏng* alone begins on the tonic. As it happens, all twenty-six
pieces in *Chŏngdaeŏp* and *Pot'aep'yŏng* begin on the tonic, and thus it
is entirely understandable that the opening note of *Ch'ŏngsan pyŏlgok*
would have been altered when the melody was borrowed for this
purpose. Other instances of such alteration occur: for example, the
twelve-measure piece *T'angnyŏng* 濯靈 in *Chŏngdaeŏp*, recorded in the
Sejong sillok, later came to be divided into half to make two separate
pieces, *T'akchŏng* 濯征 and *Chŏngse* 靖世, which are recorded in the
revised *Chŏngdaeŏp* of the *Sejo sillok*. The seventh measure of
T'angnyŏng has the melodic motion g-c'-c'; when this is borrowed as
the opening measure of *Chŏngse*, the g is changed to a, the tonic, and
the resultant line is a-c'-c'.

Thus, as *Hyumyŏng* and *Chŏngse* show, any piece borrowed for
use in *Chŏngdaeŏp* is subject to having its opening pitch changed to the
tonic pitch. The reason is that, just as the text of *Chŏngdaeŏp* has been
rendered in pure Chinese, the music is altered to begin on the tonic, as
is characteristic of music in the Chinese style.

B. Measure two:

The second measures of *Hyumyŏng* and *Ch'ŏngsan pyŏlgok* match
closely, the only difference being the change of mode. The *Ch'ŏngsan
pyŏlgok* melody is b-a-b-b, which suggests that the a might be merely
an ornamental tone; this idea is supported by the *Kyŏnggŭn chi kok*
line, which has only b-b. In the second and third stanzas of *Kyŏnggŭn
chi kok* (not shown in the example), the melody is altered slightly: b-b-b
in one case and b-a-b in the other. This further evidences the notion
that the a is an ornamental tone.

Significantly, several other instances of this phenomenon occur: in
Hyumyŏng, measures 2, 4, 6, 8, and 10, and in the corresponding
measures of the other pieces (this correlation will be established as the
discussion proceeds). For the most part, this type of phrase occurs in the
even-numbered measures of all the pieces, with the exception of the
final measure of each. The chief violation of this rule appears in
Ch'ŏngsan pyŏlgok, which has this phrase in measure 9 rather than 8;
the reason, as explained earlier, is that the fourth line of text is com-

pressed to fit into a single measure (#7) rather than into the usual two measures. The nonsense syllables of the refrain begin in measure 8. Since this sort of phrase with an ornamental tone does not occur at the very end of the pieces or at the beginning of line settings, it may be considered a form of internal half-cadence.

Another exception is to be found in measure 6 of *Kyŏnggŭn chi kok* No. 1, in which the melodic motion does not follow the norm: instead of *e-d-e-e,* it has *e-d-e-(a-b).* However, the exceptional *a-b* at the end is not the musical setting of the end of a line of text, but rather of the first two syllables of a new line; this unusual occurrence is mentioned above in the consideration of texts. Even in this exceptional instance, it is clear that the appearance of the long-held pitches and ornamental tone are characteristic settings for the ends of lines.

This conspicuous use of a consistent cadential formula for the ends of textual lines opens the way for comparison of *Hyumyŏng* and *Ch'ŏngsan pyŏlgok*; it is what gave the "impression of monotony" mentioned in the Introduction. Such internal cadential formulas are also to be found in other pieces in *Chŏngdaeŏp* and *Pot'aep'yŏng*.

C. Measure three:

Hyumyŏng, Napssiga, and *Ch'ŏngsan pyŏlgok* correspond closely in measure 3. However, while these three pieces begin with the tonic, *a, Kyŏnggŭn chi kok* No. 1 begins a fifth higher, on *e'. Kyŏnggŭn chi kok* No. 2 (not shown), on the other hand, begins on the expected *a; Kyŏnggŭn chi kok* No. 3 starts on *d'*. This suggests that the *e'* is just a change from the *a*. Other instances of this sort of alteration may be cited; the same relationship exists between standard *sijo* 平時調 and *sijo* of descending melodic contour, 지름時調 (see page 74), though the difference is a sixth rather than a fifth.

Also, *Kyŏnggŭn chi kok* lacks the quarter-note at the end of the half-measure. However, this is just a passing tone in the other three pieces, not an essential note. Similarly, *Ch'ŏngsan pyŏlgok* has *f#* as its last note, anticipating the *f#* in the following measure, but *Kyŏnggŭn chi kok* No. 1 ends with *e*, a non-essential lower auxiliary note. This lower auxiliary is also found in *Napssiga*.

D. Measure four:

All four pieces coincide.

E. Measure five:

As in measure 1, *Hyumyŏng* begins on the tonic, *a*, while the other pieces have *f#*. All four pieces are beginning a new line of text at this point, as in measure 1; all the melodic structures are also similar to those in measure 1. *Kyŏnggŭn chi kok* No. 1 varies somewhat from *Ch'ŏngsan pyŏlgok*, but the differences are not major; the second half of the measure in *Kyŏnggŭn chi kok* No. 2, as it happens, is identical to that of *Ch'ŏngsan pyŏlgok*, so that a connection is still clear.

F. Measure six:

All four pieces coincide, with the exception of the last two notes of *Kyŏnggŭn chi kok* No. 1, as described above in paragraph B. Similar examples of the early start of the final line of a verse may be found in the pieces *Ch'wip'unghyŏng* 醉豐亭 (*Sejong sillok* 145.1a) and *Chŏng-sŏkka* (*Siyong hyangak-po* 23b). The fourth line of *Kyŏnggŭn chi kok* No. 1, thus begun in measure 6, extends through measure 8 and concludes the verse.

G. Measure seven:

Ch'ŏngsan pyŏlgok and *Hyumyŏng* coincide perfectly. As in measure 6, *Kyŏnggŭn chi kok* No. 1 is somewhat different from *Ch'ŏngsan pyŏlgok;* however, while the other pieces are starting a new line of text, *Kyŏnggŭn chi kok* No. 1, as explained above, began its line of text near the end of measure 6. It would be appropriate for *Ch'ŏngsan pyŏlgok*, like *Kyŏnggŭn chi kok* No. 1, to start its line of text in measure 6, but this is not the case in the notated source; instead, it has eight syllables of the last line of its verse strangely compressed into a single measure. All the preceding odd-numbered measures of *Ch'ŏngsan pyŏlgok* have had six syllables. The textual underlay of measures 6 and 7 of *Ch'ŏngsan pyŏlgok* might be corrected as follows:

Original: 𝅗𝅥. 𝅗𝅥 𝅗𝅥. ┊𝅗𝅥. 𝅗𝅥 𝅗𝅥. │𝅗𝅥. 𝅗𝅥 𝅗𝅥. ┊𝅗𝅥. 𝅗𝅥 𝅗𝅥. │

      따   먹   고.   青 山 의   살어리랏 다

Revised: 𝅗𝅥. 𝅗𝅥 𝅗𝅥. ┊𝅗𝅥. 𝅗𝅥 𝅗𝅥. │𝅗𝅥. 𝅗𝅥 𝅗𝅥. ┊𝅗𝅥. 𝅗𝅥 𝅗𝅥. │

      따   먹   고. 青山의   살 어 리 라   따

The *a* at the beginning of the second half of measure 7 in *Kyŏnggŭn chi kok* No. 1 does not agree with the $f^\#$ in *Ch'ŏngsan pyŏlgok*, but in *Kyŏnggŭn chi kok* No. 4, *e* is substituted for the *a*, and it is apparent that the *a* is not an invariable choice for this position in measure 7.

H. Measure eight (of *Hyumyŏng*):

In *Ch'ŏngsan pyŏlgok*, the last line of text in the verse is set in measure 7, so that measure 8 begins the nonsense-syllable refrain; that is, it begins a new line of text. In *Kyŏnggŭn chi kok* No. 1, however, the music for the last line of the verse lasts through measure 8, the refrain beginning in measure 9. Measure 8 of *Kyŏnggŭn chi kok* No. 1 is a full cadence giving a sense of finality; this may be seen by comparing measure 8 with measure 12, the final measure of the piece, which is identical. *Hyumyŏng,* on the other hand, has a half-cadence in measure 8, as already discussed; this is quite different from the final cadence of *Hyumyŏng* in measure 12.

Thus, measure 8 of *Kyŏnggŭn chi kok* and *Hyumyŏng* concludes the musical setting of a line of text, unlike measure 8 of *Ch'ŏngsan pyŏlgok*, which begins a new line. Also, the melodic structure of *Kyŏnggŭn chi kok* or *Hyumyŏng* in this measure does not appear in *Ch'ŏngsan pyŏlgok*, with the possible exception of the final measure. Measure 8 of *Kyŏnggŭn chi kok* No. 1 and *Hyumyŏng*, then, is added on to the original melody of *Ch'ŏngsan pyŏlgok*; as a result, measure 8 of *Ch'ŏngsan pyŏlgok*, as noted below, corresponds to measure 9 in *Kyŏnggŭn chi kok* No. 1 and *Hyumyŏng*.

I. Measure nine (of *Hyumyŏng*):

Measure 9 of *Kyŏnggŭn chi kok* No. 1 and *Hyumyŏng* corresponds to measure 8 of *Ch'ongsan pyŏlgok*; *Kyŏnggŭn chi kok* No. 1 and

Ch'ŏngsan pyŏlgok here begin their refrains, and *Hyumyŏng* begins its third section of text. The correspondence, however, is not exact, and there are several differences of pitch in the three versions. But since all start on *d* and all coincide in the following measure, it is clear they belong in the same genealogy. Also, the general melodic shape is the same in all three.

J. Measure ten (of *Hyumyŏng*):

Measure 10 in *Hyumyŏng* and *Kyŏnggŭn chi kok* No. 1 corresponds exactly to measure 9 in *Ch'ŏngsan pyŏlgok*.

K. Measure eleven (of *Hyumyŏng*):

Measure 11 in *Hyumyŏng* has no corresponding measure in *Ch'ŏngsan pyŏlgok;* it is, however, very similar to its own measure 7 and that of *Napssiga*. In the three-part structure of *Hyumyŏng,* measures 7 and 11 perform similar functions: measure 7 sets the third line of the second part of the text, and measure 11 sets the third line of the third part of the text (see textual discussion above). Thus, it appears that in expanding the music of *Ch'ŏngsan pyŏlgok* for use with the newer text of *Hyumyŏng,* the music of measure 7 was simply used again for this corresponding textual line.

Measure 11 of *Kyŏnggŭn chi kok* also does not correspond to any particular measure in *Ch'ŏngsan pyŏlgok*. However, neither is it a repetition of its own measure 7. The low tessitura of this measure suggests a connection with the following, concluding measure; indeed, measures 11-12 of *Kyŏnggŭn chi kok* No. 1 might well be considered an expansion of measure 10 of *Ch'ŏngsan pyŏlgok,* that is, the concluding measure of *Ch'ŏngsan pyŏlgok*.

Whatever the source of measure 11 in *Hyumyŏng* and *Kyŏnggŭn chi kok,* they are additions to the original melody borrowed from *Ch'ŏngsan pyŏlgok*.

L. Measure twelve (of *Hyumyŏng*):

The final measure has a good deal of rhythmic difference among the four pieces, but all agree on the basic melodic shape and concluding note. *Napssiga* is actually the closest to the *Ch'ŏngsan pyŏlgok* original, *Hyumyŏng* and *Kyŏnggūn chi kok* No. 1 being comparatively distant.

Napssiga has not been discussed for some time and deserves a concluding comment. Up through measure 7, it corresponds to the other three pieces very closely. Since, however, it lacks a refrain, measure 8 of *Napssiga* is its conclusion and thus is derived from the concluding measure of *Ch'ŏngsan pyŏlgok* rather than from measure 8 or 9 of *Ch'ŏngsan pyŏlgok*.

CONCLUSIONS

When the melody of *Ch'ŏngsan pyŏlgok* was borrowed for use in setting the texts of *Hyumyŏng* and *Kyŏnggūn chi kok* No. 1, it was necessary to add two extra measures of music (8 and 11). The ten-measure original was thus expanded to twelve measures. More specifically, the original text of *Ch'ŏngsan pyŏlgok* was set in this fashion: four measures for the first two lines of the verse, three measures for the last two lines of the verse, and three measures for the refrain. *Kyŏnggūn chi kok* No. 1 has a similar textual form, four lines of verse plus a refrain, but it has added a measure to each of the two three-measure groups of *Ch'ŏngsan pyŏlgok*. Since *Kyŏnggūn chi kok* No. 1 has a verse-refrain structure, the end of the verse is given a full cadential phrase (measure 8) on a par with the conclusion of the refrain.

Hyumyŏng, like *Kyŏnggūn chi kok* No. 1, has been expanded to twelve measures from the original *Ch'ŏngsan pyŏlgok*; there are twelve lines in its text, with one measure of music per line. Unlike *Kyŏnggūn chi kok* No. 1, however, *Hyumyŏng* is simply a twelve-line verse, having no verse-refrain structure; a full cadence in measure 8 would be inappropriate, and therefore only an internal half-cadence is given. This is the essential reason for the differences between measure 8 of *Hyumyŏng* and that of *Kyŏnggūn chi kok* No. 1.

These sorts of later developments of a melody suggest a useful generalization. By examining the number of measures used for setting a poem, the use of internal half-cadences, and the use of a full cadence to signal the end of a verse or a refrain, clues as to the age of a piece of music may be obtained. Music divided into several sections may be viewed as pre-dating music which simply consists of a series of two-measure sets with half-cadences.

In the case of *Hyumyŏng* and *Ch'ŏngsan pyŏlgok,* just as the text has been changed from pure Korean to pure Chinese, the music has been altered to include characteristics of Chinese style: the musical phrasing has been changed from two sections (corresponding to verse and refrain) to one continuous section, with a half-cadence in every second measure; and *Ch'ŏngsan pyŏlgok* begins on the scale degree below the tonic, but *Hyumyŏng* starts, in Chinese fashion, on the tonic itself.

POSTSCRIPT

In preparing this article, I had not noticed the very brief mention of pieces derived from *Ch'ŏngsan pyŏlgok* given by Professor Chang Sa-hun in his *Kugak non'go,* page 72. He states that *Napssiga* is derived from *Ch'ŏngsan pyŏlgok,* but that measures 8 and 9 of *Ch'ŏngsan pyŏlgok* are eliminated; this is just as described here. He also states that *Kyŏnggŭn chi kok* No. 1 derives from one section of *Ch'ŏngsan pyŏlgok,* but does not identify the section; the present article may explain the details of the relationship.

Dr. Chang also points out that the piece *Taeguk* 大國, recorded in the *Siyong hyangak-po,* corresponds in full to *Ch'ŏngsan pyŏlgok.* Like *Kyŏnggŭn chi kok,* however, *Taeguk* is divided into several stanzas (three, to be precise), and only the first of these corresponds in full to *Ch'ŏngsan pyŏlgok. Taeguk* No. 2 is sixteen measures long, and is derived from *Ch'ŏngsan pyŏlgok* only in its last ten measures. *Taeguk* No. 3 requires two measures to complete the drum pattern in a single measure of *Ch'ŏngsan pyŏlgok,* and its correlation is unclear. Comparison of these three stanzas of *Taeguk* with the other pieces derived from *Ch'ŏngsan pyŏlgok* should yield more information on the method of musical variation in Korean music.

Musical Example

NAGYANGCH'UN: CHINESE TZ'U MUSIC

INTRODUCTION

The *tangak* 唐樂 ("music of T'ang") section of the music essay in the *Koryŏ-sa* 高麗史 (History of the Koryŏ Dynasty) records the text of *Nagyangch'un* 洛陽春 (Chinese: *Loyang-ch'un*) (71.16b); if we separate that undivided version into lines, it is as follows:

紗窗未曉黃鶯語
蕙爐燒殘炷
錦帷羅幕度春寒
昨夜裏三更雨

繡簾閑倚吹輕絮
斂眉山無緒
把花拭淚向歸鴻
問來處逢郎不

This text might be rendered in English in this fashion:
>*Spring in Loyang*
Gauze windows glimmer and the yellow nightingale twitters.
>In the fireplace some fire lingers still.
Silk curtain and tapestry hold me warm from spring's cold.
>Late last night it rained.
Leaning on the screen, I see light-winged seeds afloat in the air.
>I close my eyes, my mind disturbed.
Flowers in hand, drying tears, I ask the wild returning geese:
>Have you seen my love?

227

The *Koryo-sa* gives no music with the text. However, the piece *Nagyangch'un* is still played today at the National Institute of Classical Music in a purely instrumental version. Similarly, notated versions in Chapters 4 and 6 of the 18th-century *Sogak wŏnbo* 俗樂源譜 have music, but no text. It is proposed here to fit the text preserved in the *Koryŏ sa* to the music notated in the *Sogak wŏnbo*; on the basis of the combined result, an investigation into Chinese *tz'u* music and Japanese *Tōgaku* 唐樂 ("music of T'ang") is possible.

THREE MUSICAL SOURCES FOR NAGYANGCH'UN

The *Sogak wŏnbo* records two versions of *Nagyangch'un*: one, in Chapter 6, is a score for the string instruments *kŏmun'go* 玄琴, *kayagŭm* 伽倻琴 , and *pip'a* 琵琶. The original score, shown in Illustration 1, consists of seven sets of four columns each. In each set of four columns, the first (on the right) gives the melodic line in letter notation (*Yulja-po*; see p. 24); the next three columns give plucking information for, respectively, *kŏmun'go, kayagŭm,* and *pip'a.* "ㄱ" means plucking toward the player, and "I" means away from the player. This version of *Nagyangch'un* is transcribed in Example 1.

The second version of *Nagyangch'un* preserved in the *Sogak wŏnbo* is a score in Chapter 4 which gives both letter (*Yulja-po*) and scale-degree notation (*Oŭm yakpo*; see p. 28) for the melody, plus instructions for the hourglass drum, *changgo* 杖鼓, and clapper, *pak* 拍. Illustration 2 shows the first two pages of this long score [the fifth column in each set is never used]; a complete transcription is given in Example 2.

Example 1 is only seven measures in length, as compared to forty-one measures in Example 2; although these would thus appear to be different, a closer look reveals that the number of tones used is practically the same: seventy-eight and seventy-nine. Also, the melodies are virtually the same. The chief difference is one of notation: although the conversion factor is not entirely consistent, a quarter-note in Example 1 typically equals a half-measure in Example 2.

The only exceptions to the melodic identity of these two examples are as follows:

Illustration 1

洛陽春

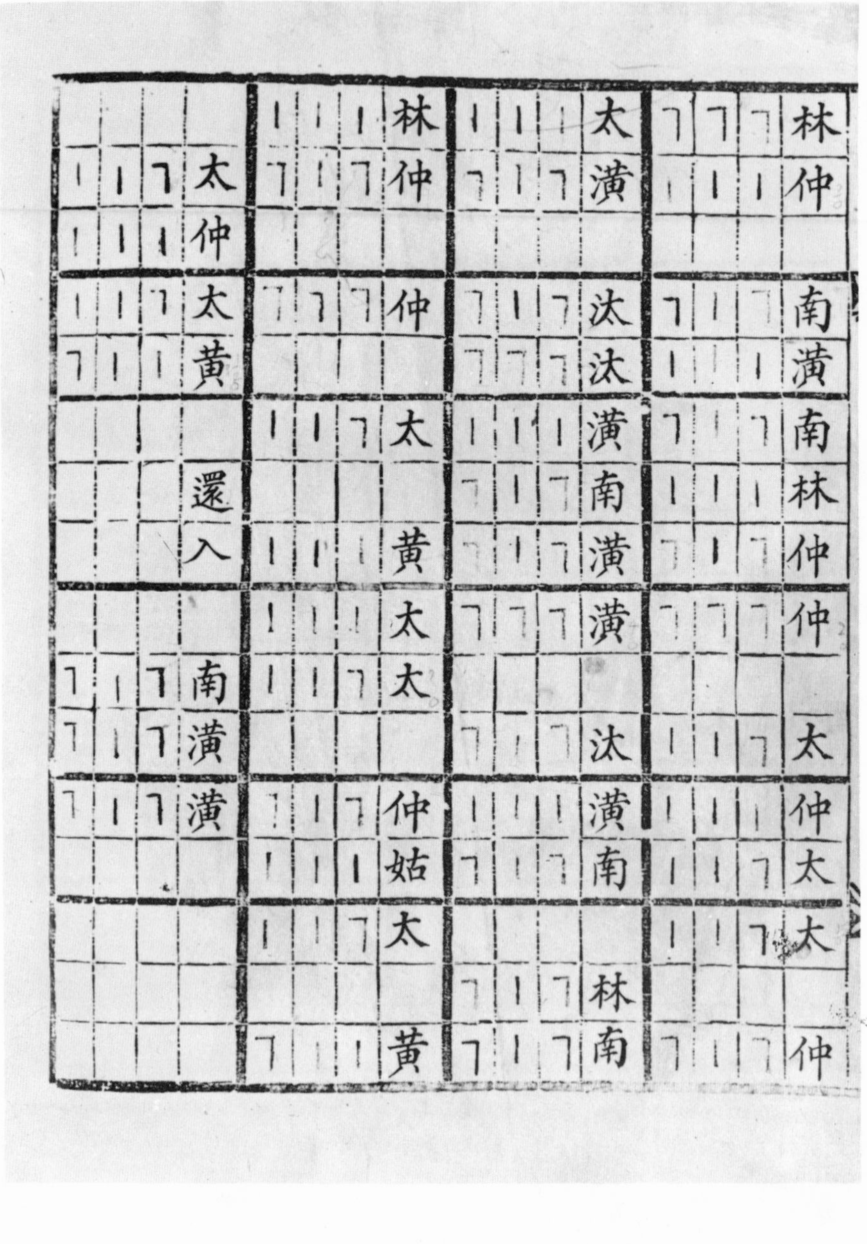
林仲南潢南林仲仲太仲太太仲
太潢汰汰潢南潢潢汰潢南林南
林仲仲太黄太太仲姑太黄
太仲太黄還入南潢潢

Illustration 2

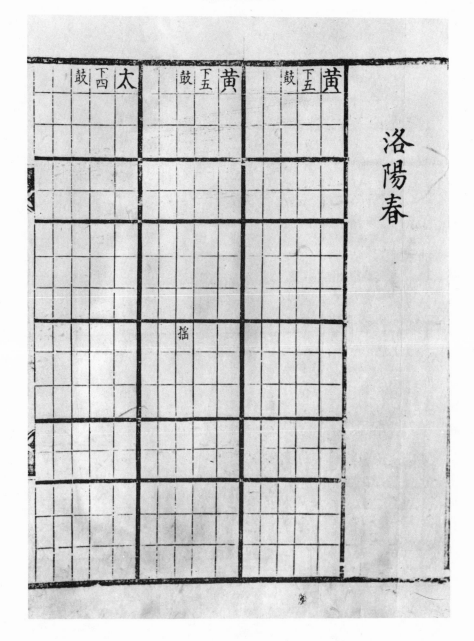

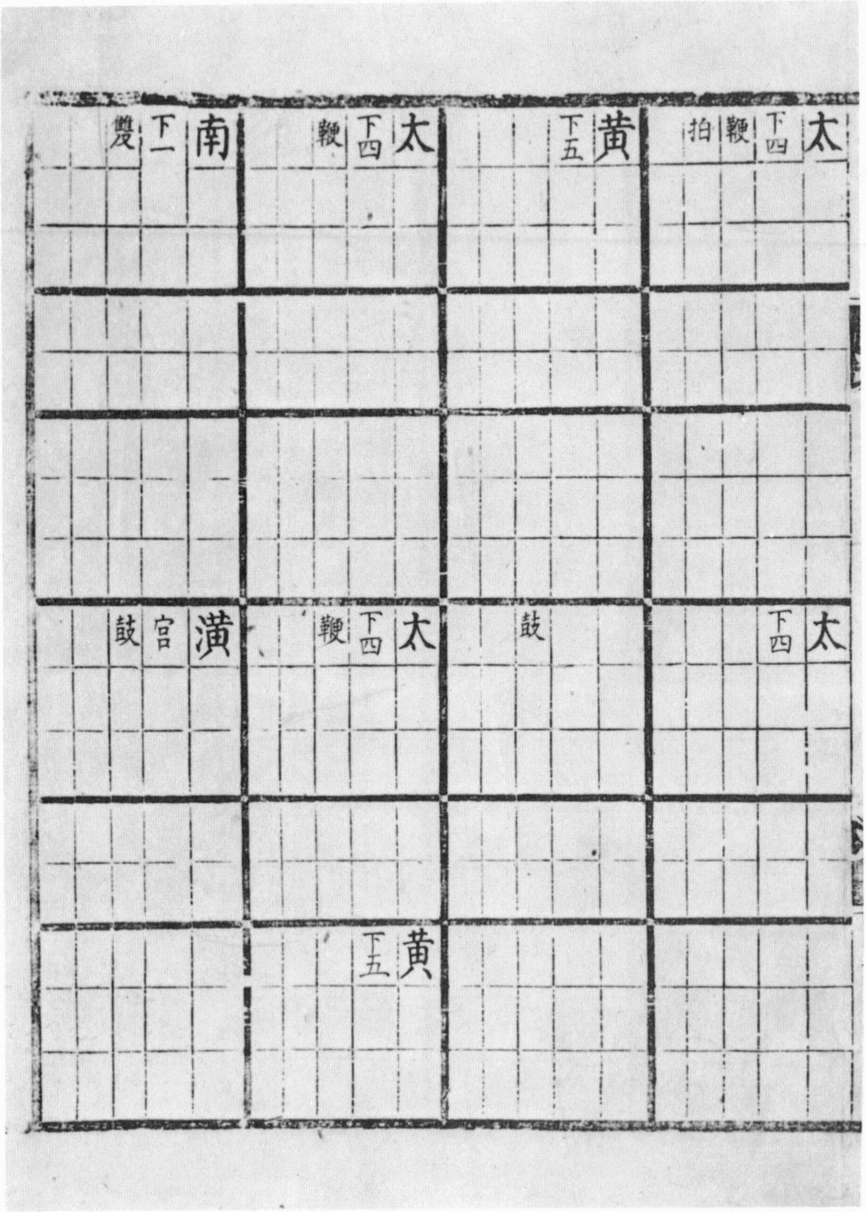
太 下四 鞭 拍
黃 下五
太 下四 鞭
南 下一 雙
太 下四
鼓
太 下四 鞭
潢 宮 鼓
黃 下五

Example 1: Example 2:
Measure 3: b^b versus Measure 13: b
Measure 6: e versus Measure 35: e^b

Example 3 gives the score of *Nagyangch'un* as presently performed at the National Institute of Classical Music. At the places corresponding to the two problematic notes in the old scores (m. 11 and m. 25), the modern performance gives b and e . Thus, all three known versions of *Nagyangch'un* have independent, albeit very close, readings of these two notes. But certainly these differences are minor, and the character of the melody is the same in all sources.

Similar cases of scores with the notational relationship of those in Examples 1 and 2 occur elsewhere. For example, scores of the piece *Pot'aep'yŏng* 保太平 in the *Sogak wŏnbo* (Chapter 6) and the fifteenth-century *Annals* of King Sejo (*Sejo sillok* 世祖實錄) (48.17a-32a) have such a relationship, as do the scores of the piece *Pohŏja* 步虛子 in the *Sogak wŏnbo* (Chapter 7) and the *Taeak hubo* 大樂後譜 of 1759 (Chapter 6).

At first glance, Examples 2 and 3 would, like Examples 1 and 2, appear to be quite different. However, if we look at the melodic line of the chimes (*p'yŏn'gyŏng* 編磬) and bells (*p'yŏnjong* 編鐘) rather than the ornamented lines of the flute (*taegŭm* 大笒) or oboe (*tang-p'iri* 唐觱篥), the two examples are very close in melodic structure. The lines of the two bowed string instruments, *haegŭm* 奚琴 and *ajaeng* 牙箏 , are even closer to the old version. The exception is that the *f* in measure 38 of Example 2 is missing in measure 27 of the modern score.

Although Examples 1, 2, and 3 coincide melodically, they are rhythmically different. The length of a measure in the modern score is variously two, three, four, five, six, or eight beats in length. However, the eight strokes of each pattern played by the drum (*chŏlgo* 節鼓) generally correspond to a single line of song text, as will be made clear in the discussions below (these drum strokes are indicated by parenthetical numbers in Example 3). Table 1 shows the number of beats contained in each drum stroke.

Thus, although the rhythmic structures of the modern score and Example 2 are not consistent, a line of text corresponds to eight strokes on the drum in one and eight measures in the other. That is, we can

(Table 1: Number of Beats)

Drum Stroke:	1	2	3	4	5	6	7	8
Text Line 1	4	2	3	3	2	5	5(3)	0(2)
2	2	7(4)	0(3)	4	6(3)	0(3)	3	5(3)
3	0(2)	7(4)	0(3)	4	8(4)	0(4)	5(3)	0(2)
4	3	8(2)	0(2)	0(4)	4	6(3)	0(3)	2
5	2	5(3)	0(2)	4	2	5	5(3)	0(2)

regard the eight strokes on the drum in Example 3 as eight measures in Example 2.

In sum, the three scores of *Nagyangch'un* are clearly versions of the same piece; the differences are insignificant. Accordingly, in the discussion that follows, *Nagyangch'un* will be examined on the basis of Example 2, which is the oldest of the three sources.

FITTING TOGETHER TEXT AND MUSIC

A. First and second verses:

The text of *Nagyangch'un,* as given above, has fifty syllables; the music of Example 2 has forty-one measures, so that a direct connection between the two is not readily apparent. A study of the textual structure itself is revealing. The text was written by Ou-Yang Hsiu 歐陽修 (1007-1072), a famous Chinese poet of the Sung dynasty. Its lines are of irregular length, having variously five, six, or seven syllables, which is to say that it belongs to the Chinese genre called *tz'u* 詞. *Tz'u* are generally composed of two stanzas; this is true of *Nagyangch'un*, which has two similarly constructed stanzas of twenty-five syllables each.

The word *hwanip* 還入, occurring at measure 39 of Example 2, is important to notice here: in Korean, this is called *todŭri* 도드리, meaning "repeat." It corresponds to *kaesitsuke* 返付 in Japanese *Gagaku* 雅樂. Reference to the *hwanip* in *Pohŏja* 步虛子 (Chinese: *Pu-hsü-tzu*), another *tz'u* preserved in Korea, sheds light on this matter: in the *Sogak wŏnbo* score of *Pohŏja* (Chapter 5), *hwanip* refers to the last three lines of the second stanza; that is, the music of the second, third, and fourth lines of the second stanza is a repeat of that for the same three lines in the first stanza. In some sources, such as the *Sogak wŏnbo* version of *Pohŏja,* the word *hwanip* is written over the score, but the repeat is written out (in slightly ornamented form); in others, such as the *An Sang kŭmbo* 安瑺琴譜 of 1572 (p. 46a-53b), the repeat is not written out. Considering this, the fifty syllables of text of *Nagyangch'un* should not correspond to the full forty-one measures of score; rather, the 25 syllables of the first stanza and seven syllables of the first line of the second stanza, totalling 32 syllables, should correspond to 38 measures of Example 2 preceding the word *hwanip*. Roughly, then, there should be one syllable of text per measure of music.

B. Role of the clapper:

There are many examples in Korean sources of pieces which have one syllable of text per measure. Among such pieces, only *Nagyang-ch'un* and *Pohŏja* are exceptional in not being strictly one-to-one. Points of particular significance are that all such pieces have a Chinese text and that as a rule in such Chinese-style music the clapper *pak* is struck every fourth measure (or four syllables). This four-measure pattern is what Chang Yen 張炎 (1248-ca. 1315), in his *Tz'u yüan* 詞源, refers to as *ling* form; his statement *"ling-ch'ü ssu k'en-yün"* 令曲 四揹勻 evidently means "the *ling* pieces have four equal beats." Table 2 shows how the clapper beats (shown as asterisks) fall with respect to the text in *Pohŏja*; this reveals that textual lines are always neatly arranged with respect to the clapper beats, not ending at random between the beats (a dash indicates a measure with no text).

This text-rhythm relationship is true not only of the clapper beats, but also of the *changgo* drum strokes. Table 3 shows a comparison of the drum strokes in *Pohŏja* (based on *Taeak hubo,* Chapter 6) with those in *Nagyangch'un*; the four possible strokes are: a left hand stroke on the open skin (o), a stroke with a stick on the right (l), a metrically unimportant roll with the stick (i), and both sides together (Φ).

The text of *Pohŏja* in Table 2 has three more syllables than *Nagyangch'un,* and for this reason the two sets of drum patterns initially appear not to coincide; the difficulty lies in the third line of *Pohŏja*. A

(Table 2: Pohŏja)

Line 1: 碧 烟 籠 曉 海 波 閑 —
                    *   *

Line 2: 江 — 上 — 數 峰 寒 —
                    *   *

Line 3: 珮 環 聲 裡 異 — 香 —
                    *   *

Line 4: 弸 絳 節 — 五 雲 端 —
                    *   *

Line 5: 宛 然 共 指 嘉 禾 瑞 —
                    *   *

(Table 3: Changgo strokes)

Nagyangch'un Line 1:	Ο	Ο¡	Ο	Ι		Ο	Ι Ι	⬤Ο	Ι
Pohŏja Line 1:	Ο	Ο	Ο¡¡	Ι		Ο	Ι¡ Ι¡	⬤Ο¡	Ι
Pohŏja Text:	碧	烟	籠	曉		海	波	閑	—
N. Line 2:	⬤Ο	⬤¡	Ι Ο	⬤		Ο¡	Ι	Ο Ι Ο	⬤
P. Line 2:	Ι Ο¡	⬤¡¡	Ι Ο	⬤		Ι ¡¡	Ι¡¡	Ο Ι Ο¡	⬤
P. Text:	江	—	上	—		數	峰	寒	—
N. Line 3:	Ο	Ο	Ο¡	Ι		Ο	Ι Ι	⬤Ο	Ι
P. Line 3:	Ο	Ο	Ο¡¡	Ι		Ο Ι¡	Ι¡ Ι¡	⬤Ο¡	⬤
P. Text:	珮	環	聲	裡		異		香	
					Ο¡¡	Ι¡ Ι¡	⬤Ο¡	Ι
					飄	落	人	間
N. Line 4:	Ι Ο	⬤¡	Ι Ο	⬤		Ο¡	Ι	Ο Ι Ο	⬤
P. Line 4:	Ι Ο¡	⬤¡¡	Ι Ο¡	⬤		Ο¡¡	Ι	Ο ¡¡	Ι
P. Text:	弸	絳	節	—		五	雲	端	—

close look at Table 3 shows that the drum beats for the last four syllables of line 3 of *Pohōja* are essentially the same as those used for the preceding two syllables; in other words, the immediately preceding pattern has been repeated in order to accomodate the extra text. Excepting this matter of musical extension, the drum patterns of *Nagyangch'un* and *Pohōja* are revealed by Table 3 to be very closely related. Similar examples of extension by repetition may be found in the *kagok* 歌曲 repertory.

Nagyangch'un and *Pohōja* thus follow each other closely in the important rhythmic matters of clapper placement and drum pattern. It is primarily in the use of the secondary drum roll that the two sets of patterns differ. Noticeable also is the close similarity of the drum pattern for lines 1 and 2 to that of lines 3 and 4.

As indicated by asterisks in Example 2, the clapper beats in *Nagyangch'un* occur strictly, once on the last of every four measures. We have seen that the lines of text in *Pohōja* align precisely with the clapper beats. In Example 2, however, the word *hwanip* curiously comes at measure 39, between the clapper beats of measures 36 and 40. In other words, it would indicate that a preceding line of text would end not in the measure with a clapper beat, but two measures earlier. It is reasonable, then, to suggest a correction of the beginning of the *hwanip,* or repeat, to the measure just after the clapper beat; that is, to measure 41. Whether or not this is a good hypothesis will be proven by the evidence presented below; we will try to fit the 32 syllables of the first five lines of *Nagyangch'un* not into 38 measures, but into 40 measures of Example 2.

C. Line 1 of the text:

It has already been suggested that, roughly speaking, each syllable of text in *Nagyangch'un* should correspond to a measure of music. More precisely, the seven syllables of the first line of text should, for the following reasons, be set to the first eight measures of music, not seven.

1. As shown by Example 2, the clapper beats occur regularly on every fourth measure in *Nagyangch'un.* As shown in Table 2, no line of *Pohōja* ever begins in a clapper measure; even when a line ends before a clapper measure, the next line does not begin until after the clapper measure is finished. Following this example in *Nagyangch'un,* it would

be inappropriate to have the second line of text, that is, beginning with the eighth syllable, start in the eighth measure, which has the clapper beat.

　2. In measure 7 of Example 2, the melodic motion is from *a* to *c* ; in measure 8, the *c '* is again played and prolonged through the entire measure. In other words, if these two measures were setting only the final, seventh syllable of line 1, then the final syllable would be long and drawn out. There are examples of just this phenomenon in *Pohŏja,* and many others in Japanese *Tōgaku.* For example, in *Shinraryō ō Kyū* 新羅陵王 急 (Example 4), *Chōgeishi* 長慶子 (Example 5), *Butokuraku* 武德樂 , *Konju no Ha* 胡飲酒破 , *Etenraku* 越天樂, *Gakkaen* 合歡鹽 , and other pieces in the four-measure rhythmic cycle called *haya-yohyōshi* 早四拍子, every eighth measure prolongs and extends the pitch of the seventh measure. This has, in Japanese, the special name *in* 引. Thus, in both *Tōgaku* and the music we are considering here, the seventh and eighth measures draw out a single tone; this corresponds to the rhyme carried by the last syllable of the first line of text in the Chinese poem, which should be sung longer than the other syllables. On the other hand, unlike Chinese or Western languages, the final syllables in Korean tend to be weak, so that the final syllables cannot be sung long, but rather short. This may be observed in Korean settings of native poetry. For these reasons, measure 8 of Example 2 must be a prolongation of the *c '* introduced in measure 7, corresponding to the end of the first line of text.

　3. Assuming for the moment that these deductions are not valid and that the second line of text starts on measure 8, difficulties arise with the *hwanip.* Measure 8 has only the pitch *c* ; whether the *hwanip,* or repeat, begins in measure 39, as originally notated, or in measure 41, as we have suggested, the pitches do not agree with measure 8. Measure 39 starts with *a* and measure 41 has it throughout, conflicting with the *c '* of measure 8. On the other hand, if we assume our deductions to be correct, with measure 8 as a prolongation of measure 7 and the last syllable of the first line of text, the *hwanip* would start from measure 9, which has the pitch *a* throughout.

　Considering the above points, the only possible setting of the first line of *Nagyangch'un* would be as follows (numbers indicate measures, asterisks the clapper beats):

1	2	3	4	5	6	7	8
紗	窓	未	曉	黃	鶯	語	一
			*				*

D. Line 2:

Unlike line 1, line 2 has only five syllables; various line lengths are characteristic of *tz'u*. The second line of *Pohŏja* similarly has five syllables, and its setting is as follows:

9	10	11	12	13	14	15	16
江	—	上	—	數	峰	寒	—
		*				*	

Using this as a model, the *Nagyangch'un* setting should be this:

9	10	11	12	13	14	15	16
蕙	—	爐	—	燒	殘	炷	—
		*				*	

Hence, it appears that each line of the text, whether seven or five syllables, equally takes eight measures of music; each eight measures has two clapper beats, and the final, rhyme syllable is prolonged into the closing clapper measure. Similarly, in Japanese *Tōgaku*, each musical phrase regularly takes eight measures (in *hayayohyōshi*) or sixteen measures (in the eight-measure cycle *hayayahyōshi* 早八拍子). Just as *Nagyangch'un* has the clapper appearing regularly in every fourth and eighth measures, the Japanese drum *taiko* 太鼓 regularly appears in the third and seventh measures in *hayayohyōshi* (see Examples 4 and 5). Also, there is the abovementioned regular occurrence in *Tōgaku* of the pitch of the seventh measure being extended into the eighth measure (in the case of *hayayohyōshi*) or the tone of the thirteenth measure being extended into the sixteenth measure (in *hayayahyōshi*) (Examples 4 and 6).

E. Line 3:

Like line 1, line 3 has seven syllables and clearly must be set in eight measures in the same fashion:

17	18	19	20	21	22	23	24
錦	帷	羅	幕	度	春	寒	—
			*				*

F. Line 4:

The closing line of the first stanza of *Nagyangch'un,* unlike the other lines, has six syllables. The same is true of the fourth line of *Pohŏja,* which can be used as a model. That is, according to the meaning of the text, the line is divided into two equal halves, the last syllable of each being prolonged (see Table 2):

25	26	27	28	29	30	31	32
昨	夜	裏	—	三	更	雨	—
			*				*

As we have seen, each line of text, regardless of whether it contains five, six, or seven syllables, is set to eight measures of music; as a result, the 25 syllables of the first verse have been set to 32 measures of music from the *Sogak wŏnbo.* The same reasoning may be applied to the first line of the second stanza, which, lke that of the first stanza, has seven syllables:

33	34	35	36	37	38	39	40
繡	簾	閑	倚	吹	輕	絮	—
			*				*

Thus, the 32 syllables of the first five lines are set to forty measures of music; the remaining three lines would be set to a repetition, *hwanip,* of the music from measure 9 through measure 32. This accords precisely with the earlier hypothesis that the *hwanip* should apply to measure 41 (= measure 9) rather than to measure 39, where it is placed in the original score.

The text has been inserted into Example 2 to show the result of this scheme.

TŌGAKU PRESERVED IN JAPAN

Up to this point we have mostly limited out discussion to *Nagyangch'un* and *Pohŏja*, pieces of so-called *tangak* 唐樂 ("music of T'ang") preserved in Korea. Now we shall examine the *Tōgaku* (same characters as *tangak*) surviving in Japan. Included in Volume I of Mr. Shiba Sukehiro's 芝祐泰 transcriptions of *Gagaku*, *Gagaku zenshū* 雅樂全集 (Tokyo: Ryuginsha 龍吟社 , 1955), are the following seven pieces:

1. *Konju no Ha* 胡飲酒破 , in the mode *Ichikotsu-chō* 壹越調 ; a *shōkyoku* 小曲 in *Hayayohyōshi* 早四拍子 , 14 *hyōshi* (dance piece) (these terms are explained below).
2. *Etenraku* 越天樂 , in *Hyōjō* 平調 ; a *shōkyoku* in *hayayohyōshi*, 14 *hyōshi*.
3. *Shukōshi* 酒胡子 , in *Sōjō* 雙調 ; a *shōkyoku* in *hayayohyōshi*, 14 *hyōshi*.
4. *Jussuiraku* 拾翠樂 , in *Ōshiki-chō* 黃鐘調 ; a *shōkyoku* in *haya-yohyōshi*, 10 *hyōshi*.
5. *Seigaiha* 青海波 , in *Banshiki-chō* 盤涉調 ; a *chūkyoku* in *hayayahyōshi* 早八拍子 , 12 *hyōshi* (dance piece).
6. *Chōgeishi* 長慶子 , in *Taishiki-chō* 太食調 ; a *shōkyoku* in *haya-yohyōshi*, 16 *hyōshi*.
7. *Bairo* 陪臚 , in *Hyōjō;* a *chūkyoku* in *hayatadayohyōshi* 早只四拍子 , 12 *hyōshi* (dance piece).

Of the above seven pieces, *Konju no Ha* and *Bairo* belong to *Rinyu-gaku* 林邑樂 , or music from India, and are both dance pieces; in these, a roll (*rai* 來) is played on the *kakko* 喝鼓 drum, corresponding to the roll (*yo* 搖) on the Korean *changgo*. *Jussuiraku* and *Chōgeishi* are "new pieces" brought to Japan in the ninth century. *Etenraku*, *Shukoshi*, and *Seigaiha* derive from T'ang (618-907).

The phrase *haya-yohyōshi* means, in Western terms, four beats to a measure, four measures comprising a *hyōshi*, or clapper or *taiko*. *Haya-yahyōshi* doubles the number of measures: four beats to a measure, but eight measures in a *hyōshi*. *Haya-tadayohyōshi* means four measures of alterating two and four beats, comprising a *hyōshi*. Examples, in addition to *Bairo*, include *Batō* 拔頭 and *Rinkokodatsu* 輪鼓褌脫 . The term "16 *hyōshi*" means sixteen occurrences of *hyōshi*.

The first point to be noticed here is that in *haya-yohyōshi,,* the drum *taiko* is regularly given a single stroke in the third measure of every four-measure group. In Mr. Shiba's transcriptions, the *taiko* is actually played twice, in the second and third of each group of four measures, but in the transcription by Professor Robert Garfias, which is based on a seventeenth-century score, the *taiko* is played only once, in the third of every four measures. In this article, we shall follow the latter source. This sort of *taiko* drum pattern is found only in Japanese *Tōgaku* (including *Rinyū-gaku*), and not in the socalled *Koma-gaku* 高麗樂 (music from Korea). In *haya-yahyōshi,* the *taiko* is struck in the fifth of every eight measures (see Example 6).

Thus, it appears, the regular occurrence of the drum *taiko* in the third of every four measures in the *haya-yohyōshi* pieces of Japanese *Tōgaku* corresponds to the regular striking of the clapper *pak* in every fourth measure in Korean *tangak,* that is, in *Pohōja* and *Nagyang-ch'un.* Five of the seven *Tōgaku* pieces listed above are in *haya-yohyoshi;* some twenty-two other pieces of *Gagaku* also have this metrical structure. A striking feature of these pieces is that virtually all of them are *shōkyoku,* or "small pieces;" this term refers, basically, to comparative length, the other possibilities being *chūkyoku* ("middle pieces") and *taikyoku* 大曲 ("great pieces"). The only exception is the piece *Gakkaen* 合歡鹽 , which is a *chūkyoku.*

In the above list of seven pieces, only *Seigaiha* is in *haya-yahyōshi,* though sixteen other examples of *haya-yahyōshi* could be cited from the repertory. Of these, one is a *taikyoku,* eight are *chūkyoku,* and seven are *shōkyoku.*

Examination of the *haya-yohyōshi* pieces shows that, in large part, in the seventh and eighth measures of every eight measures there is the tonal prolongation called *in* 引 ; in some *haya-yohyōshi* pieces a long *in* occurs in the thirteenth through sixteenth measures of every 16. These phenomena may be clearly seen in *Shinraryō ō Kyū* (Example 4) and *Chōgeishi* (Example 5). Similarly the *haya-yahyōshi* pieces have an *in* prolongation in the thirteenth through sixteenth of each 16 measures. In *Nagyang-ch'un* and *Pohoja,* every eighth measure continues the pitch begun in the seventh measure, and thus corresponds to the same event in Japanese *haya-yohyoshi.*

Korean *tangak,* that is, *Pohōja* and *Nagyangch'un,* stems originally from texted vocal pieces; in the course of time, the texts have been lost, and the pieces now survive only as instrumental orchestra pieces. Similar cases of lost text may be seen in the native Korean pieces *Yōmillak* 與民樂 and *Yōngsan hoesang* 靈山會相 . Although these several pieces lost their texts, they were used in the Korean court to accompany ceremonies and dances, so that the music itself has survived to the present. *Nagyangch'un,* for example, was used at bowing to the king in court ceremonies; *Pohōja* and *Yōmillak* were used at the entrance or exit of the king; and *Yōngsan hoesang* and *Pohōja* accompanied dancing.

By restoring the texts to pieces like *Nagyangch'un,* we are better able to understand the music. For example, it permits us to see the original phrasing and form, avoiding misconceptions derived from the surviving instrumental forms.

Also, Japanese *Tōgaku,* especially that in *haya-yohyōshi* which has the *in* prolongation in the seventh and eighth of every eight measures, may be seen as instrumental music derived from vocal originals. Those pieces comprising 64 measures may be viewed as having originally been settings of eight-line poems (eight measures per line).

It is uncertain whether the foreign dance music introduced into Japan (*bugaku* 舞樂) originally had texts which have since been lost. When the various types of foreign music were classified, the classifications were according to music and dance, ignoring song; this is shown by the following passage from the *Nihon goki* 日本後記 , Chapter 17 (809 A.D.):

> *Tōgaku* teachers, twelve; flute teachers, two
>
> *Koma-gaku* teachers, four: flute, zither, *makumo*, and dance.
>
> *Kudara-gaku* 百濟樂 [music from Paekche] teachers, four: flute, zither, *makumo*, and dance.
>
> *Shiragi-gaku* 新羅樂 [music from Silla] teachers, two: zither and dance.
>
> *Tora-gaku* 度羅樂 [unknown origin] teachers, two: drum and dance.
>
> *Gigaku* 伎樂 [masked plays] teachers, two.
>
> *Rinyū-gaku* teachers, two.

This quotation does not make it clear whether or not the dance music had vocal texts associated with it. However, the music in Silla

home country had song attached. The Korean source *Samguk sagi*
三國史記 (1145), in its section on music, gives singers in addition to
zither players and dancers in connection with Silla music.

If, then, Japanese *Tōgaku* is considered to have originally been
vocal music, it might be inappropriate to analyze it using instrumental
terminology like melodic development and episodic treatment, as in
Western instrumental music. *Tōgaku* may largely have lost its original
texts, as did *Pohŏja* and *Nagyangch'un,* with the passage of time.

CHINESE SONGS OF WHITESTONE THE TAOIST

Surviving in China are seventeen *tz'u* pieces by the Sung author
Chiang K'uei 張燮 (1155-1221), otherwise known as Whitestone the
Taoist (Pai-shih tao-jen 白石道人), in his *Pai-shih tao-jen ko-ch'ü*
白石道人歌曲 (1202). All of these have been transcribed into Western
notation by Mr. Yang In-liu 楊陰瀏, but I have had access to only one
of these, the piece *Yang-chou Man* 楊州慢, reproduced in Hsia Ch'eng-
tao 夏承燾, *T'ang Sung tz'u lun-ts'ung* 唐宋詞論叢 (Shanghai, 1956),
page 110. It is impossible to make definite statements about the copying
of mistakes in the sources of *Pai-shih tao-jen ko-ch'ü,* and consequently
it is impossible to be fully confident of the transcriptions; Mr. Hsia (p. 111)
raises questions about the accuracy of the several sources of these songs.

Yang-chou Man, the only transcribed piece I have seen, is not a
ling 令 (short-lined *tz'u*), but a *man* 慢 (long-lined *tz'u*). However, like a
ling, it is divided into two stanzas, and we can investigate the matter of
repetition in it. Example 7 shows Mr. Yang's transcription. The fourth
lines of the first and second stanzas are virtually identical; there are also
many close similarities between the two second lines and between the
two third lines.

The text of the first stanza, shown below has lines varying in
length from ten to fifteen syllables, for a total of fifty syllables.

淮左名都　竹西佳處　解鞍少駐初程
過春風十里　盡薺麥青青
自胡馬窺江去後　廢池喬木 猶厭言兵
漸黃昏 清角吹寒　都在空城

The shortest line in this *man*, ten syllables, is much longer than five syllables, the shortest line in a *ling* like *Pohŏja* or *Nagyangch'un*. Similarly, the longest line is 15 syllables, as opposed to the longest line of seven syllables in *Pohŏja* or *Nagyangch'un*.

It has been observed that in *Gagaku* pieces in *haya-yahyōshi,* there are regular phrases of sixteen measures. In Mr. Yang's transcription of *Yang-chou Man,* a single beat corresponds to a measure in a slow score like Example 4, 5, or 6; a similar correspondence has already been noted between the two sources of *Nagyangch'un*: a measure of Example 2 is nearly like a single beat in Example 1. The first line of *Yang-chou Man* is given 16 beats, the second 15, the third 16, and the fourth 17, so that the number is not quite consistent. Also, in *haya-yahyōshi,* the groups of 16 measures are regularly divided into two groups of eight measures. In these eight-measure groups, the *taiko* regularly appears in the fifth measure. In Mr. Yang's transcription, the half-line divisions are inconsistent in length, as follows:

Line 1: 16 beats (8 + 8)
Line 2: 15 beats (7 + 8)
Line 3: 16 beats (7½ + 8½)
Line 4: 17 beats (7½ + 9½)

We have seen that in *Nagyangch'un* or *Pohŏja,* a two-syllable phrase of text is set to four measures of music (for example, the first two syllables of line 2 of *Nagyangch'un*); the same is true for a three-syllable phrase (for example, the remainder of line 2 of *Nagyangch'un*). In Mr. Yang's transcription, five syllables are set as in the second line of text:

Beats:	1	2	3	4	5	6	7	
	過	春	風	十		里		
Beats:	·1	2	3	4	5	6	7	8
	盡	薺	麥			靑	靑	

Both of these phrases have five syllables, but one is set to seven beats and one to eight beats; furthermore, the internal rhythms of the two phrases differ. If we follow the model of *Pohŏja* in the setting of five syllables (such as line 2 of Table 2), the two five-syllable phrases of *Yang-chou Man* would come out this way:

1	2	3	4	5	6	7	8
過	春	風	一	十	一	里	一

1	2	3	4	5	6	7	8
盡	薺	麥	一	靑	一	靑	一

The three-syllable phrase opening line 4 of *Yang-chou Man,* in Mr. Yang's transcription, is set to five beats:

1	2	3	4	5
漸	黃	昏	一	一

According to examples of three-syllable phrases in *Pohōja,* this might be corrected to:

1	2	3	4
漸	黃	昏	一

Following the pattern of *haya-yahyōshi* in *Gagaku,* in which one musical phrase would have 16 syllables (measures) and the samples of beat settings in *Pohōja, Yang-chou Man* would come out as in Example 8. The few significant differences of time values from Mr. Yang's transcription have been indicated there with an x.

Clearly, with the lines of *Yang-chou Man* being as long as 15 syllables, Japanese *haya-yahyōshi* is the appropriate metrical structure rather than *haya-yohyōshi. Man* refers to large texts, *ling* to short ones; *ling,* then, corresponds to *haya-yohyōshi.* It is instructive to note that two versions of the *Rinyū-gaku* piece *Ryō Ō* 陵王 exist: *Ryō Ō* in *haya-yahyōshi,* a *chūkyoku* ("middle piece"), and *Shinraryō ō Kyū* 新羅陵 王急 in *haya-yohyōshi,* a *shōkyoku* ("small piece"). These differences in size correspond to differences in length of *man* and *ling* in *tz'u.*

It is hard to avoid the conclusion that *man* in *tz'u* corresponds to *haya-yahyoshi* in *Tōgaku,* and thus that a line of a *man* text should regularly be set to 16 measures of music. Those 16 measures, further, should be subdivided into two subphrases of eight measures each. In the event of a 15-syllable text line, the musical setting should expand to 16 syllables' worth, similar to the examples of such expansion we have seen in *Nagyangch'un* and *Pohōja.*

The various *tz'u* in Chiang K'uei's set, obviously, must have basically the same rhythmic structure as *Nagyangch'un* and *Pohōja,* which are also *tz'u*. As Mr. Hsia Ch'eng-tao indicates (p. 109), punctuation with small circles is missing in various sources for Chiang's *tz'u*, and consequently their rhythmic implications are also not present; he concludes that the musical setting is basically one note per syllable. In such a syllabic setting, each note requires a certain amount of time. There are, of course, cases of one syllable getting more than one pitch in Chiang K'uei's *tz'u*, as well as in *Nagyangch'un* and *Pohoja* and the *in* in *Gagaku*. Because two or three syllables are prolonged to fill out four beats, we cannot state precisely the time required for each syllable. But certainly we can say, on the basis of Korean *tangak* and Japanese *Tōgaku*, that the overall style is one note per syllable.

CONCLUSIONS

Up to now, the music and text for *Nagyangch'un* have been independently preserved: the music in the *Sogak wŏnbo* and actual performance, and the text in the *Koryŏ-sa*. By comparison with the similar piece *Pohŏja,* for which we have a written source with both music and text (*Taeak hubo*), it has been possible to reconstruct *Nagyangch'un.* On the basis of these two pieces, several conclusions may be drawn: even though the length of textual lines may vary irregularly, the music for each line of text is consistently eight measures long. Also, the eight-measure phrases must consistently be subdivided into two four-measure halves, with the clapper *pak* being struck in every fourth measure.

Japanese *Tōgaku* preserved in the metrical cycle *haya-yohyōshi* has lost its text in the course of time, but in Mr. Shiba's transcriptions of pieces in this pattern, each musical phrase has eight measures (as determined by the prolongation *in* at the end of the phrases). Furthermore, each phrase of eight measures is subdivided into two four-measure phrases (each of which is called a *hyoshi*). In Mr. Shiba's transcriptions the *taiko* drum is struck in the second and third of every four measures, but in Professor Garfias' transcription from a 17th-century source the *taiko* is played only once in each *hyoshi,* in the third measure. Clearly, then, the music for a *ling* (short) *tz'u,* such as *Nagyangch'un,* corresponds to *Tōgaku* in *haya-yohyōshi.* This also is in keeping with the *Tz'u yüan* (ca. 1300) of Chang Yen, which says that a *ling* has four equal beats.

The Japanese *hayayahyōshi,* where the *taiko* is struck once every eight measures, corresponds to the *man* (long) form of *tz'u* and the *Tz'u yüan* statement that a *man* piece has eight equal beats. Thus, the textual lines of *ling* such as *Nagyangch'un* are set to eight measures of music, and textual lines of *man* like *Yang-chou Man* are set to 16 measures of music.

In Korea, both text and music (in mensural notation) for *Nagyang-ch'un* and *Pohŏja* have been preserved. Comparison with these pieces explains the form of orchestral *Tōgaku* preserved in Japan. The Korean and Japanese music together may be used as a basis for revealing the rhythmic structure of Chinese *tz'u* (especially *ling* and *man*), such as those in Chiang K'uei's collection.

POSTSCRIPT

Since writing the above article (1960), I have had the opportunity to examine Professor L. E. R. Picken's "Secular Chinese Songs of the Twelfth Century," *Studia Musicologica Academiae Scientiarum Hungaricae,* 8 (1966), pp. 125-172. He questions (pp. 126-127) the accuracy of Mr. Yang In-liu's transcriptions, even though Mr. Yang had taken into consideration some rhythm symbols contained in early Chiang K'uei source materials. Professor Picken then gives his own interpretation and transcribes all seventeen *tz'u.* His rhythmic interpretation, of course, differs from Mr. Yang's, and it also differs from mine. I only wish to introduce this matter here and defer detailed analysis to a later date.

Example 1: *Nagyangch'un* in *Sagak wŏnbo,* Chapter 6

Example 2: *Nagyangch'un* in *Sogak wŏnbo,* Chapter 4

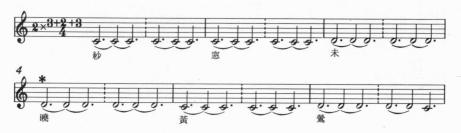

*= clapper (*pak*) beats   **D.S. 𝄋**

Example 3:
Nagyangch'un as presently performed

燒 殘 炷 錦 帷 羅 幕

(5) (6) (7) (8) (1) (2) (3) (4)

度 春 寒 昨 夜 裏

(5) (6) (7) (8) (1) (2) (3) (4)

Example 4: *Shinraryō Ō Kyū (Ichikotsu-chō)*

Example 5: *Chōgeishi (Taishiki-chō)*

Example 6: Seigaiha (Banshiki-chō)

Example 7: Yang-chou Man, Transcribed by Yang In-liu

1. 淮 左 名 都，竹 西 佳 處，解 鞍 少 駐 初 程。 2. 過

春 風 十 里，盡 薺 麥 青 青。 3. 自 胡

馬 窺 江 去 後，廢 池 喬 木，猶 厭 言 兵。 4. 漸 黃

昏， 清 角 吹 寒， 都 在 空 城。 5. 杜

郎 俊 賞， 算 而 今 重 到 須 驚。 6. 縱 荳

蔻 詞 工， 青 樓 夢 好，難 賦 深 情。 7. 二

十 四 橋 仍 在， 波 心 蕩 冷 月 無 聲。 8. 念 橋

邊 紅 藥，年 年 知 爲 誰 生。

Example 8: Yang-chou Man with Suggested Alterations

LEFT AND RIGHT MUSIC
IN KOREA

INTRODUCTION

Surviving in Korea are the so-called *tangak* 唐樂 ("music of T'ang") and *hyangak* 郷樂 ("indigenous music"); the modern Japanese *Gagaku* 雅樂 repertory is divided into *Tōgaku* 唐樂 ("music of T'ang"), also called "left" music, and *Komagaku* 高麗樂 ("music of Korea"), also called "right" music. The names would suggest a similarity of these repertories, but in fact their contents appear to be distinct. There are written sources indicating that the music of T'ang (618-907) was exported to both Korea and Japan, and that music of Samguk 三國 (the Three Kingdoms holding sway in Korea up to 668 A.D.) came to be preserved in Japan; this suggest that in origin the repertories might be the same, but connections between the surviving pieces are now difficult to find.

If the names are similar and the written sources indicate a similar musical genealogy, should we believe that these are mere fabrications and that the pieces preserved in the two countries are completely independent? Or is it that over the course of centuries so many alterations have been made that the original relationships have become obscure? These are the sorts of questions investigated in this article.

Due to the difficulty of obtaining materials, it is impossible for the author to explore the developmental changes in Japanese *Tōgaku* and *Komagaku*; the present historical discussion is limited to modifications in *tangak* and *hyangak* in Korea. Further, because of the absence of notated music, the investigation of music is largely based upon examination of instrumentation, instrument construction, and dance.

259

THE NAMES "LEFT" AND "RIGHT" MUSIC

In Japan, "left" music refers to *Tōgaku,* "right" music to *Komagaku;* this exact use of "left" and "right" is not found in the written sources of Korea. However, there is a clear dichotomy between *tang-ak* and *hyang-ak,* there being *tang-ak* court dance and *hyang-ak* court dance, *tang-ak* instruments and *hyang-ak* instruments, and so forth; this is referred to as the "two categories of music" (*yangbu-ak* 兩部樂) in an entry of the *Koryŏ-sa* 高麗史 for 1152 (17.36b). Later, in 1434, there is a record that *"hyang-ak* is set up on the east, and *tang-ak* is set up on the west" (*Sejong sillok* 世宗實錄 65.8b). Further, in the *Hsüan-ho feng-shih Kao-li t'u-ching* 宣和奉使高麗圖經 (1124) of the Chinese envoy Hsü Ching 徐兢 (1091-1153), *tang-ak* is singled out as "left" and *hyang-ak* as "right" (Chapter 40):

> Now the music is divided into two categories: the left is called *tang-ak* and consists of Chinese music; the right is called *hyang-ak* and consists of [the Koreans'] own music. For the Chinese music, the instruments are all on the Chinese system. But for *hyang-ak* there are drums, clappers, mouth organs, oboes, harps, zithers, lutes, and flutes, of which the construction is different.

These citations suggest that in Korea, as well as Japan, *tang-ak* was once considered "left" and *hyang-ak* was "right." A rather different use of "left" and "right" appears in the *Chŭngbo munhŏn pigo* 增補文獻備考 of 1908 (105.13ab): "left" is used to mean ritual music of Chinese origin, *a-ak* 雅樂, and "right" refers both to *tang-ak,* that is, entertainment music of Chinese origin, and to *hyang-ak,* native entertainment music. In other words, Chinese ritual *a-ak,* reconstructed in the early Yi dynasty, was awarded especial significance, and it gained special status as the "left" category. *Tang-ak* was moved from "left" to "right." Thus, in the Koryo period (918-1392), "left" was Chinese and "right" was native, but in Yi (1392-1910), "left" was Chinese ritual music and "right" was both Chinese and Korean entertainment music.

In sum, the historical sources show a certain relationship of terminology between Korea and Japan: the "left" (*tang-ak*) and "right" (*hyang-ak*) categories of Hsü Ching, and the west (*tang-ak*) and east (*hyang-ak*) distinction of the *Sejong sillok* correspond to the "left" (*Tōgaku*) and "right" (*Komagaku*) categories in Japanese *Gagaku.*

INSTRUMENTATION OF LEFT AND RIGHT MUSIC

Korean *tang-ak* and *hyang-ak* use, respectively, *tang-ak* instruments (*tangakki* 唐樂器) and *hyang-ak* instruments (*hyangakki* 鄉樂器); in this section, the historical instrumentation of these categories in Korea is examined and compared with instrumentation in modern Japanese *Tōgaku* and *Komagaku*.

A. *Tangak:*

Instrumentation in *tang-ak* can be traced as far back as 1076; the *Koryŏ-sa* (80.15ab) lists these instruments in a section on salary payments:

> One *saeng* 笙(mouth organ)
> Two *changgo* 杖鼓 (hourglass drum)
> Two *tangjŏk* 唐笛 (transverse flute)
> One *hyang-pip'a* 鄉琵琶 (lute)
> One *tang-pip'a* 唐琵琶 (lute)
> One *panghyang* 方響 (iron slabs)
> One *p'iri* 篳篥 (oboe)
> One *pak* 拍(wooden clapper) for song and dance
> One *Chunggŭm* 中笒 (medium-size transverse flute)

Of these, the *panghyang, saeng, tangjŏk, p'iri, pip'a, changgo,* and *pak* are mostly the same as the list of *tangak* instruments in the music section of the *Koryŏ-sa* (cited below); only four instruments are missing. The *chunggŭm* and *hyang-pip'a* are *hyangak* instruments (see next section.)

This instrumentation of 1076 is closer than any other in Korea to *Tōgaku* instrumentation (following the *Gagaku* reformations of Emperor Nimmyo (仁明) in the ninth century) *shō* 笙(mouth organ), *hichiriki* 篳篥 (oboe), *ryūteki* 龍笛 (transverse flute), *biwa* 琵琶(lute), *koto* 箏(zither), *shōko* 鉦鼓 (gong), *kakko* 鞨鼓(hourglass drum), and *taiko* 太鼓 (large drum). Both have the mouth organ (*saeng* and *shō*), oboe (*p'iri* and *hichiriki*), transverse flute (*tangjŏk* and *ryūteki*), and lute (*pip'a* and *biwa*); corresponding also are *panghyang* and *shōko,* and *changgo* and *kakko,* so that the only significant difference is the Korean lack of a zither.

If a *chaeng* 箏(zither) and *konghu* 箜篌 (harp) are added to the 1076 Korean instrumentation, the result coincides with the instrumentation of the orchestra in a painting by the T'ang artist Chou Wen-chü 周文矩 (now in the Art Institute of Chicago). In the *Shinzei kogakuzu* 信西古樂圖 , a fourteenth-century scroll depicting various kinds of entertainment, the instrumentation of *Togaku* includes iron slabs and clapper, but it is unknown when use of these was discontinued.

In 1114, the Sung emperor Hui-tsung 徽宗 bestowed the following instruments on Koryo (*Koryŏ-sa* 70.28b-29b):

> Five metal *panghyang*
> Five stone *panghyang*
> Four *pip'a*
> Two *ohyŏn* 五絃 (five-string lute)
> Four *ssanghyŏn* 雙絃(two-string zither)
> Four *chaeng* (箏)
> Four *konghu*
> Twenty *p'iri*
> Twenty *chŏk* (笛)
> Twenty *chi* 箎(small transverse flute)
> Ten *so* 簫(pan-pipes)
> Ten gourd *saeng*
> Forty *hun* 壎(ocarina)
> One *taego* 大鼓 (large drum)
> Twenty *changgo*
> Two *p'an* 板(clapper)

Of these, the *panghyang, pip'a, p'iri, chŏk, saeng, changgo,* and *p'an* (= *pak*) were also in the 1076 instrumentation; the presence of *chaeng* and *konghu*, mentioned above in connection with the T'ang painting, is significant. *A-ak* instruments (*chi, so,* and *hun*) and popular music instruments (*ohyŏn* and *ssanghyŏn*, lute and zither) have been mixed in; since these instruments are lacking in the 1076 set, the *tang-ak* set in the music section of the *Koryŏ-sa* (see below), Japanese *Togaku,* and Chou Wen-hsü's painting, they appear to have been part of the Chinese court orchestra in the Sung dynasty (960-1279).

In the music section of the *Koryŏ-sa* (71.1a and 30b-31a), the following lists of *tang-ak* and popular music (*hyang-ak*) instruments are given:

> *Tang-ak:*
>> *panghyang,* sixteen slabs
>> *t'ongso* 洞簫 (vertical flute), eight holes
>> *chŏk,* 笛 eight holes
>> *p'iri,* nine holes
>> *pip'a,* four strings
>> *ajaeng* 牙箏 (bowed zither), seven strings
>> *taejaeng* 大箏 (large zither), fifteen strings
>> *changgo*
>> *kyobanggo* 敎坊鼓 (drum in a stand)
>> *pak,* six slabs
>
> Popular music:
>> *kŏmun'go* 玄琴 (zither), six strings
>> *pip'a,* five strings
>> *kayagum* 伽倻琴 (zither), 12 strings
>> *taegum* 大笒 (large transverse flute), 13 holes
>> *changgo*
>> *abak* 牙拍 (clapper, dance property), six slabs
>> *muae* 無㝵 (dance property)
>> *mugo* 舞鼓 (drum in a stand)
>> *haegum* 奚琴 (fiddle), two strings
>> *p'iri,* seven holes
>> *chunggŭm,* 13 holes (medium-size transverse flute)
>> *sogŭm,* seven holes (small transverse flute)
>> *pak,* six slabs

This *tangak* list is essentially like the earlier ones, except that the *chaeng* has been replaced by *ajaeng* and *taejaeng,* and the *saeng* is absent. Although the *ajaeng* and *taejaeng* were not in the 1072 list, might they not be newly introduced into Korea from the Yüan dynasty (1206-1368)? The presence of these two instruments and the demise of the *saeng* shows that the *tang-ak* instrumentation of later Koryŏ increasingly differed from that of modern *Tōgaku* in Japan. But Koryŏ did distinguish between instruments for *tang-ak* and instruments for *hyang-ak*; there were no instances, such as were to occur in Yi, of *tangak* instruments being converted to *hyang-ak* instruments, or *tangak* and *hyang-ak* instruments being played together.

In the Yi dynasty, as *tang-ak* instruments were adapted for use in *hyang-ak*, the distinction between *tang-ak* and *hyang-ak* became progressively weaker. For example, when musicians were given examinations in 1430, both *tang-ak* and *hyang-ak* players had to perform on the *tang-pip'a*; the instruments examined were as follows (*Sejong sillok* 47.28b):

Tang-ak:
  tang-pip'a
  ajaeng
  taejaeng
  tang-p'iri
  tangjŏk
  t'ongso
  pongso 鳳簫 (pan-pipes)
  x *yonggwan* 龍管 (flute)
  saeng
  x *u* 竿 (large mouth organ)
  x *hwa* 和 (small mouth organ)
  x *kŭm* 琴 (small zither with seven strings)
  x *sŭl* 瑟 (large zither with 25 strings)
  changgo
  kyobanggo
  panghyang
Hyangak:
  kŏmun'go
  kayagŭm
  pip'a
  taegŭm
  changgo
  haegŭm
  tang-pip'a
  hyang-p'iri

According to the *Akhak kwebŏm* 樂學軌範 of 1493 (2.8a), 14 of the 16 *tang-ak* instruments above comprise the set of instruments used in sacrificial rites at the ancestral shrine called *Munso-chŏn* 文昭殿 ; it is clear that *a-ak* instruments (such as *u* and *kŭm*) used for other sacrificial rites have been mixed in. Except for the *a-ak* instruments (*saeng, hwa, u, kŭm,* and *sul*) and the *yonggwan,* the above list is the same as that in the music section of the *Koryŏ-sa.*

In the *tang-ak* used in banquet music in 1432, except for the *a-ak* instruments (*u, kŭm,* and *sŭl*), the instrumentations are close to those in the music section of the *Koryŏ-sa* (*Sejong sillok* 65.8b):

Hyangak on the east:

	kayagŭm	hyang-pip'a	kŏmun'go	tang-pip'a	haegŭm	
west	kayagŭm	hyang-pip'a	kŏmun'go	tang-pip'a	haegŭm	east
	hyang-p'iri	taegŭm	taegŭm	taegŭm	taegŭm	
	changgo	changgo	changgo	changgo	

Tangak on the west:

	Panghyang	panghyang	tang-pip'a	t-pip'a	t-pip'a	t-pip'a	t-pip'a	t-pip'a
	ajaeng	ajaeng					taejaeng	taejaeng
W	hwa	saeng	p'iri	p'iri	p'iri	p'iri	p'iri	p'iri	E
	changgo	changgo	changgo	changgo	changgo	changgo	changgo	changgo
	t'ongso	t'ongso	tangjŏk	t-jŏk	t-jŏk	t-jŏk	yonggwan	yonggwan
								kyobanggo

As in the 1430 instrumentation, this 1432 arrangement includes not only *hyangak* instruments in the *hyangak* orchestra, but also the *tangak* instrument *tang-pip'a.* However, it is clear from the east-west separation that *tangak* and *hyangak* were still set up as separate entities.

According to the *Akhak kwebom* of 1493 (2.13b), the *tang-ak* and *hyang-ak* orchestras for banquets were as listed below; these are basically the same as sixty years earlier. The musicians were arranged in two parts, the left part being basically *tang-ak* and the right basically *hyang-ak*; a *pak* was located between them.

Left half:

	taejaeng	ajaeng	panghyang	tang-pip'a	p'iri	
W	tangjŏk	tangjŏk	p'iri	tang-pip'a	p'iri	E
	t'ongso	t'ongso	p'iri	changgo	changgo	
			kyobanggo	changgo	changgo	

Right half:

	tang-pip'a	kŏmun'go	hyang-pip'a	kayagŭm	wolgŭm	haegŭm	
W	tang-pip'a	kŏmun'go	hyang-pip'a	kayagŭm	wolgŭm	haegŭm	E
	changgo	changgo		taegŭm	taegŭm	taegŭm	
	changgo	changgo		taegŭm	taegŭm	taegŭm	

In this later *tang-ak* instrumentation, the *yonggwan, saeng,* and *hwa* have disappeared; also, the total number of instruments has diminished by half. The *hyang-ak* instruments, on the other hand, now include the Chinese *wolgŭm* 月琴 (four-string lute) as well as the *tang-pip'a,* and the total number of instruments has increased. It is noticeable, however, that the *hyang-p'iri* is no longer included. It may be observed that, at the end of the 15th century, *hyang-ak* was comparatively thriving, and that the distinction between *hyang-ak* and *tang-ak* was becoming less pronounced than in earlier times.

By the end of the Yi dynasty, the distinction between left and right music had disappeared. In a royal banquet manual of 1901, *Chinyŏn ŭigwe* 進宴儀軌, the left and right orchestras are practically identical. In these large orchestras (not shown here), two formerly absent instruments appear: *ka* 筎 (oboe) and *yanggŭm* 洋琴 (dulcimer). Also *a-ak* instruments like the *t'ukchong* 特鐘 (single bell) and *t'ukkyŏng* 特磬 (single chime) have been incorporated. Further, since both left and right have nearly the same arrangement, the so-called "*hyang-tang kyoju*" 鄉唐交奏 must be interpreted as *hyang-tang hapchu* 鄉唐合奏, or "*hyang* and *tang* [instruments] playing together;" the distinction of left and right is gone. However, even though the *tang-ak* instrument *taejaeng* is no longer present and there is no clear division between *tang* and *hyang-pip'a* or *tang* and *hyang-p'iri,* the representative *tang-ak* instruments *t'ongso, tangjŏk, ajaeng,* and *panghyang* remain.

Summarizing the above, after the mid-Yi period the distinction between left and right music in banquets became non-existent, and *hyang-ak* and *tang-ak* instruments were played together. In the early Yi period and preceding Koryŏ, however, there was a clear division of *hyang-ak* and *tang-ak;* the *tang-ak* of the 11th century closely resembles, in terms of instrumentation, the *Tōgaku* still preserved in Japan and the depiction of an orchestra in a painting by the T'ang artist Chou Wen-hsü.

B. *Hyang-ak*:

The changes in *hyang-ak* instrumentation in Korea were closely linked to those in *tang-ak* and have already been discussed in that connection; this section, therefore, is rather shorter and simply compares the instrumentation of *hyang-ak* with that of Japanese *Komagaku*. This Japanese "right" music has the following instrumentation: *Komabue* 高麗笛 (six-hole flute), *hichiriki*, *taiko*, *san-no-tzuzumi* 三の鼓 (small hourglass drum), and *shoko*. In Japan, "left" music includes both instrumental and dance music, while "right" music is all dance music.

Korean "right" music is divided into "string music" and "wind music," as in the string version of *Yŏngsan hoesang* 靈山會相 and wind version of *Yŏngsan hoesang*. The so-called "string music" is not performed only by strings, but also includes wind instruments; it is used to accompany singing (although there are pieces which have lost their texts and are now performed as purely instrumental pieces). "Wind music" includes bowed string instruments, like the *haegŭm*, which can sustain tones in a windlike manner; this music is used to accompany dancing. At present, the ensemble for song accompaniment consists of *kŏmun'go*, *kayagŭm*, *haegŭm*, *yanggŭm*, *taegŭm*, *p'iri*, and *changgo*. Dance accompaniment is performed on *p'iri* (two), *taegŭm*, *haegŭm*, *changgo*, and *chwago* 座鼓 (large drum in a frame); this group is commonly known as *samhyŏn yukkak* 三絃六角. *Samhyon yukkak* might be compared to Japanese "right" music, since both are closely associated with dancing.

The *taegŭm* is now indispensable in dance accompaniment, but it seems that in Koryŏ times the smaller *chunggŭm* was more frequently used. In the 1076 instrumentation (p. 261 above), the *chunggŭm* is listed just after the *pak* used for "song and dance," and the *taegŭm* is not listed at all. In the popular music instruments in the music section of the *Koryŏ-sa* (p. 263 above), after three dance properties (*abak, muae,* and *mugo*) are listed *haegŭm, p'iri, chunggŭm, sogŭm,* and *pak*; the *taegŭm* is listed before the dance implements, together with the group *kŏmun'go, pip'a, kayagŭm,* and *changgo*. This grouping suggests that the *chunggŭm* and *sogŭm* were used in dance accompaniment and the *taegŭm* in song accompaniment. Because the *chunggŭm* and *sogŭm* were preferred for dance accompaniment in Koryŏ, they correspond to the *Komabue* used in Japanese "right" music.

The *haegŭm* or fiddle used in Korean dance accompaniment has no equivalent in Japanese "right" music, but was originally an imported instrument, only later incorporated into *hyangak*. The *hichiriki* used in Japanese "right" music is the same as that used in "left" music, but the *p'iri* used in Korea are divided into *hyang-p'iri* and *tang-p'iri*.

In any case, the instrumentation of modern Japanese "right" music, or *Komagaku,* is closer to that given in the *Koryŏ-sa* than to modern *samhyŏn yukkak.* If the imported foreign instrument *haegum* is excluded, the similarity becomes even greater.

INDIVIDUAL INSTRUMENTS OF LEFT AND RIGHT MUSIC

A. *Tang-p'iri:*

According to the music section of the *Koryŏ-sa* (71.1a and 31a), the oboe *tang-p'iri* had nine holes and the *hyang-p'iri* had seven. By the late fifteenth century, however, the lower of the two rear holes of the *tang-p'iri* had disappeared, leaving only eight holes (*Akhak kwebŏm* 7.12a). At the same time, the *hyang-p'iri* had its seven holes increased to eight (*Akhak kwebŏm* 7.31b-32a), so that both *p'iri* had the same number of holes.

The Japanese *hichiriki* has nine holes, two in the rear. The following table compares the *hichiriki* and *tang-p'iri:*

	c	*d*	*e*	*f*	*f#*	*g*	*a*	*b*	*c'*
tang-p'iri	黃	太	姑	仲	蕤	林	南	應	潢
	合	四	一	上	勾	尺	工	凡	六

	a	*b*	*c'*	**c#'*	*d'*	*e'*	*f#'*	*g'*	**g#'*	*a'*
hichiriki	黃	盤	神	上	壹	平	下	雙	𣲻	黃
	五	工	凡	ム	六	四	一	ユ	ユ	丁

The notes shown with an asterisk are produced by the rear holes. Thus, with all holes closed, the *tang-p'iri* produces the pitch *c,* and the *hichiriki* produces *g,* but from the standpoint of originally having two rear holes, the two instruments are similar.

B. *Tangjŏk:*

According to the *Koryŏ-sa* (71.1a), the transverse flute *tangjŏk,* a *tang-ak* instrument, had eight holes. Apparently, one was for blowing and seven for fingering. In the *Akhak kwebŏm* (7.11b), the *tangjŏk* has seven finger holes, but in fact the lowest hole was not used. The modern *tangjok* has only six finger holes, like the *hyang-ak* instrument *taegŭm.*

The Japanese *Komabue,* which is the counterpart of the Korean *hyang-ak* instrument *chunggŭm* or *sogŭm,* has six finger holes, while the *ryūteki* used in *Tōgaku* has seven. In this matter of construction, the *tangjŏk* of the Koryŏ period, with seven finger holes, is closer to the Japanese *ryūteki* than to the *Komabue.*

C. *Tang-pip'a:*

As already mentioned, by 1430 the *tang-pip'a* came to be played in both *tang-ak* and *hyang-ak.* As the *Akhak kwebŏm* (7.4b-6a) explains, only the four lowest, original frets were used in performing *tang-ak,* while eight additional higher frets were employed in *hyang-ak* performance. Since the *gaku-biwa* 樂琵琶 used in Japanese *Tōgaku* has only four frets, it corresponds to the *tang-pip'a* as used in *tang-ak* rather than as used in *hyang-ak.*

In sum, because *tang-ak* instruments came also to be used for *hyang-ak.,* they were altered. The *Tōgaku* instruments in Japan are closer to the earlier Korean *tang-ak* instruments, and thus may be considered to have retained a comparatively original form.

RELATIONSHIP OF KOREAN AND JAPANESE DANCE

A. "Left" Dance:

In the late 15th century, the Korean *tang-ak* court dances, corresponding to Japanese "left" dances, were as follows (*Akhak kwebŏm* 4):
Sung dynasty *chiao-fang* 教坊 music:

Hŏnsŏndo   獻仙挑
Suyŏnjang   壽延長

Oyangsŏn	五羊仙
*P'ogurak	拋毬樂
Yŏnhwadae	蓮花臺

Dances newly created in Yi:

*Monggŭmch'ŏk	夢金尺
Suborok	受寶籙
Kŭnch'ŏnjong	覲天庭
Sumyŏngmyŏng	受明命
Hahwangŭn	荷皇恩
Hasŏngmyŏng	賀聖明
Sŏngt'aek	聖　澤
*Yukhwadae	六花隊
Kokp'a	曲　破

The five dances deriving from Sung are described in some detail in the *Koryŏ-sa* (71.1b-13a). Those dances marked with an asterisk also appear in the *Chinyŏn ŭigwe* of 1901. All of the above dances, it should be noted, come either from Sung or early Yi, and not from T'ang, despite their appellation of "*tang-ak* dances."

Tang-ak dances in Korea all shared a basic form. First of all, two pole bearers 竹竿子 came out to musical accompaniment; then, without music, they recited a Chinese poem (*kuho* 口號) giving a synopsis of the dance. During the dance, the dancers sang an unaccompanied song (*ch'angsa* 唱詞). When the dance was finished, but before the dancers exited, the pole bearers recited another Chinese poem announcing the withdrawal from the stage. These three vocal items were used only in *tang-ak* dances, and not in *hyang-ak* dances.

The repertory of Japanese "left" dances includes fifteen dances called "new music" (*shingaku* 新樂) and ten dances of "old music" (*kogaku* 古樂). The "new music" dances mostly do not use masks and, according to Konakamura Kiyonori's 小中村清矩 *Kabu ongaku ryakushi* 歌舞音樂略史 (1906), these are dances of the T'ang dynasty. The "old music" dances, in large part, belong to the *Rinyū-gaku* 林邑樂 category (music from India), which uses masks and originates from an earlier time. The discussion below compares Korean *tang-ak* dances with the "new music" dances of T'ang preserved in Japan.

In Japanese "left" dances, there are no pole bearers, unlike Korean *tang-ak* dances. This may be because the Korean dances originated in Sung and the Japanese dances in T'ang. Apart from the entrance and exit music, the Korean *tang-ak* dances require more than one piece of music, while the Japanese "left" dances generally use a single piece of music. For example, the Korean dance *Hŏnsŏndo* uses three pieces of music: *Hŏnch'ŏnsu* 獻天壽 , *Kŭmjanja* 金盞子 , and *Sŏjago* 瑞鷓鴣 ; the Japanese "left" dance *Katen* 賀殿 , however, uses just the single piece of music named *Katen*.

Despite these differences, both the Korean *tang-ak* dances and Japanese "left" dances have the unaccompanied song by the dancers in the course of the dance (called *ch'angsa* in Korea and *ei* 詠 in japan).

B. "Right" Dance:

The late fifteenth-century Korean *hyang-ak* dances, corresponding to Japanese "right" dances, were as follows (*Akhak kwebŏm* 5):

From the Sejong 世宗 period (1418-1450):

Pot'aep'yŏng	保太平
Chŏngdaeŏp	定大業
Pongnaeŭi	鳳來儀

Other:

Abak	牙　拍
Hyangbal	鄉響拔
Mugo	舞　鼓
Hangmu	鶴　舞
Ch'ŏyongmu	處容舞

Of these, *Abak* and *Mugo* appear in the *Koryŏ-sa* (71.31ab and 32b-33a); those marked with an asterisk are also found in the *Chinyŏn ŭigwe* of 1901. As mentioned above, there are no pole bearers in these dances, but there are bows at the beginning and end. There is no dancers' song 唱詞 in the middle. An important point is that, with the exception of the *Ch'ŏyongmu*, no masks are used.

The repertory of Japanese "right" dances includes twelve dances with masks, eight dances without masks, and four dances created in Japan itself. Excluding the dances of Japanese origin, two-thirds of the "right" dances use masks. Since the modern Korean repertory has only one masked dance, *Ch'ŏyongmu*, the two repertories appear to be quite distinct. But four of the five *hyang-ak* dances of the Silla dynasty (668-935), described by Ch'oe Ch'i-won 崔致遠 (857- ?), used masks; similar dances have been preserved in Japan.

The "right" dance *Nasori* 納曽利 is paired with the "left" dance *Ryō O* 陵王. *Ryō O* corresponds to one of the abovementioned five *hyang-ak* dances, *Taemyon* 大面 , in which an evil spirit is driven away with a whip; therefore, *Nasori* has also been explained as belonging to this sort of spirit-expulsion play. The word *Nasori* may be explained as a phonetic rendering of Korean *na* (儺 , meaning exorcism) and *sori* (meaning song).

In sum, the Japanese "right" dance is closer to Korean *hyang-ak* dance of the Silla period than to that of the Yi period.

C. Sequence of left and right dances:

In the early fifteenth-century Korean court, both ritual music (*a-ak*) and popular music (*tang-ak* and *hyang-ak*) dances were performed in royal banquets. *A-ak* was performed in the first through fifth presentations of cups of wine in the course of the ceremony, and *hyang-ak* and *tang-ak* during the sixth through ninth presentations. In outline, the latter were as follows (*Akhak kwebŏm* 2.23ab):

Sixth cup of wine:	*tang-ak* dance
Presentation of food:	*tang-ak*
Seventh cup of wine:	*tang-ak* dance
Presentation of food:	*tang-ak*
Eighth cup of wine:	*hyang-ak* dance
Presentation of food:	*tang-ak*
Ninth cup of wine:	*hyang-ak* dance
Presentation of delicacies:	*tang-ak*
Continued by:	*hyang-ak* and *tang-ak* together

According to this list, when the cups of wine were presented, the dances were initially *tang-ak,* continuing with *hyang-ak*; in other words, the dances did not alternate one by one between *hyang-ak* and *tang-ak,* but rather a group of *tang-ak* dances was followed by a group of *hyang-ak* dances. However, at the end of the Yi dynasty, as shown in the *Chinyŏn ŭigwe,* no such organization remains. *Hyang-ak* and *tang-ak* dances are used in all nine of the presentations of wine and other parts of the ceremony, but no system of strict alternation or grouping is to be found.

In the *Akhak kwebŏm*, two *hyangak* dances (*Abak* and *Mugo*) have Korean-language song texts sung to the accompaniment of orchestral music. However, in an illustrated dance program of 1893, *Chŏngjae mudo holgi* 呈才舞圖笏記 , the same two dances instead use recited Chinese texts without orchestral accompaniment; this is the same as the *tang-ak* dance arrangement discussed above. Although Chinese words were thus added to *hyangak* dances in the fashion of *tang-ak* dances, the pole bearers characteristic of *tang-ak* dance were not added in the same fashion.

In the *Chinyŏn ŭigwe* of 1901, the names of many of the pieces of music have the phrase *hyang-tang kyoju* 鄉唐交奏 , which, as already suggested, evidently means *hyang-ak* and *tang-ak* played together. This and the above facts show that Korean dances, like Korean orchestrations, had lost strong *hyang-ak-tang-ak* distinctions and had become mixed by the end of the Yi dynasty.

As Konakamura Kiyonori explains, "left" and "right" dances in Japan are performed in alternation (*Kabu ongaku ryakushi*, I, Chapter 4):

> Dances are divided into 'left' and 'right'. Also, there are coupled dances: in a performance of dance music, a T'ang or Japanese-origin dance of the 'left' is performed first, and the performance concludes with the coupled dance belonging to the 'right', that is, to *Komagaku*. These two coupled dances are said to be a pair (*hitotsugai* 一番).

Konakamura also cites several examples of such pairs, including the abovementioned *Ryō Ō* and *Nasori*.

As mentioned earlier, the further back one goes in time, the more the instrumentations of Japanese "left" and "right" music resemble those of Korean music; they are nearly the same in the 11th century. Similarly, it is difficult to distinguish *tang-ak* dances and *hyang-ak* dances in 1900, but the distinction solidifies the further back one goes; in the 15th century, the two dances were set up separately and performed in successive groups (*tang-ak* first, *hyang-ak* second). Thus, like the instrumentation, the further back the Korean dances are examined the more their order of performance resembles that now practiced in Japan. According to an entry of 1409 in the *T'aejong sillok* 太宗實錄 (17.22a):

We in Korea still follow the old practice: *a-ak* is used in the Royal Ancestral Shrine (*Chongmyo* 宗廟), and *tang-ak* is used for Royal Audiences (*Chohoe* 朝會). At banquets, we alternately play *hyang-ak* and *tang-ak*.

FORM OF LEFT AND RIGHT MUSIC

The term for Korean "left" music, that is, *tang-ak,* means "music of T'ang," but as we have seen, it includes music of Sung. The inadequacy of the term was recognized in the past, as this passage from 1430 shows:

> The music is called *'tang-ak'* throughout the world. The character *tang* is that of the Chinese dynasty T'ang. How can it be right to refer to Chinese music of all ages as *'tang'*? I wish to change the name to 'Chinese popular music' (*Hwa-ak sokpu* 華樂俗部). (*Sejong sillok* 47.18b).

Indeed, in the *tang-ak* portion of the music section of the *Koryŏ-sa* (71.1a-30b), none of the forty-two pieces derives from T'ang; all but one of the pieces come from Sung. By 1430, the number of pieces of this so-called *tang-ak* had diminished to only thirty (*Sejong sillok* 47.18b). In 1448, when a notated collection of popular music was compiled, little time had passed, but only thirteen pieces of *tang-ak* were included (*Sejong sillok* 116.22b):

Hŏnch'ŏnsu	獻天壽
*Chŏlhwa	折　花
Manyŏpch'iyodo	萬葉熾搖圖
Ch'oeja	催　子
*So-p'ogurak	小抛毬樂
*Pohŏja	步虛子
P'aja	破　子
Ch'ŏngp'yŏngak	清平樂
*Oun'gaesŏjo	五雲開瑞朝
*Chungsŏnhoe	衆仙會
Paekhakcha	白鶴子
Panhamu	班賀舞
*Suryongŭm	水龍吟

The last six of these also appear in the *Koryŏ-sa* (Chapter 71). The 1448 collection does not survive; the six items marked with an asterisk later appeared in the *Taeak chŏnbo* 大樂前譜 (1759), which also does not survive. The *Taeak chŏnbo* included several different items of *tang-ak* as well (*Chŭngbo munhon pigo* 94.19a):

Pohŏja	
Nagyangch'un	洛陽春
Chŏninja	前引子
Huinja	後引子
Pohŏja for winds	
Hwanhwangok	桓桓曲
Suryongŭm	
Ŏkch'wiso	憶吹簫
Haunbong	夏雲峰
So-p'ogurak	
Oun'gaesŏjo	
Hoep'alsŏn	會八仙
Ch'ŏnnyŏnmanse	千年萬歲
Chŏlhwa	
Chungsŏnhoe	

The last nine of these appear also in the *Koryŏ-sa*.

Only two pieces of *tang-ak*, *Pohŏja* and *Nagyangch'un*, remain in the modern repertory. These two pieces of Sung music were used in court ceremonies up to the end of the Yi dynasty, and thus were able to survive. Both pieces have undergone a substantial amount of change, as can be seen by comparing the modern performances with old notated sources (on this, see the article on *Nagyangch'un* in this volume).

In sum, Sung dynasty music was imported into Koryŏ, and this music comprised the Korean *tang-ak* tradition. After the downfall of Sung in 1279, the Sung music, of course, was no longer reinforced in Korea, and the greater part of it disappeared with the passage of time. The two surviving pieces in the modern repertory have undergone substantial Koreanization.

The formal relationship between surviving *tang-ak* in Korea and *Tōgaku* in Japan is considered in some detail in the article "*Nagyangch'un*: Chinese *Tz'u* Music" on page 242; only a brief summary is given here. Although *tang-ak* derives from Sung and *Tōgaku* from T'ang, certain connections are evident. The surviving *tang-ak* is purely instrumental, but examination of notated sources allows us to reconstruct the original text-music correlation. In *tang-ak,* each phrase of music consists of eight measures and sets a single line of text; a line varies from five to seven syllables in length. The last tone of the musical phrase, that is, the setting of the last syllable in the line of text, is prolonged, typically for two measures; this corresponds to poetic rhyme in the text. Also, the clapper or *pak* is struck once in every fourth measure.

Similar characteristics may be found in Japanese *Tōgaku* in the rhythmic cycle *haya-yohyōshi* 早四拍子 ; in these pieces, a phrase occupies eight measures. A prolongation (*in* 引) of the final tone occurs in the seventh and eighth measures, and the drum *taiko* is regularly struck twice in each phrase. *Tōgaku* in *haya-yahyōshi* 早八拍子 has similar characteristics, but the phrase length is 16 measures instead of eight; this might be considered a slower version of *haya-yohyōshi,* appropriate for setting longer texts (although no such texts now survive in *Tōgaku*).

Since transcriptions of the *Komagaku* preserved in Japan have not been available to the author, it is regrettably not possible to make a similar comparison between Korean and Japanese "right" music.

CONCLUSIONS

The modern Korean *tang-ak* ("left" music) and *hyang-ak* ("right" music) do not actually use the titles "left" and "right"; indeed, because of the simultaneous playing of *hyang-ak* and *tang-ak* (*hyang-tang kyoju*), the Korean repertory appears to be totally distinct from the modern Japanese repertory. But historically, both countries had distinct "left" and "right" categories: *Tōgaku* and *tang-ak* for "left" and *Komagaku* and *hyang-ak* for "right."

The instrumentation of Korean *tang-ak* in the 11th century corresponds rather closely to that of modern *Tōgaku* in Japan. The scroll *Shinzei kogakuzu* shows that *Tōgaku* historically used an instrument like the *panghyang* iron slabs (replaced today by the *shōko* gong) and an instrument like the *pak* or clapper, so that the two traditions coincided historically, both instrumentations basically agreeing with a painting of T'ang musicians by Chou Wen-hsü.

Similarly, if the *taegŭm* flute and *haegŭm* fiddle used in modern Korean *hyang-ak* dance music are, respectively, changed to a smaller flute (*chunggŭm* or *sogŭm*) and eliminated as being a foreign instrument, then the instrumentation closely resembles that of modern *Komagaku*. Although modern *Komagaku* uses the same *hichiriki* oboe as *Tōgaku,* it is reasonable to think there may have originally been two different instruments.

Korean *tang-ak* dances used the pole bearers characteristic of Sung dynasty dances, whereas Japanese *Tōgaku* dances, like T'ang dynasty dances, employ no such pole bearers. In both traditions, however, the dancers perform an unaccompanied song in the course of the dance; this appears to be an important characteristic of traditional Chinese dance. Japanese "right" dances, stemming from a very early (*Samguk*) Korean tradition, mostly employ masks, whereas the modern Korean dances, deriving from a later tradition, almost all lack masks. There is literary evidence that masks were common in the Silla period, so that the further back one goes in history the more the traditions resemble each other.

The Korean *tang-ak* tradition, as far back as the Koryŏ period, has essentially been music from Sung, not T'ang; *Tōgaku,* on the other hand, preserves music from the T'ang dynasty. Nonetheless, connections are to be found between the musical phrasing of *tang-ak* and that of *Tōgaku*: steady recurrence of rhythmic structure and prolongation of tones at the end of a phrase are characteristic of both, and, thus, of Chinese music as well.

In sum, the evidence suggests that prior to the 11th century, and certainly during the Silla period, Korean "left" and "right" music were the same as the "left" and "right" music of Japan. Japan has preserved this ancient tradition down to the present, but Korea has gradually lost the distinction of left and right; also, Sung music replaced earlier Chinese music in Korea *tang-ak,* so that only the name, *tang-ak,* has anything to do with the T'ang period. This Sung music, of course, was no longer exported to Korea after the downfall of Sung in the 13th century, and the *tang-ak* repertory has decreased in size until only two pieces remain in the modern performance tradition.

Ritual music, *a-ak*, was revived in the 15th century and was made the sole type of music in the "left" category; the former "left" music, that is, the Sung entertainment music making up *tang-ak*, was shifted to a "right" category of "popular" music together with *hyang-ak*. Indeed, *tang-ak* and *hyang-ak* even came to be mixed in performance; by the end of the Yi dynasty, the instruments of *tang-ak* and *hyang-ak* had become mixed and transformed for double use, so that the distinction between *hyang-ak* and *tang-ak* became very weak.

Japan, then, preserves comparatively older musical traditions. Examination of the literary and musical sources in both countries promises to supply additional revealing information on the musical traditions in both countries. With the background of such a comparison of musical traditions of Korea and Japan, it should be possible to rediscover in part the music of Silla and of T'ang. This, in turn, would provide a basis for comparative study with other Asian music, including that of India; eventually, the entire Asian musical tradition might be compared with that of the West.